A BLUEPRINT COMING ARMAGEDDON

Few people today doubt that history is moving toward some sort of climactic catastrophe. As I have discussed in previous books, current events are moving toward a showdown between the major world powers. Many secular scientists, statesmen and military experts believe that the world is heading for a global holocaust, involving an all-out nuclear war. The only variable with most of these experts is *when*.

No one who takes seriously these terrible and momentous events that are soon to come upon our world can fail to feel an overwhelming sense of burden. As I wrote these things, my heart literally cried out for a sure hope. I realized that these things will almost certainly fall upon my loved ones—unless . . .

Bantam Books by Hal Lindsey
Ask your bookseller for the books you have missed

COMBAT FAITH
THE LATE GREAT PLANET EARTH
THE LIBERATION OF PLANET EARTH
THE 1980'S: COUNTDOWN TO ARMAGEDDON
THE PROMISE
THE RAPTURE: TRUTH OR CONSEQUENCES
SATAN IS ALIVE AND WELL ON EARTH
THERE'S A NEW WORLD COMING

THE RAPTURE

TRUTH OR CONSEQUENCES

HAL LINDSEY

BANTAM BOOKS

TORONTO • NEW YORK • LONDON • SYDNEY • AUCKLAND

THE RAPTURE: TRUTH OR CONSEQUENCES
Bantam Trade edition / August 1983
Bantam paperback edition / August 1985

Library of Congress Cataloging in Publication Data

Lindsey, Hal.
The rapture.

1. Rapture (Christian eschatology).   2. Eschatology.
3. Bible—Prophecies.   I. Title.
BT887.L56   1983   236   82-45959

ISBN 0-553-24301-2

Published simultaneously in the United States and Canada

PRINTED IN THE UNITED STATES OF AMERICA

O   0 9 8 7 6 5 4 3

To my beloved wife, Kim, whose encouragement, skillful advice, and patient support made this book possible.

ACKNOWLEDGMENT

I wish to thank Sondra Hirsch, a true daughter of Abraham, Isaac, and Jacob, for her tireless and dedicated help in typing this manuscript.

CONTENTS

ONE

A BLUEPRINT OF TOMORROW'S HISTORY

Few people today doubt that history is moving toward some sort of climactic catastrophe. As I have discussed in previous books,[1] current events are moving toward a showdown between the major world powers. Many secular scientists, statesmen, and military experts believe that the world is heading for a global holocaust, involving an all-out nuclear war. The only variable with most of these experts is *when*.

Of far greater significance is the fact that all the predicted signs that set up the final fateful period immediately preceding the second coming of Christ are now before us. We are on the verge of this period, which will last seven years. Students of prophecy have commonly called this time "the Tribulation" because of its awful worldwide judgments. Though the term "Tribulation" may not be the best, I'll use it for the sake of easy identification.

---

[1]*The Late Great Planet Earth, There's a New World Coming,* and *The 1980's: Countdown to Armageddon,* all published by Bantam Books, New York.

There is more prophecy pertaining to these seven years than any other comparable time period with which the Bible deals. Moses, Isaiah, Jeremiah, Ezekiel, Daniel, Zechariah, most of the so-called minor prophets, as well as almost the entire book of Revelation, prophesy about this period. The Tribulation is also the topic of Jesus' most extensive prophetic discourse (see Matthew 24 and 25; Mark 13; Luke 21:5–36).

The sheer volume of prophecy devoted to the Tribulation shows how important it is to God. Since we live in the general time of its occurrence, it is of immense importance to know what the Bible says will happen.

In this chapter I'm going to seek to arrange the events of the Tribulation in chronological order. I approach this task with a true sense of humility and reliance upon God's Spirit, for it is the most demanding of all Biblical interpretation. What is summarized here represents hundreds of hours of my own study over a period of twenty-six years, as well as the work of a number of other Biblical scholars.

The Duration of the Tribulation

The prophet Daniel gave the framework for the Tribulation era in Daniel 9:24–27. He was given a revelation concerning the main course of Israel's future. God decreed that seventy weeks of years[2] were allotted to the people of Israel. (One "week" of years equals seven years, so seventy weeks of years would be 490 years.) The prophecy is specifically concerned with the future of the Israelites and the city of Jerusalem (Daniel 9:24).

---

[2]Israel reckoned time in weeks of years as well as weeks of days (Leviticus 25:1–7). The context of this prophecy is that Israel was put in exile for failure to keep seventy Sabbatical years (2 Chronicles 36:15–23).

God's Prophetic Stopwatch

Around 530 B.C. Daniel prophesied that Israel's allotted time would begin with a decree to restore and rebuild the city of Jerusalem. This decree was given by Artaxerxes Longimanus of Persia in 444 B.C. Imagine that God had a great stopwatch with 490 years on it. He started the watch counting down the allotted time the day Artaxerxes signed the decree.

Daniel predicted that from the giving of this decree until Messiah the Prince appeared would be sixty-nine weeks of years, or 483 Biblical years, each of which are 360 days long. Scholars[3] have carefully worked out the chronology from ancient records and found that exactly 173,880 days (that is, 483 x 360 days) later, Jesus of Nazareth allowed Himself, for the first time, to be publicly proclaimed Messiah and heir to the throne of David (Luke 19:29–44).

Two Critical Historical Events

The prophecy then forecast that two historical events would take place *after* the 483 years, but *before* the final seven allotted years. First, the Messiah would be "cut off" or killed, and have nothing that was due Him as the heir to David's throne. Second, the city of Jerusalem and the temple, which was rebuilt by the Jews who had returned from Babylonian exile, would both be destroyed.

Jesus was crucified five days after being publicly presented as Messiah, and Jerusalem and the temple were destroyed some thirty-seven years later by Titus of Rome in A.D. 70.

God obviously stopped "the prophetic stopwatch" after it had ticked off 483 years. The predicted destruc-

---

[3]Sir Robert Anderson, *The Coming Prince* (Grand Rapids, Michigan: Kregel, 1975).

tion of Jerusalem happened far outside the predicted bounds of the last remaining week of years, so the clock could not have just continued ticking consecutively.

Because Israel failed to accept her Messiah and instead "cut him off" by crucifying him, God stopped the countdown seven years short of completion. During the ensuing parenthesis in time, God turned His focus to the Gentiles and created the Church.

The Last Week

It is the remaining seven years of this prophecy that shed so much light upon the Tribulation period. Daniel Chapter 9, Verse 27 tells us the following:

(1) The final seven years, or the Seventieth Week of Daniel as some call it, begins with the signing of a protective treaty between Israel and the Antichrist, who will come from the revived Roman Empire (9:27) composed of ten European nations.

(2) There will apparently be a temple rebuilt shortly before or at this time, because sacrifice and offerings will be resumed. Jews wishing to return to this type of observance of Mosaic law and worship could do so only in a temple rebuilt on its ancient site in old Jerusalem.

(3) After three and one-half years, the Roman Dictator will betray Israel and set up "The Abomination of Desolation." This refers to the desecration of the temple. The Antichrist will enter the holy of holies and will erect there a statue of himself, and proclaim himself to be God (Matthew 24:15; 2 Thessalonians 2:3–4; Revelation 13:14–15).

(4) Jesus, speaking of this event, warned that it signaled the beginning of the worst tribulation

ever seen on earth, which will continue for the remaining three and one-half years (Matthew 24:15–22).

(5) I have gone into some detail on Daniel 9:24–27 because it clearly illustrates that the final seven years, or the Seventieth Week, specifically pertains to God's unfinished business with the Israelite people and Jerusalem. It is a time when God's special focus is back on the Israelites as a people distinct from the Gentiles and the Church. It is an allotment of time in which Old Testament covenants to Israel are to be fulfilled and completed.

It therefore does not seem to be a time when the Church, with its distinct calling and purpose, could be present. For if the Church were present, there could be no distinction between Jew and Gentile as the following verses indicate are the rule for this present age:

"For by one Spirit we were all baptized into one body, whether Jews or Greeks, whether slaves or free, and we were all made to drink of one Spirit." (1 Corinthians 12:13)

"For there is no distinction between Jew and Greek; for the same Lord *is Lord of all, abounding in riches for all who call upon Him;"* (Romans 10:12)

"There is neither Jew nor Greek, there is neither slave nor free man, there is neither male nor female; for you are all one in Christ Jesus." (Galatians 3:28)

"—a renewal in which there is no distinction between Greek and Jew, circumcised and uncircumcised, barbarian, Scythian, slave and freeman, but Christ is all, and in all." (Colossians 3:11)

DANIEL'S PROPHECY OF 70 SABBATICAL YEARS
(Daniel 9:24-27)

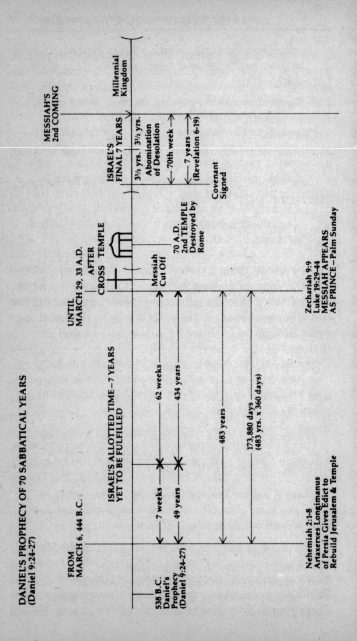

Yet in Daniel's prophecy about the Tribulation period, as well as in Revelation Chapters 6–18, the Israelites are again dealt with as a distinct, separate, and special people. Remember this very important point, for much will be said about it later.

To summarize, from the prophecy of Daniel 9:27, we know the following, as illustrated by the chart on page 6.

Now using this framework, I'm going to fit the many other prophecies together.

Events Just Before Tribulation

It is apparent that sometime before the seven-year Tribulation begins, the Antichrist will receive a mortal wound, be miraculously healed, be indwelt by Satan, and take over the ten nations of what we now know as the Common Market (Revelation 13:3). These things must first occur in order to give him the political position and power base from which to sign the protection treaty with Israel which officially begins the Tribulation.

A False Prophet, or pseudo-Messiah to Israel (Revelation 13:11–17), will be manifested before the Tribulation begins, for he is the leader of Israel who will make the covenant with the Roman Dictator (the Antichrist).

The great falling away or apostasy of the professing Christian Church also takes place before the beginning of the Tribulation which is sometimes called "the Day of the Lord" (2 Thessalonians 2:3).

The Tribulation Begins

When the Antichrist and the Israeli pseudo-Messiah sign the treaty of protection for Israel, the last seven years of Daniel's prophecy begins (Daniel 9:27 and 11:36–39). From that point final countdown resumes on God's prophetic stopwatch. There will be exactly 7 x 360 days, or 2,520 days, until the second coming of Jesus the Messiah.

In the beginning of this time frame, there will also occur the most important and incredible manifestation of God's grace for this period. One hundred and forty-four thousand Jews in Israel will be miraculously brought to faith in their true Messiah, the Lord Jesus. According to Revelation 7:1–4, this will occur before any harm comes upon the earth, the sea, or any vegetation. This means that the conversion must be right at the beginning of the Tribulation.

The context indicates that the evangelistic success of these elect and chosen people from the twelve tribes of Israel (excepting the tribe of Dan) will be awesome (Revelation 7:9-17).

Two Prophets that Shake the World

Revelation 11:3–13 traces the most unusual mission of two prophets. God sets them uniquely apart by calling them *"His* two witnesses" and by granting them *"His* own authority." I believe that these two will be none other than Moses and Elijah, who will be sent to prepare Israel for the true Messiah, and to expose the pseudo-Messiah. They will shake up not only Israel but the world for 1,260 days, or the first three and one-half years of the Tribulation.

Apparently the world at large will hate their message of warning and exposé, because all rejoice at their death.

The First Series of Judgments Begins

The first series of judgments to be unleashed on the world are called "the seven seals," and are recorded in the book of Revelation. These "seals" are fixed on a great scroll that contains God's decreed judgments. The scroll is progressively unrolled with the breaking of each seal.

THE FIRST SEAL—ANTICHRIST REVEALED

The first seal is broken at the beginning of the Tribulation. It releases the Antichrist of Rome to begin his mission of world conquest. He will bring all nations under his authority, using the European Common Market as his economic and political power base (Revelation 6:1-2; Daniel 8:23-25).[4]

General Conditions of the First Half of the Tribulation

The fear of war will apparently be stopped by the negotiating genius of the Roman Dictator. He will find solutions to such problems as the Soviet Union's desire for world conquest, the Sino-Soviet split, the enmity between the Arab and the Jew, the poverty-spawned revolutions of the third world, and the forthcoming international economic collapse.

Listen to what the Holy Spirit foretells the people of the world will say: "Who is like the beast [Antichrist], and who is able to wage war with him?" (Revelation 13:4). "While they are saying, 'Peace and Safety!'" (1 Thessalonians 5:3). In fact, Daniel shows that the Antichrist will use people's desire for peace to gain control of the world, "And through his [Antichrist] policy also he shall cause craft [deceit] to prosper in his hand; and he shall magnify *himself* in his heart, and *by means of peace* shall destroy many . . ." (Daniel 8:25, KJV).* This man will know how to use the world's desire for peace to his own diabolical ends. The Messiah-rejecting

---

[4]Hal Lindsey, *There's a New World Coming* (Eugene, Oregon: Harvest House, 1973), pp. 180-195; 228-249.

*Throughout the book, my emphases in quotes from Scripture are shown in ***boldface italics***; *regular italics* show natural emphases; and amplified word or phrase meanings are set off by square [ ] brackets.

world will be given over to his deceptions as a Divine judgment (2 Thessalonians 2:9–12).

Persecution will begin to spread worldwide upon those who believe in the Messiah during this first half of Daniel's Seventieth Week. Many false teachers and prophets will arise, and millions of true believers will be massacred. The Antichrist's apostate world religion will apparently spearhead this persecution (see Matthew 24:9–14 and Revelation 17:14).

The Midpoint of the Tribulation

Many things begin to happen quickly as the midpoint of the Tribulation is reached. This very important time is signaled by a very specific event. In the middle of Daniel's Seventieth Week the Roman Dictator will break his covenant with the Israelis and stop the offering of sacrifices and temple worship. He will then desecrate the temple by entering the holy of holies and proclaiming himself to be God (2 Thessalonians 2:4).

This act is technically known in the Scripture as the "abomination of desolation." Jesus said that this would be the sign for believers living in Israel to flee to the mountains (Matthew 24:15–20) because this would be the beginning of unprecedented catastrophes. Listen to His warning,

> "For then there will be a great tribulation, such as has not occurred since the beginning of the world until now, nor ever shall. And unless those days had been cut short, no life would have been saved; but for the sake of the elect, those days shall be cut short."
> (Matthew 24:21–22)

Jesus' warning for the believing Israelites to flee for protection coincides with the prophetic promise of protection in Revelation 12:6, 13–17.

"And the woman [Israel] fled into the wilderness where she had a place prepared by God, so that there she might be nourished for one thousand two hundred and sixty days [three and one-half years].

"And when the dragon [Satan] saw that he was thrown down to the earth, he persecuted the woman who gave birth to the male child [Jesus].

"And the two wings of the great eagle were given to the woman, in order that she might fly into the wilderness to her place, where she was nourished for a time [one year] and times [two years] and half a time [one-half year], from the presence of the serpent [Satan].

"And the serpent poured water like a river out of his mouth [symbolic of invading armies of Ezekiel 38–39] after the woman, so that he might cause her to be swept away with the flood. And the earth helped the woman, and the earth opened its mouth [great earthquake] and drank up the river which the dragon poured out of his mouth."

Most believe that this place of protection for believing Israel will be the ancient fortress city of Petra, which is carved out of the rock of a protected canyon in southern Jordan.

THE SECOND SEAL OPENED—WAR BEGINS

Shortly after the "abomination of desolation," the second seal is opened, "and another, a red horse went out; and to him who sat on it, it was granted to take peace from earth, and that men should slay one another; and a great sword was given to him." (Revelation 6:4)

Up until this point, the Antichrist has kept a pseudo-peace going on earth. But now war begins and his careful alliances are shattered. The second seal unleashes the following:

First, the Arab armies led by Egypt launch an all-out attack against Israel (Daniel 11:40). This war will probably start over a dispute concerning Jerusalem (Zechariah 12:2–3).

Second, the Soviet Union and its allies seize upon this excuse and launch an all-out invasion of the Middle East by land, sea and air (Ezekiel 38:8–17; Daniel 11:40–41). The Soviets then continue through Israel into Egypt and take it over in a classic double cross. The Soviet commander will apparently plan to take over Africa as well (Daniel 11:42–43).

At this point the Soviet invasion is stopped. News from the north troubles the commander. As he looks northward from Egypt, he faces Western Europe and sees the mobilizing of the Western armies led by the ten-nation confederacy of the Common Market.

Also, the Russian leader is troubled by news from the east. The Oriental forces led by the People's Republic of China declare war on Russia and start their thrust toward the Middle East (Daniel 11:44; Revelation 16:12).

The Soviet army returns to Israel to make a stand against the combined Western and Eastern forces. It is here that the Soviets and their satellite countries will be annihilated (Daniel 11:45; Ezekiel 38 and 39; Joel 2:20).

All of this will take considerable time, perhaps months. In the same time frame the remaining seals of Revelation are opened.

THE THIRD SEAL—GLOBAL ECONOMIC CATASTROPHE

The opening of the third seal brings worldwide economic collapse. After war breaks out in the Middle East, oil from the Persian Gulf will be halted and worldwide economic chaos will set in. Food will become scarce and very expensive (Revelation 6:5–6).

THE FOURTH SEAL—ONE-FOURTH OF MANKIND PERISHES

The opening of the fourth seal brings death to one-fourth of the world's population. The enormity of this tragedy can hardly be imagined. In the space of a few months over one billion people will perish through war, famine, epidemics and breakdown of society (Revelation 6:7–8). All of these things will be the natural repercussions of the war in the Middle East.

THE FIFTH SEAL—MASSACRE OF SAINTS

The opening of the fifth seal unleashes a horrible persecution of believers. The Roman Antichrist and the Israeli False Prophet launch a wholesale slaughter of believers (Revelation 13:5–7). They have an ingenious method of exposing believers. The Antichrist and False Prophet use economics to achieve absolute control of the people. They will institute a monetary program by which every person in the world receives a number whose prefix is 666. This begins during the first half of the Tribulation. Without this number, no one is able to buy, sell or hold a job. But to get this number, a person has to swear allegiance to the Roman Antichrist. A true believer in the Messiah cannot do this, so he is exposed and has no means of survival (Revelation 13:13–18). The persecution which begins during the first half of the Tribulation (Matthew 24:9–13) now achieves full force.

Computers have made it possible for the first time in

history to do exactly what is predicted here. Plans are already being made for a cashless society in which all people will have credits electronically transferred by computer instead of currency.

THE SIXTH SEAL—FIRST NUCLEAR EXCHANGE

The opening of the sixth seal begins what all nations fear—nuclear war. Apparently warfare has been fought conventionally up until this point. But the Soviet leaders, in a desperate situation, decide to launch a first strike. Ezekiel 39:6 says that fire is unleashed upon Magog (the cryptic name for Russia) and the "coastlands," which in ancient times referred to the great, faraway Gentile civilizations. Today the term would mean "continents." I believe that this is forecasting a nuclear exchange between the Soviet Union, Europe, United States, and China.

The world is horrified, but the worst is yet to come.

THE SEVENTH SEAL—ANOTHER SERIES OF JUDGMENTS

The seventh seal is opened and there is a lull in judgment as God gives mankind a chance to repent. The seventh seal is actually the releasing of the seven trumpet judgments which are much more severe than the first six seals (Revelation 8:1–2). It is important to note that God gives a gracious interlude between each series of judgments, which shows His reluctance to pour out more of His wrath. But each series of judgments is more severe and seem to be timed more closely together.

With the sounding of the seven trumpets judgment greatly increases in speed, scope and severity.

THE TRUMPETS—A JUDGMENT OF THIRDS

The first trumpet brings a burning of one-third of the earth's surface, one-third of the trees, and all the grains and grasses on earth (Revelation 8:7). This could be caused by fire storms started by the numerous nuclear explosions of the sixth seal.

The second trumpet gives a *foreview* of a great nuclear naval battle. Convoys of merchant ships and warships are all destroyed. It appeared to the apostle John to be caused by a great burning mountain cast into the sea. I believe this is an excellent first-century description of a twentieth-century hydrogen bomb. A third of all ships and life in the sea is destroyed by this nuclear battle (8:8–9).

The third trumpet brings a poisoning of one-third of all the world's fresh water. This could be caused by another nuclear exchange resulting in fallout, which would poison the fresh water with radiation. The burning star or meteor hitting the earth (8:10) is a perfect description of ballistic missile warheads re-entering the atmosphere.

The fourth trumpet is a judgment against light reaching the earth. Light from the sun, moon and stars is diminished by one-third. I believe this is a result of the debris spread into the upper atmosphere by the blast of hundreds of nuclear warheads. This would block out light from space. Just imagine how this will add to the panic and terror already gripping the earth (8:12).

The fifth trumpet is very difficult to discern. Whatever it is, some very vicious demons who have been bound until that time will be closely involved. Unbelievers will be so tormented by this judgment that they will seek death but be unable to find it. This will last for five months (9:1–12). This could be the result of some form of biological warfare. The Soviet Union already has a formidable arsenal of chemical weapons that could easily produce the symptoms given here.

The sixth trumpet coincides with the prophecy of Daniel 11:44 where news from the east troubles the Soviet commander. The vast Chinese army and its Oriental allies mobilize to contest the Soviet invasion of the Middle East and Africa. The activity at the Euphrates River, which was the ancient boundary between east and west, indicates that the Oriental power is incited to war by some especially powerful and vicious demons who were bound there (9:13–14).

This army numbers two hundred million. Only China could raise such an army, and has already claimed that number of men under arms. As they move toward the Middle East, they wipe out **one third** of earth's population. They do this with fire and brimstone which again seems to indicate a massive use of nuclear weapons (9:15–18).

Can you imagine the horror of these times: With one-fourth of mankind killed by the fourth seal of judgment, and one-third killed by this one, it brings the total of the earth's population destroyed to one-half. And all of this occurs in a period of less than three years. No wonder Isaiah said of this time, "The inhabitants of the earth are burned, and few men are left." (Isaiah 24:6) And again, "I will make mortal man scarcer than the gold of Ophir. Therefore I shall make the heavens tremble, and the earth will be shaken from its place at the fury of the Lord of hosts." (Isaiah 13:12–13)

An Incredible Survey of World Opinion

As terrible as all this is, the real holocaust is yet to come. It staggers the imagination to consider the hardness of the human heart reflected in the Divine survey of mankind's attitude after all these judgments take place. But listen to the Holy Spirit's preview of the world's attitude, "And the rest of mankind, who were not killed by these plagues, did not repent of the works of their hands, so as not to worship demons, and the idols of gold and silver and of brass and of stone and of wood, which can neither see nor hear nor walk; and they did not repent of their murders nor of their immorality nor of their thefts." (Revelation 9:20–21)

It is important to note that the history of the Tribulation period recorded in Revelation unfolds chronologically with the three series of judgments. The seventh seal actually unleashes the seven trumpet judgments. The seventh trumpet unleashes the seven golden bowl judgments.

Interspersed between the three series of judgments, in typical ancient Hebrew style,* are many historical sketches of the main subjects who are the prime movers during the seven years of Tribulation. These masterfully written vignettes display the wisdom and genius of the Holy Spirit who inspired them. They sometimes reach far back into history to trace why certain things occur; or they will reach into future history to show their final outcome and influence on the other events of the Tribulation.

More will be said about the framework of the book of Revelation in a later chapter. Those who wish a full exposition of the Revelation may wish to read my book, *There's a New World Coming.*

The Seventh Trumpet—Bowl Judgments Unleashed

When the seventh trumpet sounds, it is very near the end of Daniel's Seventieth Week (Revelation 11:15). There is another gracious delay of events on earth before the judgments of the seventh trumpet strike. Mean-

---

*Note that the *style*, not the *language*, is Hebrew. The language of Revelation, like all of the New Testament, is Greek.

while, in heaven the Lord Jesus, the Messiah, proclaims his right to the title deed of the earth and inaugurates His kingdom.

Mankind is given one last chance to repent before the most horrible and extensive judgments of all time hit the earth. During this time Babylon, the great worldwide religious system ruled from Rome, is destroyed by the Antichrist and his ten-nation confederacy (see Revelation 17:16–18 and 18:1–24).

There are also two "reapings" of the earth at this time. The first is a great final evangelistic movement whose purpose is to bring the last group of souls to salvation. The second will bring the rest of the unbelieving world into a final great war whose vortex is centered near Jerusalem and throughout the Jordan Valley (Revelation 14:12–20).

Apparently all those who are going to believe in the Messiah have done so by this time. The choice of whether to receive or reject the 666 mark of allegiance to the Antichrist will have been made. Only someone who believes and understands the truth about Jesus and the Bible will have the reason and courage to stand up to the consequences of rejecting this mark. Those who do receive it cannot be saved (see Revelation 14:9–12). The die is cast. At this point, the eternal destiny of every living human being will already be determined by his own choice.

THE SEVEN GOLDEN BOWLS OF GOD'S WRATH

About these final judgments John the Apostle wrote, "And I saw another sign in heaven, great and marvelous, seven angels who had seven plagues, which are the last, because in them the wrath of God is finished . . . and one of the four living creatures gave to the seven angels seven golden bowls full of the wrath of God, who lives forever and ever." (Revelation 15:1–7)

These seven horrifying judgments are all predicted in the Sixteenth Chapter of Revelation. Whereas the previous judgments had some restraint, these are worldwide and unrestrained.

The first bowl brings cancer upon all those who have the 666 mark on them. This could be a natural aftermath from the radiation of so many nuclear explosions. It appears that God will Divinely protect the believers from this plague.

The second bowl turns the sea to blood and every living thing in the ocean dies.

The third bowl turns all fresh water on earth to blood.

The fourth bowl judgment intensifies the sun's rays causing horrible heat waves. This would happen when the ozone layer of the upper atmosphere is damaged by the nuclear warfare.

The fifth bowl brings a special judgment of thick darkness upon the throne of the Roman Dictator.

The sixth bowl is terrifying indeed. The mighty two-hundred-million-man Oriental army has now reached the Euphrates River, which has dried up so that their advance can be quickened. It seems that this army will also take advantage of the confusion caused by the darkness in the Antichrist's capital. Satan, the Antichrist, and the False Prophet use demonic power to deceive all the nations on earth to gather for a suicidal war. Since by this time the Soviet bloc will have destroyed the Arab armies, and the Soviets in turn will have been destroyed (Ezekiel 39:1–6; Daniel 11:45), the last battle will be fought between the Western armies and the Chinese-led Eastern army.

The vortex of this enormous battle will be fought at the place called in Hebrew *Har-Magedon* and in English *Armageddon*. This is the area around the ancient city of Meggido, which overlooks a great valley in northern Israel.

The Death of All Cities

The seventh bowl judgment seems to be primarily against cities. The greatest earthquake in the history of mankind occurs. Then *all* the cities of the Gentile nations are destroyed (Revelation 16:19). Apparently, the earthquake will affect the whole world. Just think of it. Cities like New York, London, Paris, Tokyo, and Mexico City, all destroyed. And remember, these are not cleverly devised myths we are talking about. Four-fifths of all Bible prophecy has been fulfilled in history. The last one-fifth relates to the end times and is beginning to fit into place. Even as I write these words I am overwhelmed by the horrors that will befall this unbelieving generation.

THE SECOND ADVENT OF THE MESSIAH

Shortly after the final bowl judgment, the personal, awesome return of Messiah Jesus, the Lord of Lords and King of Kings, begins. These are some of the characteristics of his return:

First, it will be **sudden** and **instantaneous,** "For just as lightning comes from the east, and flashes even to the west, so shall the coming of the Son of Man be." (Matthew 24:27)

Second, Jesus will personally return in bodily form, and will be visible to all the world,

> "Then the sign of the Son of Man will appear in the sky, and then all the tribes of the earth will mourn, and they will see the Son of Man coming on the clouds of the sky with power and great glory." (Matthew 24:30)

> "Behold, he is coming with clouds, and **every eye** will see Him, even those who pierced Him; and all the

tribes of the earth will mourn over Him." (Revelation 1:7)

Third, His return will be with **power** and **great glory.** *Fourth*, all people will **mourn** over Him, though for most of the survivors it is not in repentance. Hearts are so hardened by this point that the armies fighting each other join forces and try to prevent the Lord Jesus' return, "And I saw the beast [the Roman Antichrist] and the kings of the earth and their armies, assembled to make war against Him who sat upon the horse, and against His army." (Revelation 19:19) This reveals the incredible truth that these men hate the Lord even more than they hate each other. So, demonstrating hardened hearts beyond comprehension, they join forces and attack the Lord Himself.

Fifth, His return will be with **violent judgment** and devastating, unprecedented destruction of those who resist Him,

*"For the Lord's indignation is against all the nations, and His wrath against all their **armies;** He has utterly destroyed them, He has given them over to slaughter."* (Isaiah 34:2)

"For I will gather all the nations against Jerusalem to battle . . . then the Lord will go forth and fight against those nations, as when He fights on a day of battle." (Zechariah 14:2–3)

*"And those slain by the Lord **on that day** shall be from one end of the earth to the other. They shall not be lamented, gathered, or buried; they shall be like dung on the face of the ground."* (Jeremiah 25:33; see also Revelation 19:11–16)

Sixth, He will return with His bride, who is already prepared and adorned with her rewards,

> " 'Let us rejoice and be glad and give glory to Him, for the marriage of the Lamb **has come** and His bride **has made** herself ready.' And it was given to her to clothe herself in fine linen, bright and clean; for the fine linen is the righteous acts of the saints.

> "And he said to me, 'Write, "Blessed are those who are invited to the marriage supper of the Lamb." ' And he said to me, 'These are the true words of God' . . . and I saw heaven opened; and behold, a white horse, and He who sat upon it is called Faithful and True; and in righteousness He judges and wages war . . . and the armies which are in heaven, clothed in fine linen, white and clean, were following Him on white horses." (Revelation 19:7–9, 11, 14)

These verses clearly show that the bride of Christ, who is already judged and rewarded before the second advent, is also the army that comes with Him when He returns to judge the earth.

Remember this, for much more will be said about *who* this bride of Christ is, and *why* she is already in heaven and rewarded *before* the second advent of Jesus.

Seventh, He will return to set up the kingdom of God on earth. This kingdom was offered and rejected in His first coming, postponed during the present age, and to be set up at His second coming (Matthew 4:17, 23:37–39; Acts 1:6; Zechariah 14:9–21; Daniel 7:26–27; Revelation 19:11–20:6).

The Enormity of the Tragedy

At this point I feel it important to take stock of the enormous loss of life during the seven years of Daniel's Seventieth Week.

First, there will be many who will die during the persecution of believers in the first half of the Tribulation (Matthew 24:9–14).

Second, there will be a minimum of over one billion people killed under the judgment of the fourth seal (Revelation 6:7–8).

Third, there will be "a multitude of believers too great to be numbered" massacred during "the great Tribulation" of the last half of Daniel's Seventieth Week (Revelation 6:9–11 compared with 7:9–17). Since there are numbers like two hundred million used in Revelation, this must be an *enormous* group, too large to be numbered.

Fourth, one-third of the remaining population will die under the sixth trumpet judgment (Revelation 9:15). Assuming that the population of the earth at the beginning of the Tribulation will be about five billion, two billion five hundred million people will die in the fourth seal and sixth trumpet judgments alone.

Fifth, in the great worldwide destruction of cities that occurs during the seventh bowl judgment, many millions more will surely be killed.

Sixth, vast numbers around the whole world will die during the actual second coming of the Messiah according to Jeremiah 25:33 and other passages.

In summary, it would appear that those who survive would be not more than fifty million. No wonder God warned through the prophets about the end, "I will make mortal man scarcer than pure gold . . ." (Isaiah 13:12); "the inhabitants of the earth are burned, and few men are left . . ." (Isaiah 24:6); and Jesus Himself said,

"Unless those days are cut short, no life will be saved . . ." (Matthew 24:22).

Why have I gone into all this? Because I believe it is of utmost importance to squarely face exactly what the Scriptures predict about this period. Those who say that the believers in the Church are going to go through all these horrors never really bring out what that means. And no wonder. It's easy to see why they minimize these things, because against the backdrop of such terrifying events, it's rather difficult to get people excited about the nearness of Christ's return.

In the light of these prophecies, very few who begin the Tribulation would live to see His coming anyway. So how could anyone inspire the hope and comfort that is promised in Paul's teaching of Jesus' imminent return (1 Thessalonians 4:15–18)? Ladd, Gundry, and other post-Tribulationists talk about the hope being the prospect of seeing and being with the Lord in eternity. That is the hope normally promised to those who will die and be resurrected. But the Rapture is a hope presented to the living, not the dead. There is an enormous difference in the hope (if you can call it that) of the post-Tribulationists and the pre-Tribulationist hope presented around the mystery of the translation (Rapture) of **living** saints.

MEANWHILE, BACK AT THE END OF THE TWENTIETH CENTURY

I have endeavored to cover briefly the main events that take place during the Tribulation. Much prayer was offered as I sought to correlate important prophecies and arrange them in chronological order.

No one who takes seriously these terrible and momentous events that are soon to come upon our world can fail to feel an overwhelming sense of burden. As I wrote these things, my heart literally cried out for a sure hope. I realized that these things will almost certainly fall upon my loved ones—unless . . .

The rest of this book will deal with whether or not we have a real hope.

TWO

CLARIFYING THE ISSUE

I decided to write this book because I see a growing confusion and anxiety developing throughout the body of Christ worldwide. This confusion and anxiety comes from an uncertainty about whether the true Church, which is composed of all true believers in Jesus regardless of denomination, will go through the Tribulation, or through the first half of the Tribulation, or will be taken out of the world by Jesus before the Tribulation begins.

In my opinion, this question is about the most important one a Christian of this generation can ask. In all probability, most of the people reading this book will live to experience the answer.

About fifteen years ago this wouldn't have even been a question because most Christians didn't know much, if anything, about this issue. But since then there has been a flood of books, movies, teachers, and so forth, which have spread the message about the imminent return of the Lord Jesus, and the events that precede it.

Teaching about these end-time prophecies has lately been met with great interest around the world.

When I set out to do research for this book, I asked the Lord to overcome any prejudice or conditioning from the past, and to help me to be truly objective under the guidance of the Holy Spirit. My goal has not been to defend a view, but to seek the truth about *when* Christ is coming for His Church. I determined that if I should find that I had been wrong on this issue, that I would write a book acknowledging it.

I think it is important to bring out that as far as my own personal faith is concerned, if the Scriptures teach that the Church is to go through all or part of the Tribulation, I can certainly trust in God for His care and protection and press on. I want the truth, and I don't want to spread false hope; to be found a liar before God. That thought is more frightening to me than the Tribulation.

But, on the other hand, if Christ is coming *before* the Tribulation for His Church, this great hope should be shouted from the rooftops. As our world continues to move toward greater and greater peril, this hope will have an explosive effect upon believers. According to the Scripture, it will bring greater purity of life, comfort and peace in the midst of a turbulent world, and a bold witness for Christ.

In the months of study that followed, my main texts were the original languages of the Bible. However, I also read carefully the books of the major scholars representing the three different views about the time of Christ's coming for His Church. Many of these I had read before, but I wanted to make sure I had been fair with them.

At this point it is necessary to introduce a few important theological terms.

The coming of Christ for the Church in which He instantly catches up all living believers to meet Him in the air and translates them into immortal bodies without experiencing physical death is called the "Rapture" (1 Corinthians 15:51–54; 1 Thessalonians 4:15–18). The word *rapture* comes from a Latin translation of the Greek word *harpazo* in 1 Thessalonians 4:17 which is translated in English as "caught up." It literally means "to seize" or "to snatch away." If I had my way, I would call the Rapture "the great snatch."

All who interpret the Bible in a literal sense believe in the *fact* of the Rapture and that it is distinct from the second coming of Christ. The dispute is over exactly *when* the Rapture occurs in relation to the Tribulation period.

Those who believe that the Church will go through the entire Tribulation and be raptured simultaneously with Jesus' return to the earth in the second coming are called "post-Tribulationists."

Those who believe that the Church will go through the first half of the Tribulation, and will be raptured and taken to heaven at the midpoint of the Tribulation, are called "mid-Tribulationists."

Those who believe that the Church will be raptured before the Tribulation begins, to be with Christ in heaven and to return with Him at the end in the second coming are called "pre-Tribulationists."

I believe the following charts may help clarify the different views:

PRE-TRIBULATION RAPTURE

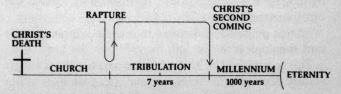

MID-TRIBULATION RAPTURE

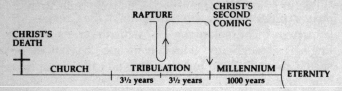

POST-TRIBULATION RAPTURE

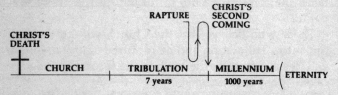

The New Protestant Purgatory

There is a fourth view concerning the Rapture of the Church which has recently been introduced. It is not widely taught, since it is unorthodox and at considerable variance with the Scripture. However, it is a view that could gain some following among those who are weak on knowledge of the Word of God and strong on experience and human viewpoint.

This view is in direct contradiction to one of the most central and important doctrines of all, that of salvation by grace through faith alone. It is commonly called the "Partial Rapture View."

There are some variations among its adherents, but generally it means the following: When the Lord Jesus comes to snatch away the true Church, only the spiritual believers will be taken. The carnal, or "back-sliden" believers, will be left to go through the Tribulation. Most adherents of this view believe that the partial Rapture will occur before the Tribulation. This view is illustrated in the following chart:

PARTIAL RAPTURE THEORY

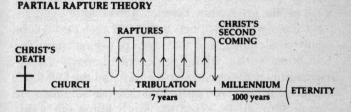

Why So Many Views?

Many, including myself, have puzzled over why there are so many conflicting views concerning a doctrine that is so important. This question becomes even more mystifying when you realize the kinds of people who are involved in the disagreement.

This has been especially hard for me, because many of those with whom I disagree on this issue are people I know and respect.

Some Areas of Common Agreement

This is the crux of the problem, that all the principal scholars and exponents of pre-, post-, and mid-Tribulationism are born again, love the Lord, believe the Bible is the Word of God, desire to teach the truth, and as far as I know live Godly lives.

Theologically, there is also a wide range of agreement. Almost all concerned hold to an orthodox view of the important central doctrines of the faith such as the person and work of Christ, justification by grace through faith, the inspiration of the Bible, and so forth.

In the field of prophecy (eschatology) there is general

agreement that there will be a literal seven years of world Tribulation, that Jesus will return visibly and personally, that He will then set up a literal 1,000-year earthly kingdom over which He will rule, that mortals will repopulate the earth, that there will be a final judgment at "the great white throne" at the end of the thousand years when all unbelievers of all ages past will be finally condemned, and that eternity begins after this.

In other words, what I've described above is a *premillennial view* of the Messiah's return and the Messianic kingdom. All the pre-, post-, and mid-Tribulationists are "premillennialists." Just so you'll know what this means, on the following page I have charted three views of the millennial kingdom.

Postmillennialists believe that the Church will overcome the world and bring the millennial period of peace and perfect environment to earth on its own. Then the Messiah will come at the end of history and receive the kingdom from the Church. This view flourished in the late nineteenth and early twentieth centuries, during a period of pseudo-optimism about the Church's missionary success and the effect of education on human nature.

But World War I seriously shook this view, and World War II all but wiped it out. It should be noted that the view is founded on a gross mishandling of the prophetic Scriptures. The allegorical method of interpretation is used throughout.

The term *"amillennial"* means no millennium, and proponents of this view believe there will be no specific period of Tribulation, no fulfillment of Daniel's prophecy about the Seventieth Week and no millennial kingdom. Jesus will simply come at the end of history, judge all people, believers and unbelievers, and start eternity.

The *only* way one can arrive at this view is by using an allegorical method of interpretation. This means that

PREMILLENNIAL VIEW

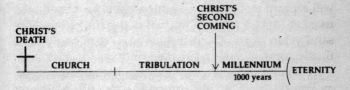

POSTMILLENNIAL VIEW

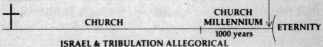

AMILLENNIAL VIEW

CHRIST'S
SECOND
COMING

CHRIST'S
DEATH

CHURCH ↓ ETERNITY

ISRAEL, TRIBULATION & MILLENNIUM ALLEGORICAL

one assigns to words a meaning other than that normally understood and accepted at the time of writing.

Amillennialists concede that if prophecy is interpreted literally (normally), grammatically, and historically it will produce a premillennial view. The literal method allows for parable, allegory, and figures of speech, but recognizes that the context will clearly indicate when this is the case.

Amillennialism has some very dangerous side effects. First, it makes God guilty of not keeping unconditional covenants and promises made to the physical descendents of Abraham, Isaac, and Jacob, whom we call Jews today. For God not only swore that there would always be a distinct race of Israelites on earth, but that there will be a true believing remnant of Jews who will be established in a literal kingdom on earth ruled by the Messiah. If you look up the following verses you will see that the covenants depend upon God's faithfulness alone, not Israel's obedience:

(1) Promise of the land: Genesis 12:7; 13:15–16; 17:7–8.

(2) Promise of the land, a kingdom, and a greater Son of David (Messiah) as king: Psalm 89:27–37.

(3) Promise of restoration to the land of Israel from worldwide dispersion and establishment of Messiah's kingdom: Jeremiah 31:31–37; Ezekiel 36, 37, 38, 39, and so forth.

(4) Promises that a remnant of the Israelites will be saved: Romans 11:25–29; Zechariah 13:8–9; Isaiah 10:20–22.

This is only a sampling of passages, but it shows how solemn God's covenants with the Israelites are. The restoration of the State of Israel in May 1948 is a literal confirmation of these promises.

Roots of Anti-Semitism

The second effect is that from the time that amillennialism began to be taught (about the fourth century, beginning with Augustine A.D. 345–430), it became a philosophical basis for anti-Semitism. Amillennialism teaches that the Church has been given the promises made to the Israelites because they crowned a history of unbelief by rejecting the Messiah. Therefore, since in this view the Israelites have no future in God's plan, and since they believe that "the Jews engineered the execution of Jesus," a subtle justification for the persecution of Jews resulted (Jeremiah 31:35–37).

There is evidence that this kind of thinking is reviving again today. There are those who are teaching that the State of Israel is filled with imposters and that there are no true Israelites today apart from spiritual Israel, which according to them is the Church.

This kind of teaching is demonic and heretical. I am thankful to say that no person who believes in the premillennial view can be anti-Semitic. In fact, the premillennialists are probably the truest non-Israelite friends the Israelites have in the world today, for they believe God will keep all His promises to the Israelites, including punishing all who persecute them.

A Disagreement Among Brothers

So it is good to remember that the pre-, post-, and mid-Tribulationists are all premillennial, with all the good qualities and areas of agreement that we have just surveyed.

Such post-Tribulationists as Robert Gundry and George Ladd fit into the above category, and I have found as I have studied their books through the years that they were careful scholars. Others who believe this view, such as Pat Robertson, Walter Martin, Jim McKeever, etc., have served the Lord well.

The same is true of the mid-Tribulationists like Norman B. Harrison and J. Sidlow Baxter who are also scholars. This view has received new interest through Mary Stewart Relfe's popular book, *When Your Money Fails*. I enjoyed reading her book, with the exception of a few uncharitably critical generalizations she made about those who disagree with her.

And among the pre-Tribulation exponents, I've never found greater scholarship than that expressed by J. Dwight Pentecost, John F. Wolvoord, and Charles C. Ryrie. The books of these men have dominated the scholarly side of prophetic study for decades, and they are virtually the standard in this field for our times.

I have found that almost all men who consistently proclaim a prophetic message in evangelism are pre-Tribulationists. My spiritual father, Col. Robert B. Thieme, Jr., a man who is still the best Bible teacher I have ever heard, is in this camp.

From Bouquets to Battle

You're probably saying by now, "If all these things are true, why is there disagreement about the time of the Rapture's occurrence?" My opinion is this: Good men disagree because God deliberately made this issue difficult to settle. Only the most diligent study and comprehensive knowledge of the whole realm of Biblical prophecy can begin to answer it.

As an example, Dr. Gundry repeatedly says that pre-Tribulationism is based largely on arguments from inference and silence.[1] This is in some measure true. But

[1] Robert H. Gundry, *The Church and the Tribulation* (Grand Rapids: Zondervan Pub. Co., 1973).

here is the big point: *All* of the views have to be developed to some degree on arguments from inference and silence.

The truth of the matter is that neither a post-, mid-, or pre-Tribulationist can point to any single verse that clearly says the Rapture will occur before, in the middle of, or after the Tribulation.

Can Anyone Offer a Sure Hope?

You may be saying, "Wow, if it's all that complicated, why bother?" I believe the first answer to that question is, "Because the Lord commanded us to seek to understand His prophetic Word." This is especially true in these last days.

Second, I believe that by comparing correlating prophecies on this issue, and by consistently adhering to the tried and proven literal method of interpretation, a sure answer to the Rapture question can be found. The most important element in this process, of course, is to consciously depend on the Holy Spirit for His guidance and illumination.

Third, as I said before, whatever the answer to the Rapture question is, *we will most likely live to experience it.* So how preeminently important the answer is for planning our lives for Jesus in this day and time!

Why Me, Lord?

There is no question in my mind that the Lord unmistakably led me to write this book. But I confess that many times I asked, "Why me, Lord?" After all, many scholars have written on and debated about this subject.

As I studied, however, I began to sense a reason. I believe the Lord has given me some fresh insight on the issue. I haven't studied as much or with such interest and excitement since my seminary days.

And one thing I will own up to, the Lord gave me the gift of "simplicity." Most scholarly works on this subject need an "interpreter." I'll never forget, as a young Christian, how chills went through me when I read the promise of God, "The entrance of Thy Words giveth light; it giveth understanding unto the simple." (Psalm 119:130) I chuckled in prayer to the Lord and said, "Well, Lord, I surely qualify for this promise, because I am simple. Will you please pour Your Word into me and give me light." You know, the Lord surely has been answering that prayer.

I prayed that same prayer again as I studied and wrote this book. The result has been wonderful. I've been blessed, reassured and given a confident and joyous hope.

May this book do the same for you.

THREE

PREDICTIONS AND PROMISES OF THE RAPTURE

I will never forget the first time that I heard about "the Rapture." It was from a young minister in Houston, Texas, named Jack Blackwell. I was so excited that I could hardly sleep for a week.

But it wasn't long thereafter before I ran into some people who called the idea of Jesus coming for the Church *before* the Tribulation "a false doctrine." They even brought a minister to straighten me out on "this dangerous teaching."

The result was a real blessing because this motivated me to search the Scriptures on the issue many hours a day. In fact this was one of my first lessons in systematic study of the Bible. In the process, the whole course of my life was changed. It was during those days that I realized that I would never be happy apart from studying and teaching the Bible. All other ambitions faded into boredom in comparison to this newfound love.

There were times during this search that I experienced the presence of the Holy Spirit in such power that I went into an ecstatic state. It was like lying in the ocean and feeling waves wash over me—only it was a physical experience of God's love moving over me.

During the course of these months I became completely convinced that the Lord Jesus would come for the true Christian *before* the Tribulation period. This conviction was not based only on what men taught me, but on a careful personal study of the Scripture.

Now, almost thirty years later, I've rechallenged all the reasons for that hope of the Lord's pre-Tribulation Rapture. As you read the following chapters, I pray that you will be motivated to also search the Scriptures, so that you'll know why you believe what you believe.

The most important place to start is with a careful examination of all the Biblical passages on the Rapture. They reveal that the Rapture has many unique factors.

THE RAPTURE IS A MYSTERY

In 1 Corinthians, Chapter 15, the apostle Paul, under the inspiration of God's Spirit, is teaching about the certainty of every believer's resurrection from the dead. He also reveals that the resurrection body will be wonderfully changed into an eternal immortal form that has real substance.

Paul clearly teaches that our new body will "bear the image of the heavenly," that is, like the Lord Jesus' resurrected body (Verse 49). In this regard, he says, "Flesh and blood cannot inherit the kingdom of God; nor does the perishable inherit the imperishable" (Verse 50).

In other words, our present body of flesh and blood, which must be sustained by elements of the earth which are perishable, must be changed to another form. This new form has material being, but it is of a kind that is suited for the spiritual, imperishable, eternal atmosphere of heaven.

The resurrected Lord Jesus is the measure of our future existence. He could appear and disappear at will (Luke 24:31; John 20:19). He could move through solid walls (John 20:19, 26). He could be seen and felt (Matthew 28:9; Luke 24:36–42). He could eat food, though it wasn't apparently necessary (Luke 24:41–43). Though glorified, Jesus could be recognized (Luke 24:30–31). Our resurrected bodies will no longer experience death, aging, crying, mourning, sorrow, or pain (Revelation 21:4).

The above are just a few of the wonders that we believers will experience in our future resurrected bodies. One thing, however, is necessary to be resurrected: We must first die! Resurrection is only for the dead. Resurrection from the *dead* was certainly a hope clearly taught in the Old Testament.

An Ancient Lesson in Hope

The earliest account of the resurrection hope in the Old Testament is recorded in the book of Job. Job actually lived before Abraham and Moses. Job took up the age-old question of resurrection when he said, "If a man dies, will he live again? All the days of my struggle I will wait [patiently trust], *until my change comes.*" (italics mine) (Job 14:14) Job responds to his own question by saying he would patiently trust until his change into a new resurrected body came.

Job states an incredible faith in his own resurrection, considering the early period of Divine revelation in which he lived, "For I know that my redeemer lives, and that he shall stand at the latter days upon the earth; and though after my skin worms destroy this body, yet in my flesh shall I see God, whom I shall see for myself, and mine eyes shall behold, and not another; though my heart be consumed within me." (Job 19:25–27, KJV) This

is particularly amazing because at the time this was declared, there was no known written revelation from
God.

This proves, along with many other Old Testament
verses that could be quoted, that resurrection was
known and believed throughout man's history of redemption, which began soon after mankind's appearance upon this earth.

I Love a Mystery

In the midst of Paul's teaching on the resurrection he
says, "Behold, I tell you a mystery; we shall not all sleep,
but we shall all be changed." (1 Corinthians 15:51)

There are many important truths taught in this verse.

First, Paul says he is introducing a *mystery*. The moment Paul uses the word "mystery," it signals that he is
going to reveal a new truth not known before. The word
in the original Greek *(mysterion)*, as used in the New Testament, means something not previously known, but
now revealed to the true believer.

So what is it that is new? In this chapter he has
summed up what was known in the Old Testament: that
flesh and blood cannot enter God's presence; that we
must first die, and then be raised in a new eternal form.

THE RAPTURE MEANS NO DEATH

The second truth in this verse, and the meaning of the
mystery, is that we Christians are not all going **to die!**
This was a totally new concept. No Old Testament believer dreamed that some future generation would enter
eternity and God's presence without experiencing physical death. Death is an absolute prerequisite to entering
immortality through resurrection.

There were two partial examples of the Rapture in the

cases of Enoch and Elijah. They were taken directly into heaven without experiencing physical death. But even Enoch and Elijah haven't yet received their immortal bodies. As for the Old Testament believer in general, no one dared to believe that there would be a future generation of believers who would be taken en masse to God's presence.

The truly electrifying fact is that many of you who are reading this will experience this mystery. You will never know what it is to die physically.

THE RAPTURE INCLUDES ALL

The third truth in this verse is that **all** believers at the time of the Rapture will escape physical death. It is not an accident, I'm sure, that God selected the Corinthians to be the recipients of this revelation. For of all the early churches the New Testament records, the Corinthian church was the most carnal.

Paul rebukes them for everything from fornication (6:15–20) to getting drunk at communion (11:20–22). Yet Paul says to them, "We *all* will be changed."

A famous Supreme Court decision defined the word "all" as follows: "All includes everyone, and excludes no one." That's a very apt definition for how many believers go at the Rapture. Some will regretfully be raptured while out of fellowship with God. This may result in a loss of rewards for service, but not participation in the Rapture. We base this on the same foundation upon which we base our salvation. It is "by grace through faith, and that not of ourselves, it is a gift of God." (See 1 Corinthians 3:10–15 and Ephesians 2:8–9.) There is no Scriptural basis for a partial Rapture. The Rapture *must* be based on the same principles as salvation.

THE RAPTURE IS A TRANSFORMATION

The fourth truth revealed in the mystery of the Rapture is that "all Christians *will be changed.*" The Greek word *(allasso)* translated "be changed," literally means "to be transformed." All Christians will be transformed in body and nature into new bodies that are suited for the eternal, spiritual, incorruptible realm in which God dwells.

All the things Paul teaches in this chapter about the resurrection body are true of the Rapture except that they are bestowed apart from death.

The extent of this transformation is the greatest thing God could bestow upon us. He transforms us into the exact likeness of His glorified Son, the Lord Jesus Christ.

> *"For our citizenship is in heaven, from which also we eagerly wait for a Savior, the Lord Jesus Christ; who will transform the body of our humble state into conformity with the body of His glory, by the exertion of the power that He has even to subject all things to Himself."* (Philippians 3:20–21)

THE RAPTURE IS INSTANTANEOUS

Paul says, "In a moment, in the twinkling of an eye, at the last trumpet; for the trumpet will sound, and the dead will be raised imperishable, and we shall be changed." (1 Corinthians 15:52). Someone said that the twinkling of an eye is about one-thousandth of a second. The Greek word is *atomos* from which we get the word atom. It means something that cannot be divided. In other words, the Rapture will occur so quickly and suddenly that the time frame in which it occurs cannot be humanly divided.

Just think of it . . . in the flash of a second every living believer on earth will be gone. Suddenly, without warning, only unbelievers will be populating planet earth.

I recently watched in awe as the space shuttle blasted off into space. Within a matter of a few minutes it was out of sight and traveling at more than six times the speed of sound. What will take place for each living believer at the Rapture surpasses this by all comparison.

In another crucial passage on the Rapture, God reveals to us what will occur while we are being instantaneously transformed into immortal bodies, "For this we say to you by the word of the Lord, that we who are alive, and remain until the coming of the Lord, shall not precede those who have fallen asleep. For the Lord Himself will descend from heaven with a shout, the voice of *the* archangel, and with the trumpet of God; and the dead in Christ shall rise first. Then we who are alive and remain shall be caught up together with them in the clouds to meet the Lord in the air, and thus we shall always be with the Lord. Therefore comfort one another with these words." (1 Thessalonians 4:15–18)

Will We See Our Loved Ones Again?

The apostle Paul wrote these words to reassure the Thessalonians who had believing loved ones who had died. They were afraid that their departed loved ones would be in some other part of God's plan. Therefore, they feared that those who were raptured would not see their dear ones again in eternity.

Paul's answer is as amazing as it is comforting. For he assures them that not only will we see again Christian loved ones who have died, but that they will receive their resurrection bodies a split second before we are transformed into immortality.

The key word is "we shall be caught up." This is the translation of the Greek verb *harpazo*. As I mentioned earlier, it literally means "to snatch out" or "to seize." When we put together the concept of "being caught up into the clouds to meet the Lord in the air" together with the idea of an instantaneous transformation, the result is spine-tingling.

We will suddenly one day just blast off into space. Faster than the eye of the unbeliever can perceive, every living believer on earth will disappear. The world will probably hear a great sonic boom from all our transformed immortal bodies cracking the sound barrier. But the rest will be a mystery.

THE RAPTURE IS A REUNION

As for us, one moment we will be going about our life here on earth; the next moment we will be hurtled into the presence of departed loved ones. And above all, we will have a face-to-face meeting with the One whose death in our place made it all happen.

Another very wonderful experience is predicted in 1 Thessalonians. The apostle Paul reveals that we will not only be reunited with all our Christian relatives and loved ones, but with all those persons who trusted in Jesus through our witness. He said of those Thessalonians to whom he had ministered, "For who is our hope or joy or crown of exultation? Is it not even you, in the presence of our Lord Jesus at His coming?" Paul says that these spiritual children of his will be "his crown of exultation in the Lord's presence when He comes." From this it appears that each one of us will have grouped around us those we have helped to believe in Jesus.

I don't know about you, but that excites me out of my mind. It makes me want to redouble efforts to witness for the Lord Jesus. To see even one person standing there before our Savior in a glorified body because I was available for the Holy Spirit to work through, will be the most wonderful "crown" of all.

A Meeting in the Air

It is very important to note that "We will be caught up in the clouds to meet the Lord in the **air.**" (1 Thessalonians 4:17) There is a major point of controversy between the pre-Tribulationists and the post-Tribulationists over what happens next.

The post-Tribulationist says that after meeting the Lord in the air we will immediately return with Him to the earth. They agree that all believers alive at the time will be instantly transformed into immortal bodies. But since this event, in their view, occurs in connection with the second coming, believers will meet the Lord in the air only to return immediately with Him to earth. In thoroughly examining this scenario, I find that it poses some unanswerable problems with other Scriptures that deal with events that immediately follow the second coming. All these problems will be pointed out later, but let's take up one here.

To the Father's House

Pre-Tribulationists believe that a very important personal promise of the Lord is fulfilled when we meet the Lord in the air. As Jesus taught the disciples at the Last Supper, He sought to comfort and reassure them concerning His imminent departure with this promise, "Let not your heart be troubled; believe in God, believe also in Me. In my Father's house are many dwelling places; if it were not so, I would have told you; for I go to prepare a place for you. And if I go and prepare a place for you, I will come again, and receive you to Myself; so that where I am, there you may be also." (John 14:1–3)

Let us make several observations about this prophecy.

First, Jesus specifically makes this promise to believers in the Church. For His whole teaching at the Last Supper (which has been designated The Upper Room Discourse) emphasized the revolutionary new privileges that would come to each believer when He ascended to the Father and sent the Holy Spirit to take up permanent residence in them. It is these very privileges that make the age in which we live unique and vastly distinct from God's previous dealing with Old Testament believers in general and Israel in particular.

Second, Jesus gives a very specific location around which the whole prophecy revolves. Jesus said, "I am going to prepare a place for you," and that place is specifically "His Father's house." We know from passages like Psalm 110:1 that when Jesus left and ascended, He went to God the Father's presence and took a seat at His right hand.

Jesus continued and said that as certainly as He was going to the Father's house to prepare a place for us, that He would come again and take us to that place to be with Him.

Third, Jesus gives us the specific time that all the above will be fulfilled. It will be at the time He returns for the true Church, for He says, "I will come again, and receive you to Myself; that where I am [in the Father's house], there you may be also."

Now if Jesus is building a dwelling place for us in the Father's house, and if we are to go there **when** He comes for the Church, how could He be speaking of an event that occurs simultaneously with the Second Advent? For at that time Jesus is specifically and personally coming to the earth (see Zechariah 14:4–9).

If the post-Tribulationists are right, then Jesus is engaged in a futile building program. For when He comes to the earth in the second coming, He will rule out of the earthly Jerusalem for a thousand years. Since He says

He is going to come in order that we may be with Him **where he is,** we would have to be with Him here on earth. Do you see the problem? The dwelling places in the Father's house would be unused. And worse by far, Jesus would be guilty of telling us a lie. For as we have seen, He is coming for the purpose of taking us to the Father's house at that time.

Post-Tribulationist Robert Gundry doesn't keep this passage in context when he says, "Jesus does not promise that upon His return He will take believers to mansions in the Father's house. Instead, He promises, '*Where I am,* there you may be also.'"[1] This makes Jesus' whole promise ridiculous. Why would He speak of preparing a place in the Father's house for us if He didn't mean that His return was to take us there? With all due respect, Gundry has violated a basic principle of interpretation here; i.e., to keep verses in context. The passage is clear to the simple folk. It takes real determination to find Gundry's interpretation in this passage.

Gundry goes on to make a truly novel allegorical interpretation of John 14:1-3, "In order to console the disciples concerning His going away, Jesus tells them that His leaving will work to their advantage. He is going to prepare for them *spiritual abodes within His own person.* Dwelling in these abiding places they will belong to God's household. This He will accomplish by going to the cross and then ascending to the Father. But He will return to receive the disciples into His immediate presence forever. Thus, the Rapture will not have the purpose of taking them to heaven. It rather follows from their being in Christ, in whom each believer already has an abode." [2]

---

[1]Robert Gundry, *The Church and the Tribulation* (Grand Rapids, Mich.: Zondervan Pub. House, 1973), p. 153.
[2]Ibid. p. 154.

This interpretation surprised me. Gundry usually tries to avoid the allegorical method of interpretation. I strongly disagree with him here because it takes a passage which gives every indication of being literal narrative and makes *part of it* allegorical.

Jesus was literally taking His physical presence away from the disciples. This is exactly why they were troubled. Jesus also literally went to take a seat at the Father's right hand. There is absolutely no indication in the context that the dwelling places He is preparing and His return to take us there are allegorical.

Later Jesus does promise that He will be with us spiritually through the indwelling Holy Spirit, and that we will experience a mystical union with Him personally. But the context is very clear that this is what is literally meant (see John 14:15–26; 16:7–25).

Once again let us remember some basic principles of interpretation. First, if the literal sense makes common sense, seek no other sense. Second, all things are intended to be taken literally unless the context clearly indicates otherwise.

PUT IT ALL TOGETHER

Let us briefly sum up what the Scriptures covered in this chapter have taught about the Rapture.

(1) The Rapture was unknown until it was revealed to the Church by the apostles, especially Paul.

(2) All believers living when the Rapture occurs will not experience physical death.

(3) The Rapture will occur suddenly, without specific warning, and will be instantaneous.

(4) In the Rapture, every living believer will be in-

stantly transformed from mortal to immortal bodies which are like Jesus' glorified body.

(5) Those raptured will be caught up in the air to meet the Lord and the resurrected church-age believers who have died.

(6) At that time, we will be taken into God the Father's presence to temporary dwelling places that the Lord Jesus is presently preparing.

The post-, mid-, and pre-Tribulationists would agree on all the points above except number 6 and part of number 3.

Academics aside, the really important issue is the wonder of it all! What a marvelous expectation exists for this generation! No wonder Paul taught after revealing the great hope of the Rapture, "Therefore, my beloved brethren, be steadfast, immovable, always abounding in the work of the Lord, knowing that your toil is not in vain in the Lord." (1 Corinthians 15:58)

We can be steadfast and immovable in the midst of a turbulent and increasingly dangerous world, because we know that it means the Lord's coming is drawing near. Prophecy of the Rapture shines ever brighter as darkness gathers about us.

FOUR

SOME DIVINE DISTINCTIONS

There is a method of interpretation that is absolutely essential for determining which view concerning the Rapture is correct. This method is called dispensationalism.

Dispensationalism (which is the Divine ordering of worldly affairs) not only helps answer the Rapture question, but helps harmonize many Scripture passages that on first observation seem to be contradictory.

Here are a few examples:

First, Jesus taught in the Sermon on the Mount, "Do not think that I came to abolish the Law and the Prophets, I did not come to abolish, but to fulfill. For truly I say to you, until heaven and earth pass away, not the smallest letter or stroke shall pass away from the Law, until all is accomplished." (Matthew 5:17–18)

But Paul said in Galatians, "Nevertheless knowing that a man is not justified by the works of the Law but through faith in Christ Jesus, even we [Jews] have believed in Christ Jesus, that we may be justified by faith in Christ, and not by the works of the Law; since by the works of the Law shall no flesh be justified." (Galatians 2:16)

Trying to reconcile those two statements as a new Christian was practically impossible. In fact it troubled me. It was obvious that something radical must have happened between the Sermon on the Mount and the ministry of the apostle Paul.

Second, later in Jesus' ministry, He made another statement that confused me, "These twelve Jesus sent out after instructing them, saying, 'Do not go in the way of the Gentiles, and do not enter *any* city of the Samaritans; but rather go to the lost sheep of the house of Israel.'" (Matthew 10:5–6) I couldn't imagine why God wouldn't allow the apostles to speak to the Gentiles and why He sent them only to preach to Israel.

Yet later in the same Gospel of Matthew, Jesus said, "Go therefore and make disciples of all the nations (Gentiles), baptizing them in the name of the Father and the Son and the Holy Spirit . . ." (Matthew 28:19).

Obviously, these two examples point out a distinguishable change in God's plan. For some reason, that was unfathomable to me as a baby Christian, God introduced some completely new revelation about how He and man were going to relate to each other. I could add many more examples like these if space permitted, but these should sufficiently illustrate the point.

What is an Age?

Another indication that there have been distinguishable changes in God's plan for man is revealed in the term *age* or *ages*. The following New Testament usages of the word reveal this clearly.

Jesus spoke of *"this age* and *the age to come"* (Matthew 12:32). He also spoke of "the end of this age." (Matthew 13:39, 40, 49; 24:3; Mark 10:30).

God revealed through the epistles many different *ages* in the history of His dealings with man. For instance, He speaks of *"ages past"* (note the plurals) in Romans 16:25, Colossians 1:26, and Titus 1:2. He speaks of *"the present evil age"* in Galatians 1:3. Again, He speaks of *"the ends of the ages"* in 1 Corinthians 10:11, and *"the consummation of the ages"* in Hebrews 9:26. In 1 Timothy 1:17, God is called the *"King of the ages."*

A very important element is added to the concept of successive ages in God's plan in Ephesians 3:9–11. It is a complex context, but the main point to this discussion is in Verse 9, "and to bring to light what is the **administration** of the **mystery which for ages** has been hidden in God, who created all things . . ."

Several observations should be made of this statement. First, the context indicates that the Church is a mystery which has been hidden in God from all ages past. Romans 16:25 indicates the same truth.

Second, Paul is now "bringing to light" the *administration* of this mystery in the present age. The word *age* as it is used here is defined as "a period of time in history or in the development of man." In the context this idea is connected with the term *administration* which is *oikonomia* in the original Greek. This term is translated "dispensation" in the King James Version. This is the word that gave the system of interpretation its name. The root meaning of *oikonomia* is "to manage a household."[1] It means "to arrange, order, plan and administrate a household."[2] As the word is used in this context where it is linked with the term *age*, it means that God has planned, ordered, arranged, and administered cer-

---

[1] F. W. Gingrich and Frederick Danker, *A Greek-English Lexicon of the New Testament* (Grand Rapids, Mich.: Zondervan Pub. Co., 1979), p. 559.

[2] Ibid.

tain purposes within the sphere of definable periods of history. The *two* terms together (i.e., administration and ages) define the world as a household that is being administered by God in growing stages of Divine revelation.

It is important to add that the closest English equivalent to the Greek word *oikonomia* is *economy*. Webster's Unabridged Dictionary shows *oikonomia* as the root of *economy* and defines it as "an art of managing a household; the management of the affairs of a group, community, or establishment with a view to insuring its maintenance or productiveness; God's plan or system for the governing of the world,"[3] so, it is in this last sense that I am using the term *economy* and its synonyms, *administration* and *dispensation*.

Third, Verses 10 and 11 reveal that "God is teaching the angels His manifold wisdom through the mystery, the body of Christ, and that it is in accordance with the purpose of the ages (literal), which is made possible through Jesus our Lord." The main point here is that the *ages* are declared to have a definite Divine purpose.

Taken literally, the Bible reveals that history from God's viewpoint has progressed through a number of ages in which there have been different revelations of God's will. For as we have seen, the Bible not only speaks of "this present *age*," but of "*ages* past and of *ages* future."

Inseparably linked with this is the revelation of God's arrangement, purpose and design within the ages via the term "administration" in the New American Standard Bible.

One of the most important verses concerning God's involvement with the ages is found in Hebrews 1:2, which literally says in the original, ". . . through whom

[3]Webster's Third New International Dictionary of the English Language Unabridged (Chicago: Encyclopedia Britannica, Inc., 1981).

also He *blueprinted* the ages." This unique declaration reveals that Jesus actually planned and designed the various stages into which man's history would flow before time and space were set into operation.

Explosive Emotion versus Reason

I realize that the subject of dispensationalism is an explosive one. A whole book could be written on this important matter which I am trying to summarize in one chapter. And on this point, I urge every serious Bible student to read Dr. Ryrie's excellent book, *Dispensationalism Today.*[4]

Whatever your theological viewpoint, you have to come to grips with the *two recurrent concepts:* the economies and the ages. Apart from these concepts, the Bible cannot be understood as a consistent and cohesive whole. The only other alternative is to allegorize large portions of Scripture, which were clearly intended to be taken as normal statements of fact, in order to keep the Bible from contradicting itself.

The theological system that most adheres to a consistent, literal, grammatical and historical interpretation of the Bible is dispensationalism.

WHAT IS DISPENSATIONALISM?

No better definition of dispensationalism can be found than that of Dr. Ryrie, "A concise definition of dispensation is this: a dispensation is a distinguishable economy in the outworking of God's purpose. If one were describing a dispensation he would include other things, such as the idea of distinctive revelation, testing, failure, and judgment. But we are seeking a definition, not a description.

[4]Charles C. Ryrie, *Dispensationalism Today* (Chicago: Moody Press, 1965).

"In using the word *economy* as the core of the definition, the emphasis is put on the Biblical meaning of the word itself (i.e., *oikonomia*). Economy also suggests the fact that certain features of different dispensations might be the same or similar. Differing political and economic economies are not completely different, yet they are distinguishably different. Communistic and capitalistic economies are basically different, and yet there are functions, features and items in these economies that are the same."[5]

Each one of the various dispensations or economies that are distinguishable in the Bible begins with a new revelation from God to man. The new revelation contains both responsibilities of how man is to relate to God, and promises which enable man to perform them.

There is then a period of testing in the new revelations. Each economy reveals human failure to both appropriate the blessings and to obey the revealed responsibilities.

Each economy ends with a distinct Divine Judgment upon man for his failure and then a new economy is introduced.

The German scholar, Erich Sauer, adds a very important observation about the succession of the various Biblical economies, "The Holy Scripture is plainly not a spiritual-divine-uniform 'block,' but a wonderful articulated historic-prophetic *organism*. It must be read organically, age-wise, according to the Divine ages.

"Thus a new period always begins only when *from the side of God* a change is introduced in the composition of the principles valid up to that time; that is when from the side of God three things occur:

"1. A continuance of certain ordinances valid until then;

[5]Ryrie, ibid. pp. 29–30.

"2. An annulment of other regulations until then valid;

"3. A fresh introduction of new principles not before valid.

"Thus with the introduction of the present period of salvation there *remains* the general moral principles ruling the realm of the earlier period (Romans 8:4; 13:8–10), even though in a completely new spirit; for the Law is a unity (James 2:10), and as such is wholly abolished."[6]

The main points that should be emphasized from Sauer's statement are that the Bible is an organic, cohesive progress of living revelation that cannot be mechanically put into a philosophical strait-jacket. But it falls into various Divinely initiated stages of history in which certain ordinances of past ages continue, certain regulations of the past are eradicated, and certain new principles are revealed and set up as the new governing force of living for God.

I wish to make it clear, however, that even though there are distinguishable economies, there has always been only one way of salvation presented by God for man. Man has always had to approach God and be forgiven and accepted by Him on the basis of faith alone. In other words, salvation always has been and always will be received by man on the basis of faith alone.

The way that a redeemed man is to live for God has changed in the various dispensations. But the way of salvation has not.

What are the Dispensations or Economies?—God's Time-Line

One of the best ways to explain further the principle of Biblical economies is to show what they are. Now it

[6]Erich Sauer, *The Dawn of World Redemption* (Grand Rapids, Mich.: Wm. B. Eerdmans Publishing Co., 1951), pp. 193–194.

really isn't of utmost importance exactly how many there are. Nor is it fatal to the validity of the system that the various economies are called different names by different people.

The important thing is that they be distinguished and recognized. Even the avowed enemies of dispensational interpretation have to make distinctions between the way God deals with mankind in the dispensation of the law, the Church and the coming Messianic kingdom.

The following list of Biblical economies is generally agreed upon by all dispensationalists. The chart at the end of this chapter will also aid greatly in seeing these things in perspective.

I. THE DISPENSATION OF FREEDOM OR INNOCENCE

God created Adam in a state of holiness which was compatible with His own character. But Adam had, as part of the image of God created in him, freedom of choice. It was through this attribute that the possibility of sin existed.

Some have said, "If God created man with the potential for sinning, then God is responsible for the failure." But what were the choices? God could have created man without freedom of choice and thus have had a robot. Man would not have been able to respond to God's love, nor could there have been fellowship. For one must be able to choose not to love in order to be able to love.

The only other possibility was for God to take a calculated risk and create a creature in His own image. That image gave man intellect by which he could understand God; emotion with which he could respond with feeling and passion; and volition or freedom of choice with which he could act upon his understanding and emotions. The other two facets of God's image in man are moral reason or conscience and everlasting existence of his immaterial being, called the soul.

God took the calculated risk and created man in His own image, as defined above, in order that man could respond to Him in true love and fellowship.

The Angelic Factor

There is one other factor that is somewhat shrouded in the mist of eternity past which has to do with why man was created and why history is organized the way that it is. The Bible reveals that the angels are vitally concerned with how man responds to God. We know that the highest being created was an archangel named Lucifer who through pride and a desire to be equal with God rebelled against God and led a revolt among the angelic creation (Ezekiel 28:11–17; Isaiah 14:12–15).

We know that Lucifer, who became known as Satan and the Devil, was instrumental in causing Adam and Eve to believe a lie about God's character, to reject the relationship they had with Him, to lose their unproven holiness, and to lose the most basic part of their being, called spiritual life. It was only through this spiritual nature that man could know God on a personal basis and understand Divine revelation (Genesis 3; John 3:1–18).

We know that all through the successive Biblical ages Satan and his angels (called demons) have relentlessly sought to prevent humans from understanding and accepting God's provision of forgiveness, and to neutralize and destroy those who do receive it (John 8:42–47; 2 Corinthians 4:3–4; Ephesians 6:10–18; 1 Peter 5:8).

We know that the angels who remained faithful to God rejoice over one fallen human being who comes to repentance and believes in God's salvation (Luke

15:7–10). We also know that the angels are learning about God's manifold wisdom by the way He is dealing with mankind through the Church (Ephesians 3:10–11). We also know that the angels stare intently at the way God's grace is being poured out upon the world through the Holy Spirit (1 Peter 1:12).

As I surmised in a much fuller way in my book, *Satan Is Alive and Well on Planet Earth*,[7] man was created in large measure for the purpose of resolving the angelic conflict. Apparently, God allowed Lucifer and his rebel angels time to repent. But after a period of grace, God brought judgment against Satan and his angels and sentenced them to eternal separation from God under a perpetual punishment. At that point Satan must have called God unjust and unloving.

Although God was under no obligation to do so, He chose to demonstrate to His angels His perfect justice and unfathomable love by means of a vastly inferior creature called man. The crowning of grace is that God is going to elevate redeemed and glorified man not only to replace the *angels* who were banished with Satan, but He is going to make him ruler over the whole angelic realm (1 Corinthians 6:3).

How God Answered a Dilemma

When the first human parents fell, God instituted a plan of redemption that demonstrates to the whole universe the perfection of His character.

God demonstrates His justice in that even though He loved man, He did not compromise that justice by simply sweeping the rebellion of Adam and Eve under the rug. Instead, God demonstrated His wisdom by devising a way for a uniquely qualified substitute (Jesus) to

[7]Hal Lindsey, *Satan Is Alive and Well on Planet Earth* (New York: Bantam Books, 1972).

fully pay our debt to His violated law and thus provide a free pardon.

God demonstrated His perfect love by coming into the world, becoming a man, living a selfless and sinless life, so that He could qualify to take upon Himself the full measure of His own wrath against sin on behalf of every human being.

All of this was done in order that rebellious man might receive a full pardon and eternal life by simply believing that the Lord Jesus died in his place.

At the final judgment, this great act of salvation will silence all of God's accusers and cause all to bow and acknowledge that they deserve their punishment.

So in the first dispensation man was free to do anything he chose, except that he was to tend the garden and not eat from one specific tree that God put off limits.

When man failed, innocence and freedom from sin was lost. The immediate judgment was loss of the relationship with God, the loss of spiritual life. Nature was cursed so that it would be very difficult to provide a living. Man was cast from the paradise garden, woman was placed under man's authority and childbearing became much more difficult.

II. THE DISPENSATION OF CONSCIENCE OR SELF-DETERMINATION

At the end of the previous economy, even in the midst of judgment upon man's failure, God introduced the way of forgiveness. Adam and Eve experienced a basic change in their being. They were still physically alive; but as God had warned, they had died spiritually the moment they decided to reject God's one commandment.

There was an immediate experience of guilt which was

evidenced by their becoming uncomfortable with being naked. They immediately tried to cover their sense of guilt with the work of their own hands. This was the first act of religion, for religion is man's attempt to cover his sin by his own works.

God graciously showed man the only acceptable way to cover his sin. God killed an animal and from its skin made coverings for their guilt. This, in very simple form, taught man that the consequence of his sin was the death of an innocent substitute of God's choosing. And from the substitutionary sacrifice God provided a covering for the effect of their sin. All they could do was receive it and throw away their own religious handiwork. This was the Gospel in childlike simplicity.

In this economy man was to recognize his need of forgiveness as well as understand how he was to live for God by the witness of his conscience. Man had conscience from the beginning, but now there was a great need for daily moral choices. Conscience now became the principal way God governed over mankind during this dispensation.

Man was responsible to respond to God through the inner promptings of his conscience. But man soon discovered the age-old art of rationalization. He soon made black white, white black and everything some shade of gray.

Finally, God evaluated the world of that day as follows: "Then the Lord saw that the wickedness of man was great on the earth, and that every intent of the thoughts of his heart was only evil continually." (Genesis 6:5)

God destroyed all mankind with the exception of eight persons who walked with Him, and believed in His provision of forgiveness.

The judgment that distinctly ended this period was a

worldwide flood. Man had failed another period of testing.

III. THE DISPENSATION OF CIVIL GOVERNMENT

Noah was the patriarch of the world after the flood. The new revelation to govern this period included making the animals fearful of man. Man became an eater of meat as well as grains. A promise was given that there would be no more world floods. And man was given the ultimate authority for human government—capital punishment.

This ultimate authority endowed human government with all lesser authority necessary for governing the world. Human civil government became the Divine means of maintaining order. It also included the way of preserving and proclaiming the message of salvation and the way to walk with God.

Man's inability to govern properly became apparent early in this economy. Noah displayed moral weakness by getting stone drunk and improperly guiding his own family.

Instead of dispersing and subduing the earth as God had commanded, the people banded together in one place. Soon, the first world dictator arose (Nimrod, Genesis 10:8–12; 11:1–9) and then led all the inhabited earth into the first system of false religion. This new religion was based on astrology and the worship of the stars.

The people built a tower at Babel (which later became the site of Babylon). This tower was an observatory for studying the stars, and was a symbol of unity. It was totally devoted to astrology. More importantly, it was also the symbol of man's rejection of God and His truth.

Man used civil government as a unifying system to bring all people into a false religion and to stamp out the truth about God. Once again unregenerate man failed by taking the very vehicle that was to lead him to God and using it to blind himself to the truth.

God knew that any form of one world government made it too easy for Satan to slip in a dictator who could then lead all mankind away from the truth.

The judgment that ended this economy was the sudden confusion of languages. This forced man to scatter and form nations. Soon afterward the nations began to deliberately erase the knowledge of God from their memory.

A Special Note

In the history covered by the first three economies, issues are not as precisely distinguished in the Scripture as they are in the following economies. There just wasn't very much written about those early periods. Several thousand years of man's relationship with God is covered in the first eleven chapters of Genesis.

I want to carefully note that this is not the case with the following economies The Scriptures from Genesis 12 to Acts 2 are specifically addressed to the special people created from one Divinely chosen man named Abraham. This portion of the Bible of course has *application* to all believers of all ages, but by strict *interpretation*, it was addressed specifically to the physical descendents of Abraham, Isaac and Jacob under two economies.

So the following dispensations that are noted are very clearly distinguishable. There is clear Scriptural differentiation of the principles that prevail in each one of the successive economies.

IV. THE DISPENSATION OF ISRAEL UNDER PROMISE

This economy is characterized by a *people* and a *promise*. The term *promise* comes from the unconditional covenants that God made with an Assyrian man named Abram whom God renamed Abraham.

God's *reason* for introducing this new economy is clear. All nations were deliberately pushing the knowledge of God and the way of salvation out of their minds. Romans 1:18–32 is certainly an applicable description of the course all nations took in that era.

So in order that the truth about God might be preserved upon earth, and the way of salvation for all mankind might not only be kept but developed, God elected to create a special nation through which all these things would be accomplished.

A Promise is a Promise

God created this nation with a series of *promises*. God bound Himself with an oath to keep each promise. The following is a catalogue of the promises, which are also called covenants:

(1) *The Promise of a Nation:* "I will make you a great nation . . ." (Genesis 12:2a)

(2) *The Promise of Preservation of Abraham and His Descendents:* "I will bless those who bless you, and the one who curses you I will curse . . ." (Genesis 12:3a)

(3) *The Promise of World Blessing Through Abraham's Seed:* "And in you all the families of the earth shall be blessed . . ." (Genesis 12:3b)

(4) *The Promises of a Specific Land:* Genesis 13:14–17; 15:18–21

These promises were confirmed to both Isaac (Genesis 26:2–4) and to Jacob (Genesis 28:13–14). Ryrie gives an excellent analysis of the general character of this economy, "The responsibility of the patriarchs was simply to believe and serve God, and God gave them every material and spiritual provision to encourage them to do this. The promised land was theirs and blessing was theirs as long as they remained in the land. But of course there was failure soon and often."[8]

The Scripture that specifically deals with this economy is Genesis 11:10–Exodus 18:27. Some have questioned whether there truly are two dispensations distinguishable in God's dealings with Israel, since the *promise* and the *law* were both given to the same people.

I believe the two dispensations are sharply distinguished in Galatians 3 in spite of the statement that the Mosaic law did not annul the promise that was previously given. The distinction between the dispensation of promise and the dispensation of law fits every principle of definition given in the early part of this chapter.

Paul summarizes the failure of the people under the promise, "Why the law then? It was added because of transgressions . . ." (Galatians 3:19). The people failed to live by faith in the promises that God had given them so He placed them under specific laws. (For God's summary of Israel's failure to believe His promises see Numbers 14:11, 22, 23.)

V. THE DISPENSATION OF ISRAEL UNDER LAW

This economy began with dramatic and frightening manifestations of God at Mount Sinai. God reviewed how He had graciously delivered them under the conditions of promise, "You yourselves have seen what I did

[8]Ryrie, op. cit. pp. 60–61.

to the Egyptians, and how I bore you on eagles' wings, and brought you to Myself." (Exodus 19:4)

Then God offered the Israelites the law, "Now then if you will indeed obey My voice and keep My covenant, then you shall be My own possession among all the peoples, for all the earth is Mine . . ." (Exodus 19:5). I believe, with many other theologians, that had the Israelites refused this offer of a law relationship, and instead asked to remain under the gracious economy of promise which depended upon God answering faith, that the Lord would not have forced the change.

But instead the people reacted with human pride and said, "*All* that the Lord has spoken we will do!" (Exodus 19:8). This confirmed the unbelieving heart which God saw and which caused the Lord to introduce the economy of law. The law was given to make man see how utterly incapable he is to live up to God's standards by human effort. This is revealed in the following verses:

> "And the law came in (for the purpose) that the transgression might **increase** . . ." (Romans 5:20)

> "Therefore did that which is good become a cause of death for me? May it never be! Rather it was sin, in order that it might be shown to be sin by effecting my death through that which is good, that through the commandment sin might become utterly sinful." (Romans 7:13)

The law was given to make sin *increase*, not decrease, because man is inherently blind to the sinful nature with which he is born. The law provokes this nature into life so that it becomes very exposed. The more *we try* to keep God's law, the more the sinful nature rebels. So man has to admit that he is inherently so sinful that he must look by faith to the Messiah Jesus to save him, and to the Holy Spirit to enable him to live pleasingly for God.

God spoke to Moses about Israel's chances of living successfully under the law at the beginning, "Oh that they (the Israelites) had such a heart in them, that they would fear Me, and keep all My commandments always, that it might be well with them and with their sons forever!" (Deuteronomy 5:29)

It is obvious that the law was not God's preferred way to deal with man, but rather was a necessary historical lesson in the development of man's understanding of his total helplessness to establish a relationship with God by his own efforts.

God clearly anticipated Israel's failure under law when He predicted, through Jeremiah in the 7th Century B.C., "'Behold, days are coming,' declares the Lord, 'when I will make a new covenant with the house of Israel and with the house of Judah, not like the covenant which I made with their fathers in the day I took them by the hand to bring them out of the land of Egypt, My covenant which they broke, although I was a husband to them' declares the Lord." In the rest of the statement, the Lord says that He will bring in three uniquely new factors: (1) "I will put My laws within them, and on their heart I will write it." (2) "All shall know Me, from the least of them to the greatest of them." (3) "I will forgive their iniquity, and their sin I will remember no more." (Jeremiah 31:31–34)

Israel's utter failure to live under law is meant to be an historical lesson for all mankind. The law was never meant to be a way of salvation, but rather to show us how good we would have to be if we were going to help God save us. This is clearly stated in Romans 9:30–10:4. Once again, the only way of salvation in every dispensation has been by faith in God's provision.

The interruption of this dispensation was predicted by the Lord Jesus, "O Jerusalem, Jerusalem, who kills the prophets and stones those who are sent to her! How often I wanted to gather your children together, the way a hen gathers her chicks under her wings, and you were unwilling. Behold, your house is being left to you desolate! For I say to you, from now on you shall not see Me until you say, '*Blessed is He who comes in the name of the Lord.*'" (Matthew 23:39) This economy was in focus from Exodus 19 to Acts 1:26.

The rejection of the often promised and long awaited Messiah caused God to set Israel aside and to *temporarily* suspend this economy. I say *temporarily suspend* because according to the previously mentioned prophecy of Daniel 9:24–27, Israel still has allotted to her seven years to complete the six Divinely given responsibilities named in Daniel 9:24. These are to be fulfilled under the same conditions that prevailed in the dispensation in which the first 483 years were acted out (or 69 weeks of years), namely the law of Moses.

This seven-year period, called the Tribulation by theologians, is actually the completion of the economy of law.

VI. THE DISPENSATION OF GRACE

This dispensation was actually a mystery in the ages of the Old Testament. It had to be, or there simply could not have been a bona fide offer of the promised Messianic kingdom to the Israelites.

One dispensational teacher calls this economy "the great parenthesis." Not because it is an afterthought of God, but because it was of necessity a Divinely-kept secret (Ephesians 3:9). No Israelite would have taken Jesus' offer of an imminent kingdom seriously if an alternate plan had already been revealed and understood in the Old Testament. This would have already concluded their failure.

A Clear Distinction

Of all the various dispensations, the most clearly revealed differences are between the economy of law and of grace.

One of the most important features of the new *modus operandi* for living under grace is the personal ministry of the Holy Spirit in and to every believer in Jesus Christ.

Since the fall of man, all the redeemed have experienced a spiritual birth when they believed. But the new ministries listed below are absolutely unique to the economy of grace. They all happen once for all at the moment of salvation.

There is the *baptism* of the Holy Spirit which joins each believer into a living union with Christ. This union is the most basic and essential meaning of the Church. The Church is the body of Christ composed of all believers. And we can only enter that body through the baptism of the Spirit (1 Corinthians 12:12–14). This first occurred in Acts 2 according to Peter in Acts 11:15–18.

There is also the *indwelling* of the Holy Spirit. The Spirit takes up permanent residence in each believer at the moment of salvation (John 14:16, 17; 1 Corinthians 6:19–20; Romans 8:11).

There is also the *sealing* of the Holy Spirit. The *presence* of the Spirit in the believer is God's *seal* or *guarantee* that we are His purchased possession and that He will certainly bring us into a glorified eternal state in His presence (Ephesians 1:13, 14; 4:30; 2 Corinthians 1:22).

There are also *gifts* of the Holy Spirit. Each believer receives at least one or more spiritual abilities (gifts) with which to accomplish God's will for his life (1 Peter 4:10–11; 1 Corinthians 12:1–33). The gifts are permanent (Romans 11:29).

Of these new ministries of the Spirit, only one is not received once and for all at the time of salvation. It is called the *filling* of the Spirit. It is a moment-by-moment ministry which must be continually appropriated by a submissive will and an aggressive faith. This is that ministry which enables the believer to effectively live for and serve God (Romans 8:1–4; Galatians 3:1–5; 5:16–18; Ephesians 5:18).

It is these new ministries of the Spirit that made it possible to remove the law principle and establish the grace principle. All of this was not possible until Jesus the Messiah completed His redemptive work at the cross. Because He satisfied all of the demands of the law against us and then paid its ultimate penalty of death in our place, God can now remove us completely from under the law's demands. The Holy Spirit under grace now works the righteousness of the law through the trusting believer (Romans 8:4).

In the economy of grace God no longer is working in a special way only with Israel. But now all nations, Jew and Gentile, are joined into a unique heavenly people called the Church. In the Church there is no national, racial or sexual distinction. All are one in Christ.

The Apostate Church

Even with such a heaven-high privilege the Bible predicts that the Church will fail, and all but a believing remnant will fall away from the faith (1 Timothy 4:1–4). Organized Christendom will have an outward facade of godliness, but will deny its power (2 Timothy 3:1–10).

Peter predicts that false teachers, masquerading as ministers of Christ, will infiltrate and take over the institutional church and teach destructive heresies. They will malign and nullify the truth which is the Bible (2 Peter 2:1–2). They will especially deny the prophetic Scripture and its claim of the Lord's return (2 Peter 3:1–7). Not to digress too much, I can testify that these prophecies have been fulfilled before my eyes and in my hearing.

How the Church Ends

This dispensation began in a unique way, and it will end in a unique way. It began with the advent of the Holy Spirit. It will end with evacuation. The Lord Himself will evacuate the Church so that the final seven years allotted to Israel under the law in Daniel's prophecy can be fulfilled.

Much more will be said in the next chapter about this very important aspect of prophecy. But it is very important to stress again that since the Church in the economy of grace was necessarily a mystery, hidden in God, from all economies past, it must be completely removed before God can finish dealing with Israel as a distinct program.

And since the focus of God is once again upon the Jew as a Jew in the seven final years of dealing with Israel (called "the Tribulation" or "the time of Jacob's trouble" in Jeremiah 30:7), the Church cannot be present. Otherwise the conditions that prevail during the time of the Church (i.e., there is no difference between a Gentile and a Jew) would make such an arrangement impossible.

VII. THE DISPENSATION OF THE MILLENNIUM

The second coming of Christ to the earth ends "the time of Jacob's distress" and ushers in the Millennial Kingdom promised to Abraham, Isaac and Jacob's descendents.

There will be an outpouring of the Holy Spirit upon all believers. Only believers will enter this kingdom. Satan will be bound for a thousand years. Jesus the Messiah will rule over the whole earth and set the atmosphere of the world system with righteousness. With all these blessings man will be expected to live out the standards of the King Messiah as described in the Sermon on the Mount of Matthew 5–7.

The curse of nature will be removed and man will have a perfect environment once more (Isaiah 11; 65:17–25; Amos 9:8–15; Micah 4:1–8; Zechariah 14:16–21).

But even with this kind of privilege some of the children of those who start the kingdom will not believe in the Lord Jesus as Savior. Evidence of unbelieving offspring shows up early in the Millennium (Zechariah 14:17–19, and so on). So at the end, God will release Satan to bring out into the open the rebellion that He sees in their hearts. Satan will quickly raise up an army of unbelievers. But God will judge them quickly and directly (Revelation 20:7–10).

At this point, time ends. All mortal believers will be translated into immortality. All unbelievers from all economies will be raised to stand before the Great White Throne for eternal condemnation.

A clear philosophy of history from God's viewpoint emerges out of these economies. Man is tested under all kinds of conditions throughout the dispensations. The first dispensation begins with a perfect environment and the last one ends with a perfect environment. Man fails in all environments, which demonstrates that environment is *not* the problem. (Thus God's viewpoint is totally the antithesis of communism, modern psychology and many other human philosophies.)

The dispensations show that the only answer is to be born again by faith so that man is changed from within. Then he masters the environment about him by God's enablement through faith.

SUMMING UP

Without an understanding and recognition of these various economies it is virtually impossible to interpret and harmonize the various stages of progressive revelation, and the distinguishable responsibilities under which man has been tested before God.

In the next chapter I will discuss more specifically how the differences between the dispensation of the Law and the dispensation of the Church bear upon the Rapture debate.

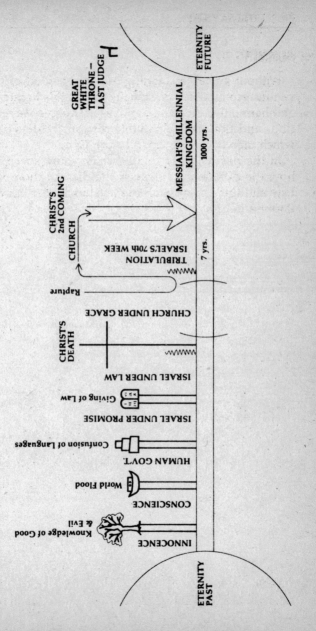

GOD'S OUTLINE OF HISTORY OR DISPENSATIONS

ETERNITY PAST

INNOCENCE

Knowledge of Good & Evil

CONSCIENCE

World Flood

HUMAN GOVT.

Confusion of Languages

ISRAEL UNDER PROMISE

Giving of Law

ISRAEL UNDER LAW

CHRIST'S DEATH

CHURCH UNDER GRACE

Rapture

CHURCH

TRIBULATION
ISRAEL'S 70th WEEK

7 yrs.

CHRIST'S 2nd COMING

MESSIAH'S MILLENNIAL KINGDOM

1000 yrs.

GREAT WHITE THRONE – LAST JUDGE

ETERNITY FUTURE

FIVE

THE GREAT HISTORICAL PARENTHESIS

One of the central questions in settling just when the Rapture occurs is whether Israel and the Church are truly distinctive and separate works of God.

In fact, Walvoord points out this critical issue when he says, "It is not too much to say that the rapture question is determined more by ecclesiology than eschatology."[1] To translate this, it means that the doctrines concerning the Church bear more on the Rapture question than the doctrines of prophecy.

Ryrie expresses a similar conviction, "Actually the question boils down to whether or not the Church is a distinct entity in the program of God. Those who emphasize the distinctiveness of the Church will be pre-Tribulationists, and those who deemphasize it will usually be post-Tribulationists."[2]

[1] John F. Walvoord, *The Rapture Question* (Findlay, Ohio: Dunham Pub. Co., 1956), p. 16.

[2] Charles C. Ryrie, *What You Should Know About The Rapture* (Chicago: Moody Press, 1981), p. 62.

I believe with these men that the question of just when the Rapture occurs in relation to the Tribulation depends to a large degree on how unique and distinct God's program for the Church is from His program for the nation of Israel.

In fact, I believe that God's purpose for Israel and His purpose for the Church are so distinct and mutually exclusive that they cannot both be on earth at the same time during the seven-year Tribulation.

If this is so, then the Church must be removed before God can deal specifically again with Israel as defined in Daniel's prophecy (Daniel 9:24–27), because today there is no such thing as a Jew remaining a Jew in the Old Testament sense after believing in Jesus as Messiah. The apostle Paul makes this very clear when he says of the believer today, "For there is no distinction between Jew and Greek; for the same Lord is Lord of all, abounding in riches for all who call upon Him." (Romans 10:12) And again Paul says, "For *all* of you who were baptized into Christ have clothed yourselves with Christ. There is neither Jew nor Greek, there is neither slave nor free man, there is neither male nor female; for you are all one in Christ [Messiah] Jesus." (Galatians 3:27–28)

From the call of Abraham until the birth of the Church, God divided the human race into two categories: Jews and Gentiles. From the birth of the Church until today, God has three categories: nonbelieving Jews, nonbelieving Gentiles and the Church. This is clear throughout the New Testament epistles which were expressly written to the Church. But the following verse makes this concisely clear, "Give no offense either to Jews or to Greeks or to the church of God . . ." (1 Corinthians 10:32).

In this present economy of God's dealing with man, there are unbelieving Jews, and there are unbelieving

Gentiles. But the believer from either category becomes known as "the church of God" at the moment of salvation.

The Scriptures from both the Old and the New Testament that apply to the Tribulation period deal with the believing Jew as a Jew and the believing Gentile as a Gentile. Even the great judgments the Messiah executes upon the survivors at the end of the Tribulation are segregated. The Gentile is judged in Matthew 25:31–46, and the Jew in Ezekiel 20:34–44. The conditions are the same as they were in the economy of Israel under law.

WHAT IS THE CHURCH?

It is very difficult to discuss the Church today because the mere mention of the word conjures up all kinds of erroneous definitions as well as various emotions.

To most the Church is the building where the Christians meet. To others it is the organizations that make up the various denominations.

I'll never forget my first lesson on the Church that I heard as a young believer. An elderly lady sitting in a Bible class I was attending in Houston interrupted the teacher and said, "Pastor, there are young people in here desecrating the church sanctuary by chewing gum." The pastor, Robert Theime, who has a knack for shocking statements, fired back, "Lady, the sanctuaries are chewing the gum."

That's probably the best lesson I've ever received on ecclesiology, because I still remember it over twenty-five years later. The thrust of the statement, though humorous, is profound. For the Church is not a building nor an organization. It is first and foremost a living organism called the body of Christ (Ephesians 1:22–23; Colossians

1:24). This body is made up of every true believer, Jew or Gentile, mystically joined in a living union with Jesus Christ Himself and with each other (1 Corinthians 12:12–28; Galatians 3:27–28).

The average professing Christian today has no understanding of this truth, and yet it is the central teaching of the New Testament. I believe that this confusion is caused by ministers who act as if the goal of the ministry is to acquire real estate and build buildings which they erroneously call churches. Sometimes in the process they drive people away from the Gospel with high-pressure fundraising programs to pay for these often unnecessarily large and palatial edifices.

Paul addressed churches that met in houses, but he never called the houses churches. (See Romans 16:5 and Philemon 2 for example.)

This concept of the Church being the body of Christ is not just an illustration, but an actual organic reality. This is made wonderfully clear in an extreme case with which Paul had to deal in Corinth.

Some of the Corinthian believers had obviously got out of fellowship (not out of relationship) with God and slipped back into their old religious ways. I have stood among the ruins of ancient Corinth and looked up the mountain to the ancient temple of Aphrodite, the goddess of love, that dominates the skyline of the old city. Part of their old worship at that temple involved having intercourse with the temple priestess-prostitutes.

It is extremely important to observe carefully how God deals with this problem among these true believers who were walking according to the flesh at this point. Listen to what God said,

> "Do you not know that your bodies are members of Christ? Shall I then take away the members of Christ and make them members of a harlot? May it never be!

"Or do you not know that the one who joins himself to a harlot is one body with her? For He says, 'The two will become one flesh.'

"But the one who joins himself to the Lord is one spirit with Him.

"Flee immorality. Every other sin that a man commits is outside the body, but the immoral man sins against his own body.

"Or do you not know that your body is a temple of the Holy Spirit who is in you, whom you have from God, and that you are not your own?

"For you have been bought with a price: therefore glorify God in your body." (1 Corinthians 6:15–20)

In the first place note that God doesn't question their salvation, but rather affirms that they are members of Christ's body.

Second, note that the whole basis of God's command for them to stop immediately their immoral behavior is: (1) "Do you not know that your bodies are members of Christ?" (2) "Do you not know that your body is a temple of the Holy Spirit who is in you, whom you have from God, and that you are not your own?"

Third, and most important, God says that when they have sexual relations with a prostitute, they are actually making the members of Christ to be members of a prostitute (1 Corinthians 6:15–16). There is only one possible way to understand the above statement. It is saying that the Christians are, in the first place, actually joined into an organic union with Christ, so that Christ is involved in whatever our bodies do (see Ephesians 5:30, KJV).

In the second place, it is saying that whenever we have sexual relations with someone, we become one flesh with that person, thus we join Christ to them. So-bering thought, isn't it?

A Very Special Word

God inspired the New Testament writers to take a common Greek word, *ekklesia*, and refine it into a highly technical and special meaning.

In its Greek usage outside of the Bible, *ekklesia* simply meant "a called out assembly of people." It is used in this sense in the ancient Greek translation of the Hebrew Old Testament, called the Septuagint.

The Lord Jesus Christ was the first to use the term *ekklesia* in its new sense when He said, "And I also say to you that you are Peter, and upon this rock I will build my church; and the gates of Hades shall not overpower it." (Matthew 16:18)

Jesus chose a very special moment to unveil "His church." Up until this moment, the word *ekklesia* had never been used in this special sense. The occasion was Peter's public confession of Jesus as "the Messiah, the Son of the living God." Peter was the first of the disciples to do this. (In the original Greek it is clear that the foundation of the church is not Peter because the word "Peter" ([Petros, masculine]) does not agree with the word "rock" ([petra, neuter]) in gender as an antecedent must do.) It is this confession of faith in Jesus that enters a person into the one true Church, the body of Christ.

This was a private revelation to Jesus' disciples. It also was a prophecy because He said, "*I will build* my church . . ." The Church couldn't be built at this point because Israel had not made its final rejection of Jesus as Messiah, and the means of forming the Church was not yet given.

The *One* Who Builds the Church

Since The Church is the body of Christ, composed of a living union of all true Christians with Christ Himself, the Church could not begin to be built until the arrival of the One who had the power to effect this miraculous union. The Bible calls that person the Holy Spirit.

Jesus predicted the coming of the Holy Spirit to inaugurate His new ministries for this dispensation, "I will ask the Father, and He will give you another Helper, that He may be with you forever; that is the Spirit of truth, whom the world cannot receive, because it does not behold Him or know Him, *but* you know Him because He abides with you, *and will be in you* . . . In that day you shall know that I am in My Father, and *you in Me, and I in you.*" (John 14:16, 17, 20)

The final seven sublime words that I have emphasized describe the essence of what the true Church is in its universal sense. *"You in Me"* describes the union of each believer with Christ Himself. Paul later described it, "For we are members of His body, of His flesh and of His bones . . . This is a great mystery, but I speak concerning Christ and the church." (Ephesians 5:30, 32, NKJV)

"And I in you" describes the permanent residence which Christ takes inside the believer at the moment of salvation. Paul later said, ". . . *that is,* the mystery which has been hidden from *past* ages and generations; but has now been manifested to His saints, to whom God willed to make known what is the riches of the glory of this mystery among the Gentiles, which is *Christ in you,* the hope of glory." (Colossians 1:26, 27)

The mystery of our union with Christ and His dwelling in us are the foundation of the true Church. For this reason, they could not have been revealed before it was obvious that Israel had rejected the Messianic claims of Jesus.

The Holy Spirit's ministry which miraculously forms the Church is defined as follows: "For even as the *body* is one *yet* has many members, and all the members of the body, though they are many, are one body, so also is

Christ." [This beautifully describes the Church universal.] "For by *one spirit* we were all *baptized* into *one body,* whether Jews or Greeks, whether slaves or free, and we were all made to drink of one Spirit." (1 Corinthians 12:12, 13)

It is the *baptism of the Holy Spirit* that forms the Church. This is not water baptism. It is the Spirit of God taking each believer at salvation and immersing him into a living, inseparable union with Christ (Galatians 3:27, 28; Colossians 2:12).

So the Church couldn't begin until the baptism of the Holy Spirit began. John the Baptist predicted that Jesus would instigate this baptism of the Spirit (Matthew 3:11). Jesus predicted that it would begin not many days from His ascension to the Father (Acts 1:5). The apostle Peter reveals that the baptism of the Spirit was first given to the Jewish believers on the day of Pentecost (Acts 11:15–16).

So the Church was born on the day of Pentecost when all of the new ministries of the Spirit that are unique to this dispensation were given.

The book of Acts reveals that God followed a specific order in initially giving the new Spirit ministries. They were first given to the Jewish believers since God previously had a covenant relationship with them (Acts 2).

Then the new ministries were initiated to the Samaritan believers who were part Jewish (Acts 8:14–17).

Next they were initially given to the non-Jews or Gentiles, who had no covenant claim to God at all (Acts 10:1–48 compared with 11:15–18).

After this transition period, the new ministries of the Spirit, for example, baptism, indwelling, sealing, gifting, and filling, were given to every believer *when* he believed. This is set forth in the epistles as the norm for every believer.

What we have been discussing is the Church *universal*.

But there are a number of other shades of meaning given to the term "church" in the New Testament.

The Local Church

The Church is often simply designated by its location. In this sense it refers to the professing believers who meet together regularly in a certain village or city. For example: ". . . the church in Jerusalem" (Acts 8:1); ". . . the church which is at Cenchrea" (Romans 16:1); ". . . the church of God which is at Corinth" (1 Corinthians 1:2).

A great many of these churches met in private homes. Twice the church that met in Prisca and Aquila's home is mentioned (Romans 16:5; 1 Corinthians 16:19). Others were mentioned as follows: "great . . . Nympha and the church that is in her house" (Colossians 4:15); "to Philemon . . . and to the church in your house" (Philemon 2).

Local churches were also described in the plural in terms of geographical regions in which they were founded. Here are a few examples: "And he [Paul] was traveling through Syria and Cilicia, strengthening the churches" (Acts 15:41); ". . . as I directed the churches of Galatia" (1 Corinthians 16:1); "the churches of Asia greet you" (1 Corinthians 16:9); ". . . the churches of Judea which were in Christ" (Galatians 1:22).

The previous references about the Church teach us the following truths:

First, though the Church assembled in various geographical locations, it is viewed as something distinct from both the building and the locale in which it met.

Second, these churches were simply designated by the name of the city, province or region in which they met.

Third, the local church was always considered to be part of the one true universal Church. For instance, it was "the Church of God which is at Corinth," and "the churches of Judea which are in Christ." Though these churches were resident in a specific location, they were viewed as belonging to God and each one directly united with Christ.

Fourth, the New Testament reveals that *not everyone* in the local church is part of the true Church universal, the body of Christ. The apostle John writes to the local churches concerning former members who have abandoned the faith,

> *"They went out from us, but they were not really of us; for if they had been of us, they would have remained with us; but they went out, in order that it might be shown that they all are not of us."* (1 John 2:19)

These are dreadful words which John says, ". . . in order that it might be shown that they **all are not of us.**"

The same apostle records the words of Jesus the Messiah to the seven churches of Revelation Chapters 2 and 3. In these letters, there are several exhortations to unbelieving individuals within those churches who are obviously not truly saved.

The clearest proof of this is the oft repeated promises to "the one who overcomes," Revelation 2 and 3. John defines this statement in his first epistle, "and who is the one who overcomes the world, but he who believes that Jesus is the Son of God . . . Whoever believes that Jesus is the Messiah is born of God . . ." (1 John 5:5 and 1a).

The Visible Church on Earth

The term "church" is also used in the New Testament to mean the totality of professing Christians without reference to locality. Used in this sense, the Church is practically equivalent to the term "Christendom." This usage embraces all the churches and individuals in them that profess to be Christian. It therefore includes true and false churches, believers and unbelievers (Romans 16:16; 1 Corinthians 15:9; Galatians 1:13, and so forth).

The Mystery of Being "in Christ"

One of the exclusive new designations given only to the believer in the economy of grace is a simple prepositional phrase that is repeated some 165 times in the epistles. This prepositional phrase is variously stated as "in Christ," "in Christ Jesus," "in Him," or "in God the Father and the Lord Jesus Christ."

These phrases describe the eternal, inseparable, personal union that each believer has with the Lord Jesus through the baptism of the Spirit. Virtually every benefit of salvation that the heavenly Father bestows upon the believer is transmitted through this union with Christ.

For example, we were given "every spiritual blessing in the heavenly places *in Christ.*" (Ephesians 1:3)

We were given the very "righteousness of God *in Him.*" (2 Corinthians 5:21) Since Jesus Christ is "the righteousness of God," when we are made one with Him, His righteousness becomes ours.

"*In Him* we have redemption through His blood, the forgiveness of our trespasses, according to the riches of His grace." (Ephesians 1:7)

Because of being **in Christ,** His death and resurrection are as much an actual fact for the believer as they are to Jesus Christ Himself. Sin and the law have no more claim on Christ because He has already died under the full penalty of the law. Just so, the same thing is true of the believer because of his total union of life with Christ (Romans 6:3–14). Just as sin has no claim on Christ's new resurrection life, so sin has no claim on the one who is in union with Him. Again, what is true of Christ is true of the believer *in* Him. This is so difficult to believe that only the Holy Spirit can make us understand and receive it.

The Lord says, "Even so *consider* yourselves to be dead to sin [the sin nature], but alive to God *in Christ Jesus.*" (Romans 6:11) If you want your life changed to a whole new sphere of victory, then begin to count as true what God says is true.

In the economy of grace, the Christian way of life is a matter of **becoming** what God **has already** made you in Christ. It simply depends upon learning what God says is true of us because of union with Christ, and then counting it true by faith. And remember, what God says is true about us *is* the most true thing there is about us.

Because of all that has been accomplished for us **in Christ,** God promises flatly, "For sin [the sinful nature] shall not be master over you, for you are not under law, but under grace." (Romans 6:14) In this new economy of grace, we are no longer under obligation to the law principle which could only demand but not enable. But we are under the principle of grace which doesn't demand, but gives new inner desires and enables (Philippians 2:13 and 4:13).

Now What?

You are probably saying, "What's all this got to do with the Rapture question?" Everything! All the unique and unparalleled ministries of the Holy Spirit to every believer make this economy absolutely distinct from all previous economies. These present ministries of the Holy Spirit also make this economy distinct from the conditions that are predicted for the seven-year Tribulation.

Robert Gundry and George Ladd seek to downplay this uniqueness in order to promote their case for a post-Tribulation Rapture.

Is the Church a Mystery?

In his effort to remove the distinction between the Church and Israel, Gundry first attacks the doctrine of the Church being a mystery, "Further, any argument for the exclusiveness (of the church) on such grounds runs up against the fact that the Church *as such* is never designated a mystery."[3]

Gundry's statement really begs the question. As discussed earlier in this chapter, Paul in the Ephesian letter said that the mystery is, ". . . that the Gentiles are fellow-heirs and fellow-members of the *body*, and fellow-partakers of the promise in Christ [the Messiah] Jesus through the Gospel." (Ephesians 3:6) All these mystery truths revolve around and are only possible because of the uniting of Jews and Gentiles into the body of Christ. Since the body of Christ is the Church and vice versa, anything that speaks of the most basic features of the body of Christ is speaking also of the Church. Therefore, the term mystery rightly applies to the Church.

But the real point is that the Church is a *new* program of God in which the Gentiles are made fellow heirs, united in one body with the Jews who believe in Jesus as Messiah. If this new program had been revealed and understood before the Messiah Jesus offered the Jews the promised kingdom and Himself as King-Messiah, it would not have been a bona fide offer. How could they have believed in an offer that assumed their unbelief and already had a known program to replace them?

Gundry levels three arguments against the pre-Tribulationist view of dispensational distinction between Israel and the Church. Gundry says that, "A partial revelation of the present age (that is, the dispensation of the Church under grace) in the Old Testament, a con-

[3]Robert H. Gundry, *The Church and the Tribulation* (Grand Rapids: Zondervan, 1973), p. 14.

nection (not necessarily identification) between Israel and the Church, and a dispensational change involving a transitional period open the door to the presence of the church during the tribulation."[4]

It is important to note at the outset that even if Gundry could prove these three allegations, it wouldn't necessarily put the Church in the Tribulation. But after carefully searching through each argument, I didn't find any evidence to prove that the Church *in its unique sense* as the body of Christ was anywhere revealed in the Old Testament. Only the Holy Spirit could interpret and apply the veiled Old Testament references to future salvation of Gentiles and make them understandable. The Israelite certainly didn't have any Old Testament revelation that would have made him comprehend this present economy of grace and the Church.

The fact remains that all Old Testament prophecies about Gentiles picture them in a subordinate role to the Jew in the Messianic kingdom. There is justification for the old rabbinic teaching of Jewish supremacy in the Millennial Kingdom,

> *"And strangers will stand and pasture your flocks, and foreigners [Gentiles] will be your farmers and your vinedressers. But you will be called the priests of the Lord; you will be spoken of* as *ministers of our God. You will eat the wealth of nations, and in their riches you will boast."* (Isaiah 61:5, 6)

The Old Testament prophecies quoted in the New Testament and applied to the Church do not prove that the body of Christ with all its unprecedented privileges was revealed even partially in the Old Testament. It was a

[4]Gundry, ibid. p. 12.

"secret hidden in God." (Ephesians 3:9 and Romans 16:25–27)

The New Testament writers used the prophetic references to Gentiles to prove that Gentiles were always included in God's plan of salvation. The false teaching of first century Judaism, which said that Gentiles couldn't even be saved, had to be refuted by the Old Testament Scriptures which they claimed to accept. This false teaching was so tenacious that it even carried over to the early Jewish believers and the apostles (see Acts 10:34–35; 11:1–18).

This error persisted in the first Church Council of Acts 15:1–29. Some of the converts from Judaism insisted that Gentiles had to become Jewish Proselytes to be saved. The apostle James quotes Amos 9:11–12 only to show that Gentiles were always included in God's purposes.

In summary, the Old Testament references to Gentiles only have meaning when parts of these prophecies were selected by the omniscient Holy Spirit and applied to certain aspects of this economy's doctrine. But none of these Old Testament prophecies revealed anything about the body of Christ, the Church, before the Holy Spirit interpreted and applied them.

Dispensational Transitions

Gundry also contends that since there have been transitional periods in changing from one dispensation to another, there will necessarily be a transition period between the dispensation of grace and the Tribulation which, according to him, will put the Church into the Tribulation.

Even if this premise could be proven, it wouldn't follow that the Church would go all the way through the Tribulation to the very end.

There was a transition period during the change from

law to grace. It was necessary because the economy of grace introduced such radically new conditions. The change from law to grace as a principle of living, from God dealing almost exclusively with the Israelites to dealing with Gentiles on an equal basis, from a selective, conditional and limited ministry of the Holy Spirit to an unconditional permanent ministry to every believer, all required some time to inaugurate. God graciously gave time for the Jews not only to understand the above changes, but to overcome the false doctrines with which they had been indoctrinated. The epistle to the Hebrews, written sometime between A.D. 66 and 69, was God's final warning to them. In A.D. 70 Judaism was no longer an option, because the temple was destroyed by the Romans. With this destruction, animal sacrifice according to Mosaic law was rendered impossible. God left those who rejected His Messiah with no pretext to continue in a system of worship that had been made null and void by His once for all atonement.

But the change from the economy of grace back to Daniel's final predicted seven years of Tribulation does not need such a transition. The reason is that it is not the introduction of new conditions, but rather a return to old conditions previously known. The only hint of a transition is the prophetic signs that telegraph the approach of the era that precedes Christ's second advent.

The Close of the Parenthesis

Since this economy was not understood in the Old Testament times, and since there was only an expectation of a time of Tribulation and the coming of the Messiah to set up the promised Messianic kingdom, the interim economy of grace with its main feature of the Church, has to be removed even more suddenly and miraculously than it began. The Word of God certainly promises just that in the form of the mystery of the translation of living saints through the Rapture.

God's great parenthesis of history, that was hidden in God, will be closed in "the twinkling of an eye." The whole body of Christ on earth, composed of every living believer in Christ, will suddenly "be snatched out" of the earth to meet the Lord in the air. Without experiencing physical death, we will be instantly translated into immortality.

There, we will be joined by the rest of the body of Christ composed of all believers who have died from the day of Pentecost until that moment. There has never been such a family reunion as this one for which we are bound!

The Restrainer Must Go

More will be said about this later, but the removal of the Church is synonymous with the removal of "the Restrainer" of 2 Thessalonians 2:4–12.

As I will demonstrate later, the Restrainer of lawlessness who prevents the Roman Dictator called the Antichrist from being unveiled, can only be the Holy Spirit. Since the day of Pentecost, the Spirit of God has been resident in the world through the indwelling of the body of Christ which is composed of every believer.

Because of this special residence in the world the Holy Spirit has been restraining "the mystery of lawlessness" as well as the Antichrist, "the man of lawlessness." But when the body of Christ is removed, the Spirit of God in His present ministry is "taken out of the way" (2 Thessalonians 2:7).

In the first place, the Tribulation is characterized by the most rampant human lawlessness of all time. The present restraint of the Holy Spirit is obviously removed.

There is ample evidence that the Holy Spirit does minister according to the conditions of the previous economy of law during the Tribulation.

It is important to note that in the Old Testament the Holy Spirit did convince people of their need for salvation, give the new birth and work through certain chosen vessels such as prophets. The Scripture predicts that He will work in the same way during the Tribulation.

Second, one of the clear examples of the limited ministry of the Spirit during the Tribulation is the severe lack of spiritual perception on the part of the believers at the judgment that occurs just after the second advent of Christ (Matthew 25:31–40). Certainly a believer who is indwelt by and filled with the Holy Spirit would understand what Jesus meant when He says, "I was hungry, and you gave Me something to eat; I was thirsty, and you gave Me drink; I was a stranger, and you invited Me in; naked, and you clothed Me; I was in prison, and you came to visit Me."

A believer today in the dispensation of grace understands through the Spirit's teaching the verse that says, ". . . he who receives whomsoever I send receives Me." (John 13:20a) The Tribulation believer, however, doesn't manifest this rather simple spiritual insight.

I praise God for a man like John Darby who in the early nineteenth century through diligently studying the Scripture found that the Church of his day had completely overlooked the large body of revelation about the uniqueness of the Church as the body of Christ.

It was his study of this doctrine that led him to believe that the Church must have as unique an ending as its beginning. But more will be said about Darby later.

The next chapter will help define how the Church and the Tribulation relate to each other. It will also help establish God's chronology of the Tribulation—Daniel's Seventieth Week.

SIX

REVELATION'S CHRONOLOGY AND THE RAPTURE

Down through history, the book of Revelation has inspired more wonder, curiosity, bewilderment and sometimes even fear, than any other book of the Bible. It is unquestionably the most difficult to analyze and interpret.

But no other book gives us more clues as to how to find the meaning. There are certain keys given in the book itself that are of enormous help to us in interpreting it.

However difficult it may be, the book of Revelation is the most important factor in understanding the events of the seven cataclysmic years immediately preceding and leading to the second coming of the Lord Messiah Jesus. It is the only extended portion of Scripture that systematically deals with this topic. Chapters 4 through 19 deal exclusively with the Tribulation period. Revelation is the "Grand Central Station" of all the prophecies that deal with the Tribulation. It puts them all together into perspective.

WHY REVELATION IS RELEVANT TO RAPTURE

No other single book is more important to the issue of when the Rapture occurs. Revelation's chronological sequence establishes just when and upon whom "the wrath of God" falls. Both the mid-Tribulationist and post-Tribulationist must establish that "God's wrath" only falls at or near the very end of the Tribulation. They *all* admit that the Scripture does say that God's wrath will not be poured out upon the Church.

The following are some of the important keys to interpreting Revelation:

The first key is the use of Old Testament symbols. Most of the symbols used in Revelation are either explained somewhere else in the Bible, or, as we will see in the second key, they are explained in the context itself.

For example, the symbols used in Revelation 12:1 and 2 are explained in Joseph's dream of Genesis 37:9 and 10. Jacob, Joseph's father, interprets the dream as follows: the *sun* is Jacob; the *moon* is Rachel; the *eleven stars* are the sons of Jacob who fathered the tribes of Israel; the *twelfth star* is Joseph. So the symbols show that the "woman" of Revelation Chapter 12 is Israel, composed of the twelve tribes descended from Jacob's twelve sons.

The second key is that symbols are often explained by the immediate context. The great dragon and the serpent of Revelation 12 is identified in Revelation 12:9 as the Devil and/or Satan. Another example is the great harlot, called Babylon the Great, of Revelation 17:3–7, which is identified in 17:18. She is the great city that **is reigning** over the kings of the earth. When the apostle John wrote this, the great city reigning over the kings of the earth was **Rome.** So Rome is clearly labeled "mystery Babylon" by the prophetic symbol of Revelation.

Parenthetically, the above use of symbols illustrates

one of the reasons for the symbols in the time of Revelation's writing. Had the apostle openly labeled Rome as the center of all heresy and corruption, the Roman Emperor would have had him and all the Christians executed for treason.

The third key is John's testimony of how he actually **saw** and **heard** the things about which he writes in his prophecies.

At the beginning of the book, John records the vision given him by the Lord Jesus Christ,

> *"I was in the Spirit on the Lord's day, and I heard behind me a loud voice like* the sound *of a trumpet, saying,* '**write** *in a book what you* **see,** *and send* it *to the seven churches . . .'"* (Revelation 1:10–11a)

All of the way through the rest of the book the apostle continually testifies that he **saw** and **heard** the things about which he wrote. And then at the end of the book John bears his final solemn testimony about how he received the content about which he wrote, "And he said to me, 'These words are faithful and true'; and the Lord, the God of the spirits of the prophets, sent His angel to show to His bond-servants the things which must shortly take place . . . and I, John, am the one who *heard* and *saw* these things . . ." (Revelation 22:6, 8).

The key is this: John heard and saw things that would happen on earth some nineteen hundred years later. How in the world would a first century man describe the highly advanced scientific marvels of warfare at the end of the twentieth century? John had to use phenomena with which he was familiar to give visual and audible illustrations of what he was witnessing.

John was hurtled by God's Spirit through time up to the end of the twentieth century, shown the actual cataclysmic events of the Tribulation, then returned to the first century and told to write about what he had witnessed.

An example is the judgment of the second trumpet,

> *"And the second angel sounded, and* **something like** *a great mountain burning with fire was thrown into the sea; and a third of the sea became blood; and a third of the creatures which were in the sea and had life, died; and a third of the ships were destroyed."* (Revelation 8:8–9)

I believe that the apostle was giving an accurate description of a thermonuclear naval battle in terms of his first century experience. Many more examples could be given of this key, but space doesn't permit. (My book on Revelation called *There's A New World Coming* gives a verse-by-verse analysis.)

The Divine Outline

The fourth key to interpreting Revelation is the outline that Jesus gave John at the time He commissioned him to write it. Actually, the Lord Jesus instructed the apostle exactly how he was to structure the book,

> *"Write therefore the things you* **have seen,** *and the things which* **are,** *and the things which* **shall take place after these things."** (Revelation 1:19)

In checking commentaries on the book of Revelation written from some two centuries ago until the present, I found that the vast majority of writers recognized that Revelation 1:19 is intended to be the outline of the book. It is obvious to any interpreter who takes the book normally and believes it at face value. This is of considerable importance because most post-Tribulationists try to explain this outline away so that they can strengthen their case for the Church being in the Tribulation.

The Things Which You Have Seen

This covers Chapter 1 where John describes the risen Lord Jesus' appearance to him and the phenomena that occurred during that visitation. It is described with a past tense.

The Things Which Are

This describes Chapters 2 and 3. These chapters are described by a present tense of the verb for being (*eimi* in the Greek) which stresses the present state of things in history. I believe, along with many scholars, that these seven letters were not only written to seven literal churches with real problems, but also that they have a prophetic application to Church history.

Many factors convinced me of this interpretation. First, why were these seven churches selected? There were hundreds of other churches in Asia at this time. There were thousands of churches worldwide. So why just these particular seven?

Second, why were these seven churches arranged in this order?

Third, why were the conditions in the churches arranged in such a way that they describe discernible, successive epochs of Church history accurately?

Fourth, why place seven practical letters of instructions to churches in this book and in this position if they have no prophetic application?

I believe that these seven churches were selected and arranged by our omniscient Lord because they had problems and characteristics that would prophesy seven stages of history through which the Church universal would pass.

The Things Which Shall Take Place After These Things

This third division of the book's Divinely given outline is clearly intended to convey *future things* to the events covered by the first and second divisions. The future tense of the verb *ginomai* contrasts sharply with the present tense of the verb *eimi* used for the previous section. The idea is "what shall come to be after these things." This statement obviously describes things that will occur after the first two sections.

"These things" is the translation of the Greek words *meta tauta*. This phrase is first used in Chapter 1:19, and not used again until Chapter 4, Verse 1. It clearly indicates that there is a shift into future things under different conditions from those described in the first three chapters, and that this is the place where the outline begins in its futuristic phase.

That this is a shift to things future to the Church age described in Chapters 2 and 3 is apparent because of these factors:

First, as I just mentioned, Chapter 4, Verse 1, is the first place that *meta tauta* is used after it is given the special meaning in Chapter 1, Verse 19. Therefore, as the antecedent of that special meaning given in Chapter 1, Verse 19, it must be understood as the place where the outline shifts to things that are future to the first two parts of the outline.

Second, in Chapter 4, Verse 1, *meta tauta* is used twice. A voice from heaven leaves no doubt as to its meaning in the latter part of Verse 1, "Come up here, and I will show you *what must take place after these things.*"

Third, John is caught up to heaven to see things that are definitely *future* to our present experience.

Fourth, not one reference is made again concerning the Church on earth until after the second coming of the

Lord Jesus Christ. Since the Church is mentioned nineteen times in the first three chapters under the divine outline of "the things which are," and since the Church is not mentioned or implied as being on earth even once after the statement "Come up here, and I will show you what must take place *after these things,*" I conclude that it is the end of the Church age that is meant here, and that the Church is in heaven thereafter until it returns as the bride of Christ in Revelation 19:7–14.

An Amazing Similarity

The similarity of the terminology used in both 1 Thessalonians 4:16–17 and Revelation 4:1–2 supports the contention that the Church is taken to heaven here. Both passages speak of a trumpet sounding, of a shout of command, of being caught up to heaven, and of an instantaneous translation of the believer. I believe, along with many scholars, that the apostle John's experience here is meant to be a prophetic preview of what the living Church will experience in the Rapture.

Revelation's Order of Judgments

By far the most important aspect of interpreting Revelation is just how the seven **Seal** judgments, **Trumpet** judgments and **Bowl** judgments relate to each other.

If the judgments occur in consecutive order, then it tends to support the pre-Tribulation Rapture. The following chart illustrates the way I believe they occur.

If the judgments are concurrent, then it tends to support the mid- and post-Tribulation views. The chart below illustrates Gundry's view of the order of judgments.[1]

[1]Robert Gundry, *The Church and the Tribulation* (Grand Rapids, Zondervan Pub.: 1973), p. 75.

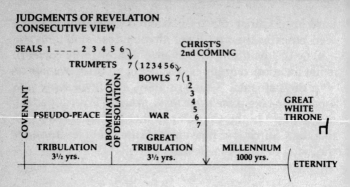

JUDGMENTS OF REVELATION
CONSECUTIVE VIEW

Since the post-Tribulationists agree that the Church cannot suffer Divine wrath, they have to jam as many of the severe judgments as possible into the short time-frame of the actual second coming. If it can be demonstrated that Divine wrath falls on the earth prior to the second coming, then, their theory contradicts itself.

Gundry states, "Thus, God's wrath will not stretch throughout the whole Tribulation. Those passages in Revelation which speak of divine wrath deal, rather,

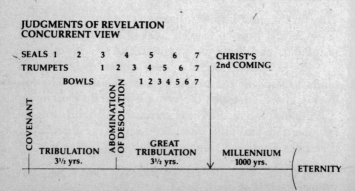

JUDGMENTS OF REVELATION
CONCURRENT VIEW

with the close of the Tribulation."[2] "Not until the final crisis at Armageddon, when Jesus descends (and the church is caught up if post-Tribulationism is correct), will God pour out His wrath upon the unregenerate."[3]

Whatever is the order of judgments, it has to fit into the *whole* pattern of Tribulation events predicted in the other prophetic passages of the Bible. I do not believe that the post-Tribulationists' scheme of Revelation's chronology can be harmonized with either the rest of the Biblical Tribulation prophecies or those of Revelation.

Let us first observe that all the judgments in the book of Revelation are presented as judgments of God on a Christ-rejecting world no matter who or what the agency of judgment may be.

The scroll of seven seals, which contains the judgment of the seals, is presented as so dreadful in Chapter 5 that no one in heaven or on earth is worthy to open them except the Lord Jesus, the Messiah Himself. So the authority and source for the unleashing of the seal judgments is the Lord. So how can anyone say that they are not God's wrath upon man?

The *first seal* unleashes the Antichrist to go forth and establish his control upon the earth. He will begin the seven years of Tribulation by signing a covenant guaranteeing Israel's security and the Middle East's peace (Daniel 9:27).

During this seal the Antichrist will apparently conquer through ingenious plans for world economic recovery and prosperity and world peace. In Daniel's prophetic description of this Roman Dictator, he says, "and by means of *peace* [he] shall destroy many . . ." (Daniel 9:25b KJV).

[2]Gundry, ibid. p. 77.

[3]Gundry, ibid. p. 48.

No one can read 2 Thessalonians, Chapter 2, Verses 9 through 12, and fail to see the clear connection between the Divinely permitted unveiling of the Antichrist, attended by Satanic miracles and a deluding influence from God, and the resulting condemnation of all on earth who reject God's truth. This passage clearly shows the Antichrist to be the chief vehicle of God's judgment on the world. The Antichrist himself is one of the greatest expressions of God's wrath, for he is the one who will slaughter believers and lead the whole world to destruction.

World Peace for Three and One-Half Years

There are several indications that the first half of the Tribulation will be a time of world pseudo-peace established by the Antichrist of Rome. In addition to the verse just quoted, Revelation records the progress of the Antichrist, ". . . and they worshipped the beast [Roman Antichrist], saying, 'Who is like the beast, and *who is able to wage war with him*?'" (Revelation 13:4). This verse reveals at least two profound insights into world conditions during the first half of the Tribulation.

First, the people will give absolute authority to the Antichrist because of fear of war and anarchy caused by economic catastrophe.

Second, the Antichrist will stop war so that the world will extol him because they believe that no one can make war against him.

Another very important clue is in Ezekiel's prophecy of Israel's condition just before the great northern power (the Soviet Union and allies) invades, "Thus says the Lord God, 'on that day when My people Israel are living *securely*, will you not know it?' And you [the USSR] will come from your place out of the remote parts of the north [extreme north], you and many peoples with you, all of them riding horses, a great assembly and a mighty army." (Ezekiel 38:14–15)

For those who say God doesn't pour out his wrath (even on the unregenerate, as Gundry said) on the world till the very end, listen to God's response to this invasion: "'It will come about on that day, when Gog [USSR] comes against the land of Israel,' declares the Lord God, 'that My *fury* will mount up in My *anger*. And in My zeal and in My *blazing wrath* I declare *that* on that day there will surely be a great earthquake in the land of Israel' . . . 'with pestilence and with blood I *shall* enter into judgment with him; and I shall rain on him, and on his troops, and on the many peoples who are with him a torrential rain of hailstones, fire, and brimstone. And I shall magnify Myself, sanctify Myself, and make Myself known in the sight of many nations; and they will know that I am the Lord.'" (Ezekiel 38:18, 19, 21–23)

Now when does all this happen? We know the following factors:

(1) Israel will be at peace under the Antichrist's protection (Daniel 9:27; Ezekiel 38:11, 14).

(2) Israel has reinstituted the sacrifices of the Mosaic law and rebuilt her temple (Daniel 9:27 cp. Matthew 24:15–20).

(3) The world is at peace (Revelation 13:4).

(4) **War** begins when the Pan Arabic army attacks Israel because of a dispute over Jerusalem (Zechariah 12:2–3), and then the Soviet Union with its allies (King of the North) immediately launch an overwhelming attack against the Middle East (Daniel 11:40–45).

(5) This war has to begin when "the abomination of desolation" predicted by Daniel in 9:27 is set up in the holy of holies of the Jerusalem temple

(Matthew 24:15). Jesus Christ is the one who says to the believing Jew of that day to flee the city to a prepared place of safety (Revelation 12:6, 13–17) because "there will be a *great tribulation,* such as has not occurred since the beginning of the world until now, nor ever shall. And unless those days had been cut short, *no life would be saved."* (Matthew 24:21–22)

We know absolutely that "the abomination of desolation" is set up in the middle of the seven-year Tribulation (Daniel 9:27). Therefore, the great *war* of Ezekiel 38 and 39 must begin in the middle of the Tribulation.

The *second seal* must, therefore, occur at the middle of the Tribulation. Because the second seal specifically "takes *peace* from the earth, and men begin to slay each other with a *great sword."* (Revelation 6:3, 4)

Therefore, the opening of the second seal must be the same as the great Russian invasion of Israel predicted in Ezekiel 38:8–16; Daniel 11:40–45 and Joel 2:20.

Parenthetically, the second seal also proves that the earth was in a period of pseudo-peace prior to its opening, because it "takes *peace* from the earth." You can't take away something that wasn't there.

Armageddon isn't One Battle, but a War

The battle plan given in Daniel 11:40–45 definitely reveals that the war that begins in the middle of the Tribulation escalates into a global conflict. Ezekiel 38 and 39 indicate the same thing.

Dr. Pentecost accurately states the issue, "It has been held commonly that the battle of Armageddon is an isolated event transpiring just prior to the second advent of Christ to the earth. The extent of this great movement in which God deals with 'the kings of the earth and of the whole world' (Revelation 16:4) will not be seen unless it is realized that the 'battle of that great day of God Almighty' (Revelation 16:14) is not an isolated battle, but rather a campaign that extends over the last half of the Tribulation period. The Greek word *polemos*, translated 'battle' in Revelation 16:14, signifies a war or campaign, while *mache* signifies a battle, and sometimes even single combat. This distinction is observed by Trench (*New Testament Synonyms*), and is followed by Thayer (*Greek-English Lexicon of the New Testament*) and Vincent (*Word Studies in the New Testament*). The use of the word *polemos* (campaign) in Revelation 16:14 would signify that the events that culminate in the gathering at Armageddon at the second advent are viewed by God as one connected campaign."[4]

Looking at war in terms of today's unbelievably destructive weapons, it is easy to understand the horrible carnage and devastation that is predicted in the prophecies about this period. These prophecies indicate something that is very important from a military perspective. The war that begins with the Pan Arab and Soviet invasion of the Middle East is portrayed as beginning with *conventional* weapons. It is only after the Soviet army is beginning to lose that the prophecies begin to intimate the use of nuclear weapons. And most important of all, the nuclear war escalates in stages until it becomes an all-out worldwide nuclear holocaust. This is the exact sort of military strategy that is being planned by the major powers today, that of a case-by-case escalation.

The seal, trumpet and bowl series of judgments in Revelation harmonize perfectly with this scenario if they are interpreted as unfolding successively. The judgments increase in frequency and severity with each new series. This is consistent with God's revealed character,

---

[4] J. Dwight Pentecost, *Things to Come* (Findlay, Ohio: Dunham Publishing Co., 1958), p. 340.

for He is slow to anger, not willing that any should perish. Therefore, the progressive increase in severity is consistent with the successive scenario of judgments in the Old Testament prophecy.

The Seventh Seal and Trumpet

The seventh seal and seventh trumpet give very important insight as to whether the seal and trumpet judgments occur successively or concurrently.

A close examination of the opening of the seventh seal reveals that it isn't the same kind of judgment as the previous six seals. There is an interlude of silence mingled with the prayers of the saints in heaven and a temporary restraint of judgment on earth. God gives the earth a chance to repent before the next series of judgments.

But the crucial thing to observe is that the seventh seal actually unleashes the next series of judgments which are the seven trumpets. Any normal reading of the following verses clearly reveals the idea of succession,

"And when He broke the seventh seal, there was silence in heaven for about half an hour. **And** *I saw the seven angels who stand before God; and seven* **trumpets** *were given to them."* (Revelation 8:1–2)

Likewise, the sounding of the seventh trumpet does not send forth a single specific judgment as the first six trumpets did. Instead there is another interlude in heaven and a lull in judgments upon earth. In heaven, God announces His claim of ownership over the earth and that His Messiah is about to begin His reign over it. Then there are more of the combined historical-prophetical cameos in Chapters 12 through 14.

We find that the next chronological movement of Tribulational events takes place in Chapter 15. Here we are introduced to the seven angels who have the seven **last plagues** which **finish** God's **wrath** (15:1).

From this, observe first that these seven bowl judgments are the direct result of the sounding of the seventh trumpet. This is true because these are the next and only judgments which occur after that trumpet is sounded.

Second, observe that it says the seven bowl judgments are the **last** ones. This indicates that they are the last in a series of previous judgments.

Third, observe that it says in these seven bowl judgments "the wrath of God is finished." (15:1) This indicates clearly that the wrath of God doesn't begin with these judgments, as Gundry and the post-Tribulationist crowd contend, but rather that they *finish it.* From this, it is evident that all the judgments of Revelation are considered God's wrath against man.

The bowl judgments occur in very rapid succession. In terms of magnitude and scope, they are unprecedented. Whereas the trumpet judgments, for instance, destroyed a third of life in the sea, the bowl judgment destroys **all** life in the sea (16:4).

I believe that a normal analysis of the structure of Revelation leads to the conclusion that the three series of judgments are consecutive to each other, and that the seventh judgment of the first two series simply introduces the next series. In other words, they are somewhat telescopic to each other as previously illustrated in my chart on page 106.

There is a strong Semitic style of writing in the book of Revelation. This is evidenced by the many historical-prophetic cameos that explain why certain things happened in history and culminate in the Tribulation.

These cameos are interspersed in the chronological unfolding of the seven years in the form of the three series of judgments. In true Semitic style, history is moved forward a bit, then explanatory sections that flash both backwards and forwards in time are added. Then history is moved forward again, etc.

A WORD FROM THE OTHER VIEW

What are the evidences to support a concurrent view of the three series of judgments?

The Semitic Style Argument

Gundry says, "The universally acknowledged Semitic style of Revelation favors the second view, according to which the seals, trumpets, and bowls will find somewhat concurrent fulfillment."[5]

As we have seen, the Semitic style is evident in the historic-prophetic cameos. But it doesn't require a concurrent arrangement of judgments. This has to be established on other grounds, because it assumes the conclusion.

The Final Catastrophe Argument

Gundry again says, "Several specific considerations positively require us to believe that the seventh seal and the seventh trumpet bring us to the end of the Tribulation and that the seven bowls are clustered at the end. The sixth seal leads us to the final catastrophe of judgment when Christ returns, for the wrath of the Lamb is just about to strike the wicked, who are calling upon the rocks and mountains to hide them (6:12–17)."[6]

A careful comparison of the events of the seventh seal, seventh trumpet and seventh bowl reveals that nei-

[5]Gundry, op. cit. p. 75.

[6]Gundry, ibid. p. 76.

ther the last seal nor the last trumpet is at the end of the Tribulation.

To be sure, there are some terrible things that happen in the judgment of the sixth seal. The kings, the great men, the military commanders, the rich, the strong, the slave, and the free man do hide in the caves and mountains from God who sits on the throne, and from the wrath of the Lamb (Revelation 6:15-16).

But this very description proves that it cannot be the end of the Tribulation. Because at the end, men's hearts will be so hardened, and they will be so blinded by demonic influences (see 16:13-14) that they no longer hide in fear. As incredible as it is, the Scripture says that they will not hide, but they will unite their armies and *attack* the Lord Jesus Himself as He returns (19:17-19).

The scenes of Revelation 6:15-17 and 19:17-19 cannot happen anywhere near each other, because it will take considerable time for men's hearts to become so hard that they no longer fear God, but actually attack Him.

The seventh trumpet also does not take us to the absolute end of the Tribulation. Remember, the seventh trumpet introduces the seven bowl judgments. The previous six trumpet judgments before are still restrained to some degree.

The bowl judgments which God expressly says "finish" His wrath, and are the "last" of the judgments, are totally unrestrained and bring back the Lord Jesus.

Even if Gundry could prove the concurrent view of Revelation's judgments, he still faces a problem with Chapter 6, Verse 17, which says, ". . . for the great day of their wrath *has come;* and who is able to stand?"

This verse places God's wrath before the post-Tribulational Rapture, which fouls up Gundry's whole post-Tribulational scheme.

In order to overcome this embarrassing verb tense (the "has come" of Revelation 6:17), Gundry comes up with a very novel interpretation, "At first glance we might think that the divine wrath is placed in the past by a historical aorist. But if the wrath has already fallen, how could the wicked be yet fleeing for refuge? (The answer is because they know that there is more wrath to come. H.L.) Rather, the wrath is at the inception of its breaking forth (ingressive aorist) or on the verge of doing so (dramatic aorist)—'has just arrived' or 'is here'."[7]

It is true that an aorist tense verb in the Greek language, which pictures an action as happening at a point of time, can be viewed from three perspectives (past, near past, or occurring). However, to give an aorist a meaning other than past action is highly subjective on the interpreter's part and cannot be used as proof for a major argument. At best, it would be a supporting point.

I majored in New Testament Greek, had five academic years of study in it, and have studied it on my own for the past twenty-three years. So I know that Gundry's interpretation of this verb is not only highly subjective, but also not in accord with the mainstream of translators and commentators on this verse who had no axe to grind.

Ryrie comments on Gundry's interpretation of Revelation 6:17,

"To counter the force of this statement, posttribulationists have to understand the aorist as meaning that the wrath is on the verge of breaking forth, that is, it will not have started before the end. Now this is a possible use of the aorist, but highly unlikely in this verse. As Alford indicates, 'the virtually perfect sense of the aorist *elthen* here can hardly be questioned.' (Henry Alford, *The Greek New Testament*, 4 vols. (London: Rivington, 1875, 4:622)). He explains this sense of the aorist as 'alluding to the result of the whole series of events past, and not to be expressed in English except by a perfect' (4:665). Thus supported by reputable scholarship, the meaning of this verse is *not* that the wrath of God is on the verge of being poured out (as posttribulationists *must* understand it or spoil the system), but that the wrath has already been poured out with continuing results."[8]

SUMMARY

So we find that both the overall chronology of prophecy concerning the Tribulation, as well as the chronology of the book of Revelation, does not fit the post-Tribulational Rapture view. There is no way to cram all of the Divine wrath into the last moments of the Tribulation.

I believe, therefore, that we can trust God's promise in these days of ever-increasing turmoil, "For God has not destined us for *wrath*, but for obtaining salvation [deliverance] through our Lord Jesus Christ." (1 Thessalonians 5:9)

So we are to keep on believing God's promises, "and to wait for His Son from heaven, whom He raised from the dead, that is Jesus, who delivers us from the *wrath* to come." (1 Thessalonians 1:10)

[8]Charles C. Ryrie, *What You Should Know About The Rapture* (Chicago: Moody Press, 1981), p. 97.

SEVEN

OTHER RELEVANT REVELATION PASSAGES

I discussed in the last chapter the many complex issues that are related to establishing the chronology of the book of Revelation. In this chapter, several other specific passages in the book which contribute to answering the Rapture question will be analyzed.

The Promise to the True Church

In Revelation 3:10 there is an extraordinary promise given to the church of Philadelphia. As is the case with all seven of the letters to the churches in Revelation Chapters 2 and 3, this letter obviously has an application which goes far beyond the time of the original addressees.

The *context* indicates that the promise applies to the end times of the Church. This is true first because the next verse says, "I am coming quickly; hold fast what you have, in order that no one take your crown." (Revelation 3:11) This verse has to refer to the coming of Christ for the Church because it uses a warning that is

119

consistently associated with it in this book (see 22:7, 12, 20).

Second, Verse 11 also mentions rewards and the receiving of a crown. This is definitely to be given at the "Bema" or judgment seat of Christ. Paul speaks of receiving a crown on "that day" (2 Timothy 4:8). Peter speaks of the "unfading crown of glory" that will be given to faithful elders "when the Lord comes" (1 Peter 5:4). This definitely ties the context to the time of Christ's coming for the Church.

The third reason why this promise must apply to the end times of the Church is given in Verse 10 itself. The promise is said to apply to "that hour which is about to come upon the whole world, to test those who dwell upon the earth." So the time period concerns a test which God will send upon the whole world. It is obvious that such a global "test" has not yet occurred.

The What, Who, and Why of the Test

It is important to understand just *what* the original Greek word translated "test" means. The original word is *periazo*. Dr. Gingrich says that the word is used here in the sense of "to try, to make trial of, to put to the test, in order to discover or reveal what kind of a person someone is."[1] Often the purpose of the trial is to bring out the evil that is in someone. For this reason it is sometimes translated "temptation."

In this context it is best understood as putting the world under severe trial to reveal its evil heart. The trials are launched against "the whole inhabited earth," which is further defined as "those who dwell upon the earth." The apostle John makes this a technical descriptive clause to mark out a certain class of people.

[1] F. Wilbur Gingrich and Frederick Danker from Walter Bauer's 5th Edition, *A Greek-English Lexicon of the New Testament and Other Early Christian Literature* (Chicago: Univ. of Chicago Press, 1979), p. 640.

Listen to what John says about *"those who dwell upon the earth"*: (1) They are the ones who murder the Tribulation believers (6:10). (2) The wrath of God contained in the judgments called the "three woes" will specifically fall upon them (8:13). (3) They will murder the two special prophets of God (whom I believe will be Moses and Elijah) and rejoice over their deaths (11:10). (4) The message given by these two prophets will torment them (11:10). (5) They will worship the Roman Antichrist, and their names are not in the Lamb's book of life (13:8, 12). (6) They will be deceived by the miracles of the False Prophet from Israel (13:14). (7) They will be intoxicated and blinded by the false one-world religious system (17:2).

From this survey we can easily see *why* God is going to have *an hour* of testing for this group. It is to so demonstrate the hard, evil hearts of "those who dwell upon the earth" that God's judgment of them will be shown as totally just.

There is also a very important contrast in Revelation between "those who dwell upon the earth" and another special group called *"those who dwell in heaven."*

Let us first consider who "those who dwell in heaven" are. First, they cannot be angels because of a statement made in Revelation 12:12 about this same group of "heaven dwellers." It says, "For this reason, rejoice, O heavens and *you who dwell in them,* woe to the earth and the sea, because the devil has come down to you, having great wrath, knowing that his time is short." God's angels would not be exhorted to rejoice because they are not dwelling on earth during the devil's unrestrained wrath. Satan couldn't hurt them.

Second, this is not a reference to the departed souls of those massacred during the Tribulation. Though a non-resurrected believer's soul does go to be consciously with the Lord after he dies, he is never said "to dwell in heaven" until after he receives a resurrection body. Furthermore, it would make no sense for the devil to blaspheme the souls of those whose bodies he has just murdered.

Third, there is a direct contrast made between "those who dwell on earth," who are unbelievers, and "those who dwell in heaven." The implication is that the "heaven dwellers" are believers.

So the question is: If they are not angels, and they are not the souls of departed believers, who are they?

I believe the answer is that they are the translated (Raptured) saints of the Church who are now dwelling in heaven in glorified bodies. This explanation gives an intelligent reason for why the devil would take the time to blaspheme them. After all, he couldn't very well hide or sweep into a corner the news of millions of "Jesus freaks" disappearing. So Satan must give an explanation to his followers lest they slip into the other camp.

I believe the Holy Spirit has given us here a clear clue as to the whereabouts of the missing Church.

The Church of Philadelphia

The prophetic application of the letter to the Church in Philadelphia is to the *true Church* in the last stage of church history. It is contrasted with the Laodicean church which depicts the predominant *apostate church* of the last stage of church history.

It is to the true Church that God says, "Because you have kept the work of My perseverance, I also will keep you from the *hour* of testing, that *hour* which is about to come upon the whole inhabited earth [literal], to test those who dwell upon the earth." (Revelation 3:10)

Gingrich, quoting the great Greek scholar Walter Bauer, brings much light to the meaning of "the word of My perseverance." He says that it literally means "because you have kept the word concerning patient expectation of Me."[2] This would mean that the promise is to those who patiently expect the Lord's coming. If that is correct, it certainly would fit the context.

However, I believe that it also means that they have persevered in clinging to the truth of God's word under much opposition.

Now because of this perseverance, God promises, "I will keep you from the hour of testing that is coming upon the whole inhabited earth." The post-Tribulationist vigorously disputes the meaning of this promise. Some even try to make it have no clear meaning at all.

There are three important aspects to analyze in this promise. First, what does the word *keep* mean? Second, what does it mean to be kept *from the hour* of testing? Third, what length of time is meant by the term *"hour"*?

The verb "to keep" (*tereo* in Greek) means "to protect," in this instance according to Bauer.[3] God makes a solemn promise to those who are faithful to His Word. He says, "I will protect you . . ."

This protection is not just from the testing, but from the *time* of the testing. This is often overlooked by those who dispute the application of this verse. The major area of dispute is over the exact meaning of the preposition translated "from" which is the word *ek* in the original.

The Greek preposition *ek* in most circumstances means a separation from within something. There are only two instances in the New Testament where *ek* is used with the verb *tereo*. Both of them are in the writings of the apostle John.

The first instance is in John 17:15 where Jesus prayed for His disciples, "I do not ask Thee to take them out of

[2]Ibid. p. 846 (2).
[3]Ibid. p. 815.

the world, but to keep *(tereo)* them from *(ek)* the evil one." The idea is that Jesus wants the believer to be protected from falling under the authority of the evil one (Satan). It is clear that the disciples were not in Satan's clutches at the time Jesus prayed the prayer. So in this case *ek* used with *tereo* means to be protected from coming under Satan's power.

The only other instance these words are used together is here in Revelation 3:10. The same author, John, is expressing the same idea. He is saying that God will protect the believer **from the time** of the testing, not just from the testing.

The meaning of "the hour of worldwide testing" must be understood in the light of the main focus of the book of Revelation. Revelation specifically details the judgments, events and personalities of the seven years of Daniel's Seventieth Week. It begins with the worldwide deception and takeover by the Antichrist of Rome. It ends with the worst holocaust of all time. Its purpose is to bring the sons of Abraham, Isaac and Jacob to faith in the true Messiah and to judge the unbelievers from all nations called "those who dwell upon the earth." So "the hour" must apply to the whole seven-year Tribulation where all these things fall upon the world.

Search for the Missing Church

I mentioned briefly in the last chapter a very important piece of evidence in Revelation which supports that the Church is translated before the beginning of the Tribulation period.

The book of Revelation, which, as I've said, is the only book in the Bible specifically written to detail the events and phenomena of the Tribulation, nowhere mentions the Church as present on earth during the Tribulation. This point gains even more significance in the light of the fact that the Church is mentioned nineteen times in Chapters 1 through 3.

After the voice from heaven says to the apostle John, "come up here, and I will show you what must take place after these things" (Revelation 4:1), the Church vanishes from these earthly scenes.

Revelation makes continual reference to the believers who are on earth during this time, so there is every reason to expect that the term Church would be mentioned if these believers were the Church. There is one striking case where the Church certainly should have been mentioned if it were on earth.

There is a formula that is addressed to the Church seven times in Chapters 2 and 3. It says, "He who has an ear, let him hear what the Spirit says to the *Churches.*" (Revelation 2:7, 11, 17, 29; 3:6, 13, 22) This exact formula is repeated again during the Tribulation in Revelation 13:9 and 10, "If anyone has an ear, let him hear. If anyone *is destined* for captivity, to captivity he goes; if anyone kills with the sword, with the sword he must be killed. Here is the perseverance and the faith of the saints."

This is an extremely strong evidence for the Church's absence. In Chapter 13:9 the formula is given to alert Tribulational believers to hear and take heed to the life and death instructions to them of 13:10. In Verse 10, believers of that period are instructed not to resist being taken captive for their faith by the Antichrist, nor are they to resist with weapons. If they use weapons, God says that they will be killed by them.

Instead the believers are instructed to persevere in their faith in Jesus Christ and leave whether they die as martyrs or survive until the second advent up to the Lord.

Now this is a very clear situation where the term "church" should have been used because it is speaking to all the believers of that time about vital survival instructions. But even though the formula is exactly the same as the one given in Chapters 2 and 3, the word *"church"* is left out of Verse nine.

Church Appearances in Heaven

When the apostle John is caught up to heaven in Revelation Chapter 4, he sees *seven lamps of fire* burning before the throne of God (Verse 5). Those seven lamps first appeared on earth in Chapter 1, Verses 12 through 20. In Verse 20 they are identified as the seven symbolic churches. I believe that these seven lamps are the Church which has just been raptured into heaven. Here they are called the seven spirits of God because John is emphasizing that the Spirit indwells the churches.

The Bride in Heaven

The Church doesn't specifically reappear until just before the second coming of Christ to the earth in Revelation 19:7–16. As previously mentioned, the bride is in heaven already rewarded and prepared for the great wedding feast. The Lord Jesus Christ begins His second coming to earth.

The bride of Christ then accompanies Him to the earth on white horses wearing the white robes of her righteous deeds.

The post-Tribulationists have to go all out to try and explain away the sequence of events in this passage. Concerning this passage Ladd says, "So the vision of the bride prepared for the wedding feast is prophetic. *In vision,* John sees the bride ready for the marriage; but this is not a vision depicting either the saints in the intermediate state or the Church in heaven prior to the return of Christ. It is a vision of what shall be after Christ returns. Then will occur the resurrection of the dead in

Christ, both saints and martyrs (20:4). The final proof that this is a prophetic vision is the fact that the dead in Christ are not yet raised; their resurrection occurs after the return of Christ (20:4)."[4]

Ladd has not only to do violence to the immediate context of Revelation 19:7–16 to come up with such a farfetched interpretation, but he also has to do damage to the whole structure of the book of Revelation.

First of all, there is a chronological sequence of events in Revelation Chapter 19. The bride of Christ not only is seen in heaven already prepared for her wedding feast, but afterward the same bride returns with Christ in His second advent to earth (19:4).

Second, the book of Revelation moves through the Tribulation in a definite chronological order except for the interludes where the cameo sections explain the history and future of the personalities, organizations and events that culminate in the book. When Ladd says that John sees "the bride of Christ [the Church] *in vision*," he seems to think that this eliminates any necessity for following the normal, logical, chronological and temporal sequences that are established throughout the book. What Ladd doesn't recognize here is that the whole book of Revelation is a vision. But that doesn't remove the fact that the visions have a definite chronological sequence. If this logic were followed throughout the book, it would reduce it to an illogical, incoherent collection of visions that cannot possibly be understood.

Third, Ladd's own quote brings out the error of his interpretation. In fact, it is an extremely strong evidence for the Church's Rapture long before the second advent of Christ.

[4]George E. Ladd, *The Blessed Hope* (Grand Rapids: Wm. B. Eerdmans Pub. Co., 1956), p. 102.

An Embarrassing Resurrection

As previously quoted, Ladd says, "The final proof that this is a prophetic vision is the fact that the dead in Christ are not yet raised; their resurrection occurs after the return of Christ (20:4)."

Ladd seems to be so determined to prove his view that he must not have carefully evaluated the implications of the above statement.

First, if God intended for this book to be intelligible at all, Chapters 19 and 20 have a very definite chronological sequence: (1) Christ returns with His bride, the Church (19:7–16). (2) The armies of the Antichrist, the False Prophet and all the kings of the earth unite to fight Christ's return (19:19). (3) The Antichrist and the False Prophet are both taken and cast alive into the lake of fire (19:20). (4) All the rest of the armies with their kings are slain by Christ and given to the scavenger birds (19:21). (5) Satan is bound for a thousand years (20:1–3). (6) The martyred **Tribulation believers** are resurrected.

There is absolutely nothing in this context to indicate to an unbiased reader that this passage is anything other than a consecutive narrative of future history.

Now here is the point. Ladd agrees that this resurrection of **Tribulation saints** takes place **after** the return of Christ. If the Church is on earth during the Tribulation, and if the Church is raptured immediately *before* the second coming of Christ, then how is it that these Tribulation believers (who are the Church according to his view) are resurrected after the second coming? The Scripture says that "the dead in Christ shall rise first, then we who are alive and remain until the coming of the Lord shall be caught up together with them in the clouds to meet the Lord in the air." (1 Thessalonians 4:16–17)

If the Church were on earth and raptured just before the second coming (as post-Tribulationists must say), then all martyred Tribulation saints would be part of the Church and, therefore, have to be raised **before** the living believers could be translated into immortality. And all of this, according to post-Tribulationists, occurs just *before* the second advent.

This is a major evidence that the Church must be snatched up to meet the Lord long before the end of the Tribulation and the second advent.

Is God a Bigamist?

Gundry argues, "Israel is sometimes likened to a bride (Isaiah 49:18; 16:10; 62:5; Jeremiah 2:32; Hosea 2:19, 20) and the Church is likened to a wife (Ephesians 5:22-23). We should not expect to find rigid consistency in the Biblical use of metaphors. To press woodenly the marital relationship of both Israel and the Church to the Lord would be to say that God is a bigamist."[5]

Gundry's whole argument is misleading because Israel is never once said *to be* the bride of the Lord Jesus Messiah. God's attitude toward Israel is illustrated by various aspects of a bride's jewelry, by a bridegroom's excitement over his bride, and so forth.

But the Church is actually said to be the bride of Jesus Christ. In Ephesians 5:22-32, God says that though it is a great mystery, marriage is intended to be an earthly illustration of the believer's heavenly union with Christ. God says, ". . . because we are members of His body, of His flesh and of His bone. For this cause a man shall leave his father and his mother, and shall cleave to his wife; and the two shall become one flesh. This mystery

[5]Robert H. Gundry, *The Church and the Tribulation* (Grand Rapids: Zondervan Pub. House, 1973), p. 85.

is great; but I am speaking with reference to *Christ and the Church.*" (Ephesians 5:30–32, NKJV)

The Hebrew marriage custom underlies the New Testament declaration of the Church as the bride of Christ. Ryrie traces the steps of the Hebrew marriage custom of that era,

> "*First,* betrothal (which involved the prospective groom's traveling from his father's house to the home of the prospective bride, paying the purchase price, and thus establishing the marriage covenant); *second,* the groom's returning to his father's house and remaining separate from his bride for twelve months during which time he prepared the living accommodations for his wife in his father's house; *third,* the groom's coming for his bride at a time not known exactly to her; *fourth,* his return with her to the groom's father's house to consummate the marriage and to celebrate the wedding feast for the next seven days (during which the bride remained closeted in her bridal chamber).

> "In Revelation 19:7–9 the wedding feast is announced, which, if the analogy of the Hebrew marriage means anything, assumes that the wedding has previously taken place in the father's house. Today, the church is described as a virgin waiting for her bridegroom's coming (2 Corinthians 11:2); in Revelation 21 she is designated as the wife of the Lamb, indicating that previously she has been taken to the groom's father's house. Pre-Tribulationists say that this requires an interval of time between the Rapture and the second coming."[6]

[6]Charles C. Ryrie, *What You Should Know About The Rapture* (Chicago: Moody Press, 1981), pp. 60–61.

All of the symbols and imagery used in the New Testament were based upon the common Hebrew culture of the day. Otherwise there would be no hope of understanding the rich use of parable, allegory and illustrations. Therefore, the standard Hebrew marriage tradition of that time gives insight into the Church as the bride of Christ, particularly in Revelation Chapters 19 and 21.

SUMMARY

I believe that these passages we have examined contribute significantly toward the case for a pre-Tribulation Rapture. The promise of being kept from the hour; the identity of those who dwell in heaven; the Church's absence from earth in Chapters 4 through 19; the bride's presence in heaven before the second coming, all fit into the pattern of a pre-Tribulation Rapture scenario.

Now let us look at the evidence in First and Second Thessalonians.

EIGHT

FIRST THESSALONIANS AND THE RAPTURE

The two New Testament letters that mention the Rapture most were both written to the same people. These letters are First and Second Thessalonians.

These were the apostle Paul's earliest epistles. Both letters were written from Corinth in about the year A.D. 50, shortly after Paul's departure from Thessalonica (Acts 17:1–15 and 18:1–11).

Many important insights come from these early letters. *First*, it is nothing short of amazing how many Christian doctrines Paul taught these people who formed the church located in Thessalonica. He brought them from being idol-worshipping pagans to understanding the following major theological subjects in about four weeks: *election* (1 Thessalonians 1:4); *Holy Spirit* (1:5, 6; 4:8; 5:19); *assurance of salvation* (1:5); the *Trinity* (1:5, 6); *conversion* (1:9); the *Christian walk* (2:12; 4:1); *sanctification* (4:3; 5:23); *the day of the Lord* (5:1–3); the *three dimensions of man's nature* (5:23); *resurrection* (4:14–18); *Rapture of the Church* (1:10; 2:19; 3:13; 4:14–17;

5:9, 23); the *coming apostasy* (2 Thessalonians 2:3), the *advent of the Antichrist* (2 Thessalonians 2:3–12); the *second advent of Christ and world judgment* (2 Thessalonians 1:7–10).

These are only part of what Paul must have taught to them. Can you imagine today someone going to a city dominated by false religion, winning many to faith in Christ, founding a church, and then communicating all the above truths in four weeks? No wonder Paul said concerning his ministry there, "For our Gospel did not come to you in word only, but also in power and in the Holy Spirit and with full conviction . . ." (1 Thessalonians 1:5).

A *second* insight is that even though Paul had such a short time with them, he fully taught the whole scope of prophecy as it relates to the Rapture, the second coming of Christ and the world events that precede and follow. This fact alone should silence the many critical theologians and ministers who say that this subject is irrelevant to Christian living and shouldn't be taught. Paul had so thoroughly taught eschatology (prophecy) that he could refer to some advanced concepts and say, "Do you not remember that while I was still with you, I was telling you these things?" (2 Thessalonians 2:5).

The whole underlying occasion for writing these two letters sprang from the area of prophetic subjects. In First Thessalonians, Paul primarily answers the questions of whether believers who have died will be reunited with those who are still living at the time of the Rapture and are translated (1 Thessalonians 4:13–18).

In Second Thessalonians, Paul primarily writes to reassure the Thessalonian believers that they are not already in "the day of the Lord" and/or the Tribulation or the Seventieth Week of Daniel. (The first seven years of "the day of the Lord" coincides with the Tribulation period.)

The Problem of Lazy Brethren

A second occasion for writing both letters was the problem of those who misapplied the practical meaning of Paul's teaching concerning the "any moment" possibility of Christ's return which is commonly called the doctrine of imminence.

Two things should be observed about the way Paul dealt with this error. First, Paul doesn't deny or tone down his teaching that Christ's coming for the Church could be near. Some people think that no one should teach that Christ's coming could be very near because it could cause some to drop out of jobs, school, get married prematurely, and so forth, becoming generally irresponsible. However, the possible misapplication of a truth is never a justification for not teaching it. Some people misapply the truths of salvation, but we should continue to teach them.

Second, Paul shows that even if Christ were to come today, we should live responsibly and maintain a good testimony to the end. It has been my experience that most believers are motivated to greater dedication, faith, and spiritual production by the hope that the coming of the Lord Jesus approaches in their lifetime.

In 1 Thessalonians Paul reminds these idle believers of his example before them (2:9–10). He exhorts them to work, supply their own needs and maintain a testimony to the nonbelievers (4:11–12). Paul's first priority was to win people to Christ and to build them up in the faith. This, he tells us, is the proper response to the expectation of the Lord's imminent return.

The Rapture is mentioned in every chapter of 1 Thessalonians. The amazing emphasis of this doctrine in the earliest epistles underscores its importance.

The Rapture Delivers from Wrath
(1 Thessalonians 1:10)

Paul says in Chapter 1, "And to wait for His Son from heaven, whom He raised from the dead, that is Jesus, who delivers from the wrath to come." (1:10)

Dr. Morris comments on the term, *wait*, "The word for 'to wait' is found only here in the New Testament. And Grimm-Thayer (Greek dictionary) suggests that in addition to the thought of waiting for someone expected, it includes 'the added notion of patience and trust.' Findlay thinks it implies 'sustained expectation.'"[1]

This emphasizes that the believer is to constantly expect and await Christ's return. It is to be a primary motivating hope that inspires us to live for God and sustains us in adversity. The Thessalonians were undergoing extreme persecution. Paul reminds them that even though the present conditions are severe, the Lord will deliver us from the coming wrath of God upon the unbelieving world, which will be much more severe.

The purpose of this coming of "the Lord from heaven" is *to deliver* the true Church, composed of all believers, from this prophetic wrath to come. The verb "to deliver" is *ruomai* in the Greek. It means to deliver, rescue or save someone from a terrible situation in which he is helpless. This same term is used, for example, in Matthew 6:13 ("*deliver* us from evil") and in Colossians 1:13 ("He [Christ] *delivered* us from the domain of darkness"). This is a perfect term to describe the Rapture because it truly is a deliverance from human history's worst period of suffering.

---

[1]Leon Morris, *The First and Second Epistles to Thessalonians* (Grand Rapids: Eerdmans Pub. Co., 1959).

Rapture, Reunion, and Crown (2:19–20)

In Chapter 2, Paul says concerning the Rapture, "For who is our hope or joy or crown of exultation? Is it not even you, in the presence of our Lord Jesus at His coming? For you are glory and joy." (2:19, 20)

The apostle speaks of those whom he has introduced to Christ as his crown of exultation when the Lord Jesus comes in the Rapture. I believe that when the Rapture occurs we will be reunited with all those we helped come to faith in Christ. They will be part of our reward and crown at the Rapture. What a joyous thing to contemplate!

Rapture and an Unblamable Heart (3:12–13)

Paul says of the Rapture at the end of Chapter 3, ". . . May the Lord cause you to increase and abound in love for one another, and for all men, just as we also do for you; so that He may establish your hearts unblamable in holiness before our God and Father at the coming of our Lord Jesus with all His saints." (3:12–13)

If we allow the Holy Spirit to produce God's kind of love in us now, then we will have an unblamable heart of holiness when the Lord Jesus comes for the Church.

Paul also adds that all of the believers of the Church who have died will be with the Lord when He returns. This is explained in more detail in Chapter 4.

The Great Body Snatch (4:13–18)

Paul gives the basic reason for writing 1 Thessalonians at the end of Chapter 4. Since these verses have been commented on previously, it is sufficient to simply list the main points here.

First, believing loved ones who have died will not only join us in the Rapture, but will receive their resurrection bodies a split second before our translation. The Thessalonians were confused about whether they would see their loved ones again (4:13–15).

Second, the living believers will be snatched up bodily to meet the Lord and the departed saints in the air (4:16–17).

The Day of the Lord (5:1–11)

Paul answers another prophetic question that bothered the Thessalonians. He introduces this important section with the Greek phrase *peri de* ("Now as to" in NASB) which literally means "but concerning" or "now concerning." This was Paul's standard form for answering the questions of the ones to whom he was writing (see 1 Corinthians 1:11; 7:1; 7:25; 8:1; 12:1; 16:1). It always introduced a new subject and a new answer.

Let us read carefully the entire passage:

> *"Now as to the times and the epochs, brethren, you have no need of anything to be written to you. For you yourselves know full well that the day of the Lord will come just like a thief in the night. While they are saying, 'Peace and safety!' then destruction will come upon them suddenly like birth pangs upon a woman with child; and they shall not escape. But you, brethren, are not in darkness, that the day should overtake you like a thief; for you are all sons of light and sons of day. We are not of night nor of darkness; so then let us not sleep as others do, but let us be alert and sober. For those who sleep do their sleeping at night, and those who get drunk get drunk at night. But since we are of the day, let us be sober, having put on the breastplate of faith and love, and as a helmet, the hope of salvation. For God has not destined us for wrath, but for obtaining salvation through our Lord Jesus Christ, who died for us, that whether we are*

awake or asleep, we may live together with Him.
Therefore encourage one another, and build up one
another, just as you also are doing." (1 Thessalonians
5:1–11)

The question concerned the "times" *(chronoi)* and "seasons" *(kairoi)* of prophetic events that precede and lead up to the Second Coming of the Lord (5:1). *Chronoi* refers to the specific times of prophetic events in chronological order. *Kairoi*, on the other hand, views the characteristics of the events themselves.

Paul's Answer

First, Paul reminds them that they already "know perfectly" about this subject (5:2). This stands in contrast to their ignorance about the subjects of the previous section (4:13–18).

Second, Paul groups their entire question about specific prophetic events and their characteristics under one all-inclusive prophetic period—"the day of the Lord." He had obviously taught them that the day of the Lord included all of the specific events that count down to the Lord's return once it began. So Paul focuses his answer on *how* and *under what world conditions* "that day" will begin. The following is a brief survey of what the Bible teaches about the day of the Lord.

Day of the Lord in Old Testament

This phrase is used about twenty times in the Old Testament. The parallel terms, "the last days" and "in that day" occur fourteen times and more than one hundred times, respectively. Walvoord says, "A study of numerous Old Testament references to the Day of the Lord and 'the Day', as it is sometimes called, should make it clear to anyone who respects the details of prophecy that the designation denotes *an extensive time of divine judgment on the world* (emphasis mine). Among the texts are Isaiah 2:12-21; 13:9-16; 34:1-8; Joel 1:15-2:11; 28-32; 3:9-12; Amos 5:18-20; Obadiah 15-17; Zephaniah 1:7-18." After a thorough study, Walvoord concludes, "Based on the Old Testament revelation, the Day of the Lord is a time of judgment, culminating in the second coming of Christ, and followed by a time of special divine blessing to be fulfilled in the millennial kingdom."[2]

Day of the Lord in the New Testament

Almost all the teaching concerning the Day of the Lord in the New Testament is in this passage and in 2 Thessalonians 2:1-12. The following is a summary of what these two passages teach about "the Day of the Lord."

First, it will come "like a thief in the night" upon the unbelieving world. This metaphor means that it will come with *surprise* and *suddenness*.

Second, it will come when the world is saying "peace and safety." When the Antichrist is revealed by being miraculously raised from a mortal wound (Revelation 13:3), he will give superhuman answers to the world that will be in a state of chaos. They will almost instantly receive him as world leader and rest in his pseudo-peace and safety.

Third, sudden destruction is associated with it. The judgments of the Day of the Lord will be like birth pangs seizing a pregnant woman (5:3). Once they begin, there is no escape. But they increase in frequency and severity until the birth is over. So it will be with these judgments which are also set forth in the book of Revelation.

Fourth, it begins shortly after the Antichrist is revealed, which is immediately after the removal of the

[2]John F. Walvoord, *The Blessed Hope and the Tribulation*, pp. 111, 113.

Holy Spirit's restraining ministry (2 Thessalonians 2:1–12). This passage connects the beginning of the Day of the Lord closely to the Antichrist's revelation.

Fifth, the Day of the Lord *will not* take the believers by surprise for two reasons. The first reason is because the believer is a child of light and of the day. This means that he has the illumination of the Holy Spirit and the prophetic Scripture (Daniel 12:8–10). Peter spoke of this very illumination, "For we did not follow cleverly devised tales when we made known to you the power and the coming of our Lord Jesus Christ, but we were eyewitnesses of His majesty . . . and so we have the prophetic word *made* more sure, to which you do well to pay attention as to a *lamp shining* in a dark place, until the *Day* dawns and the morning star arises in your hearts." (2 Peter 1:16, 19) So the believer will not be taken by total surprise. As I have taught many times, the believer will not know the day or the hour, but in these last days it has been revealed that he will know the general time (Matthew 24:32–36). However, if the believer of this economy were left in the Day of the Lord with all of its specific signs, he could calculate the day of the Lord's return.

The second reason that the Day will not overtake the believer like a thief is because "he is not destined for wrath, but for the obtaining of salvation through our Lord Jesus Christ" (5:9). We will be delivered from the wrath that begins with the Day of the Lord by the Rapture.

The post-Tribulationists have more problems than a one-armed paperhanger trying to fit the beginning of the Day of the Lord in at the very end of the Tribulation.

First, they have the problem of holding off all the Divine judgments until after the Rapture (which they say is simultaneous with the Second Advent), and then having them all fall before the Second Coming. This means that at least most of the trumpet and seal judgments, plus all of the bowl judgments, would have to occur in less than five minutes. This view would also have to compress the invasion of the king of the North (Daniel 11:40–45; Ezekiel 38–39) and the kings of the East (Revelation 16:12) into that short period.

Second, they have to explain why the unbelievers of that time will proclaim "peace and safety" (5:3) in the midst of all the concentrated wrath from God. "Peace and safety" is contrasted with the sudden destruction that follows. So Gundry's interpretation that they are only wishing for peace and safety doesn't make sense.

Third, the fear and concern the Thessalonians have about being already in the Day of the Lord (2 Thessalonians 2:1–5) cannot be reconciled with the post-Tribulation view. Unless "the Day" started near the time of the Antichrist's unveiling, the passage wouldn't make sense. It would have been obvious to the Thessalonians that they could not be in the Day of the Lord if it were only at the very end.

All of us must admit that there are some things that are difficult to reconcile on this issue. But the pre-Tribulation view harmonizes all of the scriptural evidence best, and answers the most questions satisfactorily.

Sanctified and Complete at the Rapture (5:23–24)

Paul mentions the Rapture again in his closing prayer for the Thessalonians.

Paul prays, "May God Himself, the God of peace, sanctify you through and through. May your whole spirit, soul and body be kept blameless at the coming of our Lord Jesus the Messiah. The one who calls you is faithful and he will do it." (5:23, 24 NIV)

Paul reveals a beautiful truth in this prayer. It is God who sanctifies us. The verb "to sanctify" (*hagiazo* in the

Greek) has a common root with the term "holy." It literally means to set something apart as God's possession and for God's use. The word was used in ancient Greece even to describe inanimate objects that were offered to the ancient temple gods.

Paul's prayer is that God will progressively set apart our whole being to Himself. Paul then gives a promise of assurance that God will see that this is accomplished in our lives because *He* is faithful. The end result is that we will be blameless when we are caught up to stand before our Lord Messiah in the Rapture.

SUMMARY OF 1 THESSALONIANS

In conclusion, the following principles are taught in 1 Thessalonians concerning the Rapture:

(1) The doctrine of the Rapture was taught even to young believers.

(2) The Rapture will deliver believers in the Lord Jesus from the predicted time of wrath which is part of the beginning of the "Day of the Lord" (1:10; 5:9).

(3) All living believers will be suddenly caught up to meet the Lord in the air, and will be reunited with loved ones who have died.

(4) The believer will have an awareness of the general time of the Rapture's approach (5:4–5).

(5) The Day of the Lord will come with sudden destruction upon the unsuspecting, nonbelieving world while it is proclaiming peace and safety (5:2–3). The Rapture delivers believers from this period of destruction, as we noted in (2).

(6) The hope of the Rapture and its deliverance

from wrath is to be a source of comfort and encouragement to the believer (1:10; 4:18 and 5:11).

As the world spins virtually out of control from crisis to crisis, this hope burns ever brighter. May the impact of the incredible promises of deliverance from wrath we have just studied not be lost in the technical details.

NINE

LIGHT FROM A FORGED LETTER

Second Thessalonians contains a very important passage with regard to the chronology of events related to the Rapture. Whether you are a pre-, mid-, or post-Tribulationist, the interpretation of this letter is crucial.

The apostle Paul clearly states his main reason for writing the letter in Chapter 2, Verses 1 and 2:

> "Now we request you, brethren, with regard to the coming of our Lord Jesus Christ, and our gathering together to Him, . . .

> "That you may not be quickly shaken from your composure or be disturbed either by a spirit or a message or a letter as if from us, to the effect that the Day of the Lord has come." (2 Thessalonians 1–2)

The phrase "as if from us" brings out the real problem that this letter seeks to correct. Someone had brought a message to them, representing it as from Paul, which said that the Day of the Lord had already begun.

Paul begins to correct this grave error by appealing to "the coming of the Lord Jesus Christ." He specifies carefully which aspect of His coming by the qualifying clause "and our gathering together to Him . . ." This could only refer to the Rapture when all Christians will be caught up to be with Christ.

Because Paul begins this important section of the letter by holding up the promise of the Rapture first, it is obvious that it has an important bearing on whether the Day of the Lord has indeed already come.

The fact that Paul holds up the Rapture as yet to occur seems to remind the Thessalonians of its chronological relationship to the Day of the Lord. Since the Rapture hasn't occurred, the Day of the Lord could not already be present.

The Terrifying Forgery

Two words describe the Thessalonians' reaction to the forged message. The first is the verb *saleuo*, which is translated "shaken." It means to shake or agitate something. It is a violent term that is used sometimes to describe an earthquake. We have a slang expression today that captures this idea. We say, "He's all shook up," meaning that someone is thoroughly shaken from his emotional moorings. The people had been shaken from what they had been taught and become thoroughly confused.

The second term describing the impact of the forgery is translated "disturbed." The original Greek word (*throeo*) means "to be frightened." It is in the present tense which means that they were in a *continuing state* of fear.

Gundry disagrees with this premise. He says that the Thessalonians were only a little agitated, not fearful. He also says that their agitation was due to some believers who had erroneously understood that the Lord's coming was near and had quit their jobs. This misses the point of the context altogether. The Thessalonians were in a state of fear, not just agitated. They were confused and fearful because they thought they were already in the Tribulation, not because a few quit their jobs.

A CRUCIAL QUESTION

The following question helps reveal what Paul must have taught them. If Paul had told them that the Rapture followed the Day of the Lord, these people would not have been troubled but rather rejoicing because the Lord's coming for them would have been very near. They would have faced the Tribulation with hope and steadfastness, knowing that the Rapture was less than three and one-half years away, if Paul had taught a mid-Tribulation Rapture, or less than seven years away if he had taught a post-Tribulation Rapture.

But, if Paul had instructed them that the Rapture preceded the Day of the Lord, and afterwards a forged message was received that said they were already in that Day, then their panic becomes completely understandable.

I believe this scenario best explains the conditions that underlie this epistle. This whole context reflects that Paul had taught them a pre-Tribulation scenario for the Rapture.

Paul sets up a threefold denial of any message from himself which said that the Day of the Lord had come. He lists the three different ways that a false message could have been communicated, and denies them all. He sent neither a spirit, nor a verbal message, nor a written letter with such a teaching. Paul's usual way of communication was a written letter. For this reason he urges them to check out any letter presented as being from him by verifying his handwritten greeting and signature (3:17–18). He also wanted them to know that this letter correcting the forgery was not itself a forgery.

Two Imperative Historical Signs

Paul reminds them of two world-shaking events of prophecy which must happen just before the Day of the Lord can begin. He obviously selects these two events because they are of such magnitude that they could not occur unnoticed. About this Paul says,

> *"Let no one in any way deceive you, for it [the Day of the Lord]* will not come *unless* **the apostasy** *comes first, and* **the man of lawlessness** *is revealed, the son of destruction, who opposes and exalts himself above every so-called god or object of worship, so that he takes his seat in the temple of God, displaying himself as being God.*
>
> *"Do you not remember that while I was still with you, I was telling you these things?"* (2 Thessalonians 2:3–5)

The Great Apostasy

The first event which precedes the Day of the Lord is "the apostasy." This word (*apostasia* in Greek) means to deliberately forsake and rebel against known truth from and about God.

The definite article before the term "apostasy" clearly indicates that it is a definite event, not just a progressive rebellion. The article also points out that this fact had been taught to them before.

There are many New Testament warnings about a progressive apostasy in the last days which would grow in intensity within professing Christendom. Apostasy was perceptible even in the early Church as shown in Verse 7 where it is called "the mystery of lawlessness." But "the apostasy" is a reference to a climactic event when the professing church will completely revolt against the Bible and all of its historical truths.

This ultimate act of apostasy on the part of professing Christendom sets the stage for the second great sign, which apparently happens almost simultaneously.

The Unveiling of the Antichrist

With all restraint of lawlessness removed (that is, the rejection of God and His Truth), the door is opened for Satan to reveal his masterpiece, the Antichrist. He is called here "the man of lawlessness" and "the son of destruction." The exact meaning of these titles is "the man who brings lawlessness" and "the son who brings destruction."

What accurate insight these two descriptive titles give us. The Antichrist, who will spring forth from the modern remains of the ancient Roman culture and people, will cause the worst period of lawlessness and destruction the world has ever seen.

Daniel's prophecies about this world dictator give more insight into this aspect of his awesome career,

> "And he will speak out against the Most High and wear down the saints of the Highest One, and he will intend to make alterations in **times** and in **law**; and they will be given into his hand for a time, [and two] times, and half a time [three and one-half years]."
> (Daniel 7:25)

> "And in the latter period of their rule [Gentile world power], when the transgressors have run their course, a **king** will arise insolent and skilled in intrigue.

*"And **his** power will be mighty, but not by his own power [he will have Satan's powers], and **he** will **destroy** to an extraordinary degree and prosper and perform his will; he will destroy mighty men and the holy people.*

*"And through his shrewdness he will cause deceit to succeed by his influence; and he will magnify himself in his heart, and he will **destroy** many **by means of peace** . . ."* (Daniel 8:23–25a)

These Scriptures teach us that the Antichrist will alter times and laws to his own purpose. He will also be a master of deceit, and will deceive the whole world into following him. While capitalizing on the world's desire for *peace* and *security* (1 Thessalonians 5:3), he will bring them under his control and to ultimate destruction.

Paul gives a threefold summary of this Messianic counterfeit.

First, he opposes and exalts himself above every so-called god or object of worship. The Antichrist will seek to destroy all truth about God and even the gods of other religions.

Second, he will take his throne into the holy of holies of the third Jewish temple which must be rebuilt upon its ancient site.[1] This act will fulfill Daniel's and Jesus' prophecy concerning the "abomination of desolation" which officially begins the last three and one-half years of the Tribulation period (Daniel 9:27 compared with Matthew 24:15).

Third, he will proclaim and display himself as being God. This is the ultimate blasphemy. He will take secular humanism into the religious sphere by deifying man.

---

[1] It has recently been discovered that the holy of holies lies approximately 100 meters north of the Dome of the Rock. This means that the third temple could now be built without disturbing the third holiest Muslim shrine.

He will not only deceive the world into accepting him as the supreme political dictator, but will also demand worship (Revelation 13:4 and 15).

A Necessary Prelude

Another line of prophetic chronology makes it absolutely necessary for these two events to precede the Day of the Lord. This was previously mentioned briefly, but bears repeating here.

The Roman Dictator must be unveiled a short while before the actual beginning of Daniel's Seventieth Week, which also begins the Day of the Lord. This is necessary because, as stated before, it begins with the signing of a guarantee of protection for Israel between the Roman Dictator of the revived Roman Empire, and the leader of Israel called the False Prophet. The Roman Antichrist must have time to be revealed, take over the ten-nation European confederacy and establish himself as a world leader before he can have a power base from which to make the convenant with the Israeli leader.

Such momentous events necessitate an interlude between the revelation of the Antichrist and the official beginning of the Day of the Lord.

The Restrainer

After reminding the Thessalonians of the two signs just mentioned, Paul takes up another prophetic personality of whom he assumes their previous knowledge.

The apostasy and the Antichrist refer to future events. The conditions described by "the Restrainer" relate to the present time and to what is holding back these two fateful events.

Paul admonishes them by saying,

"And you know **what restrains** *him [Antichrist] now, so that in his time he may be revealed.*

"For the mystery of lawlessness [apostasy] is already at work; only **He who now restrains** *will keep on doing so until* **He** *is taken out of the way.*

"And then that lawless one will be revealed . . ."
(2 Thessalonians 2:6–8a)

The apostle had taught this subject so well that he could say "you know." Then he refers to the most critical subject of the whole context, "the Restrainer."

The term for "restrainer" *(katexo)* literally means to hold down or suppress something. It is translated in this sense in Romans 1:18 where it speaks of the unbeliever suppressing the truth.

In Verse 6, the Restrainer is called an influence by the use of the neuter gender in the participle form of the verb to restrain. But in Verse 7 a singular masculine gender is used to describe the Restrainer, thus showing that he is also a person.

The Duration of the Restrainer's Mission

The apostle Paul said that the Restrainer would keep on restraining both the mystery of lawlessness and the advent of the man of lawlessness continuously until **He** literally "takes Himself out of the midst." (This translation is demanded by the middle voice of the Greek verb.) Immediately after the Restrainer removes Himself from His mission, the Antichrist will be revealed.

Now let us list the characteristics of the Restrainer.

First, the Restrainer must be both a worldwide influence and a person. This suggests omnipresence.

Second, the Restrainer must be a supernatural person to be able to restrain from Paul's time to the present hour.

Third, the Restrainer must be a powerful person to

hold back two such mighty forces as worldwide apostasy and the Antichrist's advent.

Fourth, the Restrainer must have some logical reason for *terminating* the restraint of lawlessness and the Antichrist's advent, which agrees with the Biblical record.

Fifth, the Restrainer must have a logical reason to restrain *lawlessness* and the man of lawlessness.

WHO IS THE RESTRAINER?

There have basically been three different major views as to who or what "the Restrainer" is.

Is the Restrainer Human Government?

Some have said that the Restrainer is *human government.* Those who held this view in past history were not generally noted for their adequate view of the prophetic Scripture.

Mary Stewart Relfe is one of the modern-day Bible teachers who holds this view. She says,

"The Church was already in severe persecution at the hands of Rome, so Paul chose not to invite more suffering by naming the Roman power. He had previously in person identified it. Rome was so powerful that Paul knew *another* Super World Dictator professing to be above all could not rise to power until Rome was removed. Likewise, we know this power which has prevented the revealing of the Wicked One has been subsequent government structures.

"When the government of the world becomes unable to enforce law and order (or "is taken out of the way"), this condition will give rise to the revelation of this Wicked One World Leader, who will himself bring about some semblance of law and order. He will be revealed to the Christians in 2 Thessalonians 2:3 at the outset of the last seven years, but his wickedness will not be revealed to the world until midweek."[2]

There are a number of problems with this view. In fact Relfe's statement quoted above has some inner contradictions. This view must be rejected for the following reasons:

(1) It doesn't adequately explain the use of the masculine gender for the Restrainer in Verse 7 (*o katechon* in Greek). If the Restrainer were an impersonal force, the neuter gender would have continued to be used as in Verse 6. The deliberate switch to the masculine singular in Verse 7 indicates that the Restrainer is definitely a person.

(2) Human government doesn't have enough power to restrain Satan, who is second in power and intelligence only to God. Nor does it have the power or a logical reason for restraining "the mystery of lawlessness" which we have previously seen is that progressive development of the rejection of God and His truth. To say that the wicked Roman Empire, or any other form of human government, has restrained Satan's relentless attack against God's truth borders on the preposterous.

Furthermore, the Scripture teaches that Satan and his demons rule over this present world system, and apart from God's gracious restraint, they manipulate and guide unbeliev-

[2]Mary Stewart Relfe, *When Your Money Fails*, p. 216.

ing government leaders (see Ephesians 2:1–3; cp. Daniel 10:12, 13).

The thing that truly baffles me is how Relfe can say, "Rome was so powerful that Paul knew *another* Super World Dictator professing to be above all *could not rise* to power until Rome was removed."[3] This doesn't make sense. First of all, Satan could have simply taken possession of the Caesar of that day and made him the Antichrist. How in the world could the Roman government, a human power, have prevented Satan, a superhuman person with awesome powers, from doing this? Second, the government that the coming Dictator will take over is a revived form of the old Roman Empire.

(3) This view doesn't explain adequately the reason for "the restrainer getting Himself out of the midst." Human government will reach its zenith under the Antichrist. Human government doesn't end until the second coming of Jesus the Messiah to set up God's kingdom on earth. And, human government can't get itself out of the way as the translation of the verb's middle voice requires.

This view just doesn't harmonize with the Bible as a whole, nor answer the demands of this context.

Is the Restrainer Satan?

Another view is that the Restrainer is Satan. This would fit the need of the Restrainer to be both an influence and a person. It could also explain the purpose clause of Verse 6 which says, "so that in his [the Antichrist's] time he may be revealed." The idea (in this

[3]Ibid.

view) is that Satan would restrain the Antichrist's revelation until the most opportune time in order to insure his successful reception.

Hogg and Vine, who hold this view, interpret Verse 7 as follows,

> *"Until he be taken;* as shown in the notes, there is nothing in the text to justify *taken. Ginomai* means to become, to come to be.
> Naturally then, the meaning of the phrase is to come into being, or to appear, rather than to be removed, or to disappear."[4]

Hogg and Vine go on to make the following amplified translation of Verses 7 and 8 to support their view,

> "For the secret of (the spirit of) lawlessness is already working; only (there is) the Controller at present (who will hold it in check) until he (the man of lawlessness) may become (successfully manifested) out of the very midst (of the situation that will develop, so not risking defeat by a premature attempt to capture the key position). And then (but not until then) the Lawless One shall be revealed whom the Lord Jesus shall slay, etc."[5]

There are serious flaws in this view. First, the normal meaning of the Greek term, *katecho*, is to restrain or suppress something that is in active opposition to the restraint.

Second, the clear meaning of Verse 7 is that the Restrainer is an obstacle to "the mystery of lawlessness," not an ally holding it in tactical check.

---

[4]C. F. Hogg and W. E. Vine, *The Epistles to the Thessalonians*, p. 242.
[5]Ibid.

Third, the antecedent of *"He* is taken out of the way" is clearly the Restrainer. To make the "he" refer to the Antichrist rather than the natural antecedent is grammatically extremely improbable.

This view doesn't agree with the simple meaning of the context. The most serious flaw of this view in the light of the context is that it makes Satan be in opposition to himself. About that situation Jesus said on another occasion, "Every kingdom divided against itself will be ruined, and every city or household divided against itself will not stand. If Satan drives out Satan, he is divided against himself. How then can his kingdom stand?" (Matthew 12:26–27, NIV)

Is the Restrainer the Holy Spirit?

The third major view is that the Restrainer is *the Holy Spirit*. Relfe takes strong exception to this, "The recent pre-trib doctrine teaches that this 'he' is the Holy Spirit. There are many blatant inconsistencies which render this untrue."[6]

With due respect, this is not a *recent* view. Some noted early Church leaders believed that the Holy Spirit is the Restrainer. Alford, in Volume III of his scholarly commentaries, mentions the following men on pages 57 and 58 (I am indebted to Gundry for this insight). The first was John of Constantinople who was also known as Chrysostom (A.D. 347–407). He was called Chrysostom (golden mouth) because of the eloquence of his preaching. He is known to history as the greatest Greek-speaking Christian preacher of all time.[7] A second early Church leader who believed this view was Theodore of

---

[6]Relfe, op. cit. p. 216.

[7]Earle E. Cairns, *Christianity Through the Centuries*, pp. 151–153.

Mopsuestia (A.D. 350–428).[8] And another was Theodoret, Bishop of Cyprus (A.D. 390–457).[9]

Gundry says in favor of the Spirit's restraining role, "Far from being novel, the view just might reflect apostolic teaching . . . the charge of novelty against this view, as we have seen, does not survive investigation. We may ask why Paul should not have openly mentioned the Holy Spirit. But what reason would have prompted him to do so? For they knew what he was writing about (Verses 5 and 6a). No other passage of Scripture teaches that the Spirit holds back the appearance of the Antichrist. But neither does any other Scripture teach that Satan, the Roman Empire, or human government holds back the Antichrist."[10]

Interpreting God the Holy Spirit as the Restrainer best answers the grammatical, contextual and theological questions involved in 2 Thessalonians for the following reasons:

(1) It best answers the usage of both the neuter and masculine singular gender to describe the Restrainer. The Spirit is a worldwide restraining power, which explains the use of the neuter gender. Furthermore, since the Greek word for spirit *(pneuma)* is neuter, the neuter pronoun is regularly used to refer to Him. However, the distinct personality of God the Spirit is also frequently emphasized in the same context with the neuter by referring to Him with the masculine singular gender (see John 15:26 and 16:13–14).

(2) The Holy Spirit is almost always referred to by

[8]Ibid. p. 153.

[9]Henry Bettenson, *The Early Christian Fathers*.

[10]Robert H. Gundry, *The Church in the Tribulation*, pp. 125–126.

a title that describes His particular function or ministry. For instance, He is called "the Spirit of Truth" (John 14:17); "the Helper" (John 16:17); "the Spirit of life in Christ Jesus" (Romans 8:2). These titles mean the Spirit who teaches truth, gives us help and empowers us with the life of Jesus. So it is very normal for Paul to simply refer to Him as the Restrainer to people that he had thoroughly taught on the matter.

(3) This view is also the most consistent with the Holy Spirit's historic role revealed in the Bible. Theologically, the third person of the Trinity, the Spirit of God, is the active agent in implementing the common plan of the Triune God. For instance, He is the active agent in God's program of creation and salvation.

(4) It takes a person of superior power to restrain a supernatural person and his superhuman program. Jesus called Satan "the *ruler* of this world [-system]" (John 14:30). And in another place it says that the unbeliever is under Satan's authority and control, "In which you formerly walked according to the spirit of this age, according to the *prince* of the power of the atmosphere [of thoughts and customs], of the *spirit* that is now energizing the sons of disobedience." (Ephesians 2:2, literally translated.)

Satan has a highly organized army of fallen angels that are called demons. It is through this means that he exercises worldwide power in programs such as "the mystery of lawlessness." God reveals about this world-governing system, "For our struggle is not against flesh and blood, but against the *rulers,* against the *powers,* against the *world forces* of [behind] this darkness, against the *spiritual forces* of wickedness in the heavenly places." (Ephesians 6:12)

Satan even has his own corps of dedicated ministers within the Church who are spreading the mystery of lawlessness, "For such men are false apostles, deceitful workers, disguising themselves as *apostles* of Christ. And no wonder, for even Satan disguises himself as an angel of light. Therefore it is not surprising if his *servants* also disguise themselves as *servants of righteousness* . . ." (2 Corinthians 11:13–15)

To say that human government could restrain these things is ludicrous. Satan has no logical reason to do so. The person of the Spirit of God is the only one with the motive and the power to confront such a person and his system.

(5) This view best explains the purpose clause, "so that in his time he [Antichrist] may be revealed" (Verse 6). The verb "to be revealed or unveiled" *(apokalupto)* is used three times in this context, each time in the passive voice. This indicates that the Antichrist is revealed by God's permission into his fateful historic role.

ANOTHER PROBLEM

Even though the Holy Spirit is definitely the Restrainer of 2 Thessalonians Chapter 2, there is another issue to settle.

There are two possible ways of viewing the Holy Spirit's ministry as Restrainer. One is that He restrains directly and personally apart from the Church. The other way is that He restrains through the agency of His present personal residence in the Church.

As might be expected, Gundry leads the few who hold to a personal and direct restraining role of the Spirit apart from the Church. (I think it is important to say to the reader at this point that though I have taken personal exception to Gundry throughout this book, it is done with a healthy respect for his evident spirituality and scholarship.)

Gundry observes, "We have no warrant to infer from the residence of the Holy Spirit in the Church that He cannot work independently from the Church or that He limits Himself to the Church as His sole sphere or medium of activity. Neither in the present passage nor in any other do we catch so much as a hint that restraint of the Antichrist and of the mystery of lawlessness forms one of the purposes for the Spirit's residence in the Church."[11]

Actually, I believe that Gundry misses part of the issue in his statement. I agree that the Holy Spirit, being an omnipresent and omnipotent person, cannot be limited to working *only* through the Church in which He personally dwells.

The Holy Spirit through the Church does exercise a restraint upon the world. We are both the *salt* that preserves and the *light* that illuminates the world.

But equally important is whether there are certain ministries the Holy Spirit performs in the world because the Church *is still in the world*. When Jesus first predicted the birth of the Church, He promised, ". . . upon this rock [that is, the profession of faith in Him as the son of God and Messiah] I will build My church; and the gates of Hell shall not overpower it. I will give you the keys of the kingdom of heaven; and whatever you shall bind on earth shall be bound in heaven, and whatever you shall

[11]Ibid. pp. 126–127.

loose on earth shall be loosed in heaven." (Matthew 16:18–19)

If the post-Tribulationists are correct, and the Church does go through the seven years of Tribulation, then this promise cannot be kept. First, the Holy Spirit stops restraining Satan and his activities. Second, the mystery of lawlessness is allowed to go rampant and the great apostasy takes place. Third, the Roman Antichrist is unveiled. Fourth, the Antichrist is given complete authority over believers: "And it was given to him [Antichrist] to make war with the saints and to *overcome* them: and authority over every tribe and people and tongue and nation was given to him." (Revelation 13:7)

There is no way to reconcile the above prophecy with the promise given to the Church, if these saints are from the Church. If the Church is on the earth during this period, Satan and his Antichrist will totally overpower it.

Furthermore, Jesus made another solemn promise to the Church that is even stronger, "All authority has been given to Me in heaven and on earth. Go therefore and make disciples of all the nations, baptizing them in the name of the Father and the Son and the Holy Spirit, teaching them to observe all that I commanded you; and *lo I am with You always, even to the end of the age."* (Matthew 28:18–20)

In the light of this promise, it is a Divine necessity for the Holy Spirit to restrain apostasy and the Antichrist until the end of this Church age, which terminates with the evacuation of the Church. Otherwise, the Church would have been wiped out long ago.

All of the things which occur during the Tribulation are consistent with this view. The Tribulation becomes the hour of the power of darkness. The false apostles and ministers within the false church throw away all truth from God's Word and embrace the Antichrist as their leader. There is no more restraint. The world will be totally under Satan's authority.

The Holy Spirit will still work as He did in the Old Testament. He will not be gone from the world, but His unique ministries in, through and for the believer will be removed with the Church.

Relfe erects a straw man concerning this issue and then tears it down in her abrasive style, "If the church is to be raptured before the Tribulation, and 'he' the Holy Spirit is taken out at this time, as pre-trib espouses, how would those many Tribulation Saints with whom Antichrist makes war (Daniel 7:21; Revelation 13:7) get converted?"[12]

No informed exponent of pre-Tribulationism believes what she attributes to them. The Holy Spirit will endow the 144,000 chosen Israelites with the same kind of power He did the prophets in the Old Testament. In fact, two of the mightiest prophets from the economy of law will return to shake up the world. The Holy Spirit will convince men of their need of salvation, bring them to faith and regenerate them as He did from the beginning of man's sin.

But the unique Church economy ministries of indwelling, baptizing, sealing, gifting and filling of every believer will be removed with the Church. This is consistent with all that is revealed of the average Tribulational believer's level of spiritual insight, knowledge and maturity.

Gundry rejects this idea of a "reversal of Pentecost." He says that since all these ministries of the Spirit were given on the basis of the finished work of Christ, they cannot be removed.

But there is nothing in Scripture that says the conditions of one economy cannot be removed for a greater

[12]Relfe, op. cit. pp. 216–217.

Divine purpose that has been predicted, and then returned at a later date.

This point is graphically illustrated by another similar Divine action. The whole system of animal sacrifice required by the Mosaic Law economy is set aside in this present economy. The writer of the epistle to the Hebrews shows point by point how this system was fulfilled in the one sacrifice of the Messiah Jesus. Yet we find in Ezekiel Chapter 40 that animal sacrifice will be reinstituted in a memorial sense during the one-thousand-year millennial kingdom.

Since the Tribulation is the final seven years of Daniel's prophecy of seventy weeks of years, and since the first sixty-nine weeks of years were under the conditions of the Mosaic Law economy, it stands to reason that the same conditions must return for the final week. Thus the present ministries of the Spirit must be removed.

The Purpose of the Day of the Lord (2:8–12)

The purpose of the Day of the Lord is the last part of Paul's argument that proves it has not yet come. Paul says, "And then [after the Restrainer and the Church are removed] the lawless one will be revealed, whom the Lord Jesus will overthrow with the breath of his mouth and destroy by the splendor of his coming. The coming of the lawless one will be in accordance with the work of Satan displayed in all kinds of counterfeit miracles, signs and wonders, and every sort of evil that deceives those who are perishing. They perish because they refused to love the truth [the Bible] and so be saved. For this reason *God sends them powerful delusions* so that they will believe *the lie* and so that all will be condemned who have not believed the truth but have delighted in wickedness." (2 Thessalonians 2:8–12, NIV)

After the Restrainer is taken out of the way, Satan will be allowed not only to bring in the Antichrist, but to counterfeit the miracles of Messiah Jesus through him. The same three words that are used to describe our Lord Jesus' miracles throughout the Gospels are used in Verse 9 to describe Satan's activity through the Antichrist.

The Beginning of God's Wrath

Both the mid-Tribulationists and the post-Tribulationists argue that God's wrath doesn't come upon the world until late in the Tribulation. As mentioned before, all three views agree that God promised the Church would not experience His wrath.

Because of this, the mid-Triber says that God's wrath doesn't begin until the last three and one-half years of the Tribulation. The post-Triber maintains that God's wrath doesn't fall until the very end of the Tribulation. Both of these positions are predicated on the assumption that God's wrath is only expressed *in a physical judgment*.

I believe that this passage predicts the wrath of God is poured out in *the spiritual realm* to a horrifying degree with the very outset of the Tribulation. (Physical wrath follows shortly after.)

Just look at the terrifying direct judgments of God noted in this passage:

(1) Satan is allowed by God to counterfeit the miracles of the Lord Jesus in order to deceive the world into following the Antichrist. (If this isn't an expression of Divine wrath, what is?)

(2) The unbelieving world will be opened to "every sort of evil that deceives those who are perishing" (Verse 10).

(3) *"God sends* them a powerful delusion so that

they will believe *the lie."* (Verse 11) "The lie" probably refers to the Antichrist's claim to be God. This is a direct expression of wrath from God upon the whole world.

These expressions of God's wrath in the spiritual realm are much more terrifying to me than any of those predicted for the physical realm. Those who disagree need to hear the words of Jesus who said, "And do not fear those who kill the body, but are unable to kill the soul; but rather fear Him who is able to destroy both soul and body in hell." (Matthew 10:28)

PAUL'S FINAL PROOF

Paul assures the Thessalonians that they are not in the Day of the Lord because its purpose is to deceive and bring to destruction all those who rejected his truth and the Gospel. Since they have received and believed the truth, that Day is not for them. They will be removed with the Restrainer before the two events that set the stage for the Day of the Lord to begin.

Paul closes his argument with God's purpose for the believer, "But we should always give thanks to God for you, brethren beloved by the Lord, because God has chosen you from the beginning for salvation through sanctification by the Spirit and faith in the truth. And it was for this He called you through our gospel, that you may gain the glory of our Lord Jesus Christ." (2 Thessalonians 2:13–14) We should always be praising the Lord for His grace that has delivered us from the wrath that is soon to come.

In conclusion, the Thessalonian letters teach believers that God has not destined us for wrath, for Jesus is going to deliver us from the wrath to come (1 Thessalonians

5:9 and 1:10). But God has called us to gain the glory of our Lord Jesus Christ (2 Thessalonians 2:14).

In these days of growing darkness, what greater hope can we focus our hearts upon than these promises. The Rapture, thank God, is not a hope for the dead, but for the living.

INTERLUDE BETWEEN RAPTURE AND BEGINNING OF THE TRIBULATION

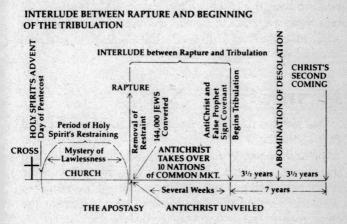

TEN

WHO WILL POPULATE
THE KINGDOM?

The most difficult question for post-Tribulationists to answer is: Who will populate the Millennial Kingdom? The answer is critical in establishing just when the Rapture takes place. There are a few important prophetic themes that converge and bear upon the answer to this question.

The *first prophetic theme* that bears upon this question has to do with whether the citizens of the Millennial Kingdom are mortals or immortals. The following outline of Scriptures clearly answers that question:

(1) They will bear children (something immortals can't do) (Isaiah 65:20–23; Jeremiah 23:3–6; 30:19–20).

(2) There will be marriage (also a no-no for immortals) (Isaiah 4:1–3).

(3) There will be labor (Isaiah 62:8, 9; 65:21–23; Jeremiah 31:5). One of the first tasks of the

Kingdom citizens will be to clean up the debris of war and bury the dead (Ezekiel 39:9–16).

(4) There will be disobedience and discipline. Even though the Millennial Kingdom begins with only believers, there will be unbelievers among their offspring (Zechariah 14:16–19).

(5) Though longevity will be greatly extended, there will be aging and death (Isaiah 65:20–23).

All of these things are characteristic of mortals, not immortals.

The *second prophetic theme* that relates to this question of who populates the Kingdom concerns *two* great judgments of the Tribulation survivors which takes place on earth immediately after Christ's return. These judgments are the Lord's first major act after returning to the earth.

There is an extremely important condition on earth which is demonstrated by the Lord's judgment of the survivors. These survivors are segregated into two judgments: one of Jews and one of Gentiles. This clearly indicates that the conditions by which God deals with mankind during the Church economy are not operative during the Tribulation. As previously noted, there is no distinction between Jew and Gentile believers in this economy (Galatians 3:27–28; Colossians 3:11). However, the judgments at the end of the Tribulation are completely segregated regardless of whether a Jew or a Gentile is a believer or an unbeliever.

This condition strongly indicates the absence of the Church during the Tribulation, or there would not be this distinction again between Jew and Gentile. These are conditions that prevailed during the time when God's special dealings were with Israel. As I mentioned before, I believe that Old Testament conditions will return when Daniel's Seventieth Week begins. These were in force when this decree was given allotting seventy sabbatical weeks of years for Israel. So since the first sixty-nine weeks of years were under Old Testament conditions, it follows that the Seventieth Week will be too.

The Judgment of Surviving Israelites

Throughout the Old Testament, prophecies were made about the coming of the promised Messianic Kingdom. Many of these spoke of a judgment of the physical descendents of Abraham, Isaac and Jacob to determine who would enter. Paul warned that not all who are called Israel are Israel (Romans 9:6).

Ezekiel clearly forewarned what would immediately precede the Messiah's founding of the Kingdom. In Chapter 20 he said that the Messiah would become king over them with great judgment upon the earth (Verse 33); that He would bring them out of the lands where He had scattered them (Verse 34); that He would bring all living survivors of Israel into the wilderness (probably the Sinai Desert) and judge them face-to-face (Verses 35 and 36); that the judgment would be made according to the covenant He made with them (which demanded faith in His provision for sin) (Verse 37); that He would purge from them all rebels who had transgressed against Him (Verse 38); and that those who remained would be established in the Kingdom (Verses 40–44).

The prophet Zephaniah predicts the same sequence of events. First, he predicts the terrible judgment of the Tribulation (1:14–18); then, the coming of the Lord to earth with great worldwide destruction and judgment (3:8). Next, he predicts a judgment of survivors in which all proud and exulting ones, and all deceitful and lying people, will be removed from their midst (3:11). He also said that only a humble and lowly people who take refuge in the name of the Lord will remain to enter the Kingdom and land of Israel (3:12–13). Finally, the Lord will become the king of Israel and remain in their midst (3:15–17).

These two passages make it very clear that all Jewish survivors will be gathered for judgment "face-to-face" with the Messiah Jesus, and that the believers alone will enter the Messiah's Kingdom.

The Judgment of the Gentile Survivors

After the Lord Jesus judges the Israelites (illustrated by the parables of Matthew 25:1–30), He will then gather all Gentiles to Jerusalem (the place of His glorious throne of Matthew 25:31) and conduct a very personal judgment of all those who survive the Tribulation (Matthew 25:31–46).

This passage very clearly indicates when and upon whom this judgment takes place, "But when the Son of Man comes in His glory, and all the angels with Him, then He will sit on His glorious throne. And all the nations [Gentiles] will be gathered before Him; and He will separate them from one another, as the shepherd separates the sheep [believers] from the goats [unbelievers]; and He will put the sheep on His right, and the goats on the left." (Matthew 25:31–33)

At the end of the judgment and separation the Lord Jesus says, "And these [that is, the goats on the left] will go away into eternal punishment, but the righteous [that is, the sheep on His right] shall go into eternal life."

The word "nations" in Verse 32 should be translated "Gentiles" for two reasons. First, the Greek original *ta ethne* can be translated either way with equal correctness. Second, since those judged are either taken into the Kingdom or cast into eternal judgment, it must be translated "Gentiles," because only individuals can be judged as to eternal destiny. No nation ever has been totally saved or totally lost.

The Lord uses a unique test to determine whether these Tribulation survivors are true believers in Him. This is evaluated on the basis of how they treated a very special group that the Lord Jesus calls "these brothers of mine" (Matthew 25:40, 45). Judging by the unusual survival of this group in spite of hunger, thirst, estrangement, lack of adequate clothing, sickness and imprisonment, it seems certain that they are the 144,000 Jewish witnesses.

They are apparently supernaturally converted just before or at the very beginning of the Tribulation much like the apostle Paul (Revelation 7:1–3). They are separated to Christ in a special way as bond-slaves (*doulos* in Greek) and are sealed with the seal of God. This usually means the indwelling presence of the Holy Spirit (compare 2 Corinthians 1:22; Ephesians 1:13; 4:30).

Because of the salvation report of untold numbers of people from every nation being placed right after the call of the 144,000, it is obvious that the Holy Spirit is indicating the results of their witness (see Revelation 7:9).

At the end of the Tribulation, the same 144,000 are pictured standing with Jesus the Messiah on Mount Zion in Jerusalem (Revelation 14:1–5). The indication is that they all survived the Tribulation and are in *unresurrected* bodies.

Now with that in mind, think of the incredible sufferings these 144,000 evangelists will have to endure. They will be marked men because they are believers from the beginning and preach the message of salvation. They will be hunted, imprisoned, and have no means of economic survival because they will expose the Antichrist and the False Prophet for what they are.

They will have to depend upon their converts to sustain and help them. And since these are going to be men with a price on their heads, only a true believer will risk death to help them. And in the light of Revelation 7:14–17, great numbers of these will be martyred for just such a faith.

But since the 144,000 can't die, they will continue to experience the hunger, thirst and exposure revealed in Revelation 7:16 and Matthew 25:35–40.

So just as Rahab the prostitute proved the genuineness of her faith by helping the Hebrew spies escape from Jericho, so the Tribulation saints will prove theirs by helping the 144,000 evangelists escape the Antichrist.

Finally, with both the unbelieving Israelites and Gentiles removed in judgment, the Kingdom begins with only believers. It is established with justice and righteousness and governed perfectly by the Messiah (Isaiah 11; 65:17–25; Micah 4:1–13). It will last for a thousand years (Revelation 20:4).

THE POST-TRIBULATION ANSWER

With these prophetic themes in mind, let us see how the post-, mid- and pre-Tribulationists answer the question of "Who will populate the Kingdom?"

The *post-Tribulation* view faces the greatest difficulty in answering this question for the following reasons:

(1) The Scriptures specify that only believers who survive the Tribulation will enter the Millennial Kingdom.

(2) Those surviving believers must be mortals with unresurrected bodies.

Yet, as I've said before, in the post-Tribulation scheme for the Rapture, the Rapture occurs simultaneously with the Second Advent of the Lord Jesus at the very end of the Tribulation. Since in the Rapture every living believer on earth will be instantly translated from mortal to immortal, from where will the believing survivors come? The only survivors left in mortal bodies after the Rapture would all be unbelievers.

Furthermore, if the Rapture occurs simultaneously with the Second Advent, how could there be a judgment immediately afterward? The Rapture would have already separated the sheep from the goats. As we have seen, the Lord divides the survivors into two groups. The sheep he calls "the righteous." They have eternal life and enter the Kingdom as mortals. The goats are cast directly into eternal punishment (Matthew 25:46).

Some post-Tribulationists ineffectively try to answer this dilemma by saying that some of the unbelievers will believe immediately after the Rapture, when they see the Lord Jesus returning to the earth. But this is impossible because the basis upon which the Messiah will evaluate genuine faith is determined by how they treated "His brothers" (literally Jesus said, "these brothers of mine" Matthew 25:40) *during the Tribulation.* It is not a "last-second" faith that He speaks of in either Ezekiel 20:33–39 or in Matthew 25:31–46.

The vast majority of post-Tribulationists do not attempt to answer these questions related to who will populate the Kingdom. Most of them do not get into the fine points of the prophetic Scriptures. They rather content themselves with taking potshots at the pre-Tribulationists, contending that pre-Tribulationists base their belief on wishful thinking and hearsay rather than on careful study of the Scriptures. But I'll have more to say about this later. Most of the post-Tribulationists with whom I have had private interaction have not even considered the question discussed in this chapter.

I once had a short debate with Robert Gundry before

the student body at Westmont College. This was sprung on me as a surprise at the end of a series of lectures on prophetic messages I had given for chapel during the spring of 1967. I recall that at that debate I hit Dr. Gundry with the question of who will populate the Kingdom, and he had no answer for it.

This is not the case today though. Gundry is one of those few "post-Tribs" who has wrestled with the fine points of the prophetic system. In his book, published in 1973, Gundry has sought to answer this question.

Gundry believes that the progenitors of the Millennial Kingdom will come from the 144,000. But to arrive at this view, Gundry had to do some fancy allegorical interpretation.

First, Gundry says that the 144,000 evangelists of Revelation Chapters 7 and 14 contain both women and men.[1]

Second, and farther out into the mist of allegorical interpretation, Gundry contends that the 144,000 Israelites are not believers until they see the Lord Jesus coming in the Second Advent. This ingenious but doubtful theory explains how there will be believing Israelites in untranslated bodies still on earth after the Rapture.

Gundry summarizes this view by saying, "Thus, the 144,000 will include both men and women who will populate and replenish the millennial kingdom of Israel. If they resist the Antichrist but remain unbelievers in Christ until the second coming, the reason for their sealing at once becomes apparent: their unconverted state will require special protection from the wrath of God and persecution of the Antichrist."[2]

I reject Gundry's view for the following reasons:

First, it is extremely improbable that the 144,000 con-

---

[1] Robert H. Gundry, *The Church in the Tribulation*, p. 82.

[2] Ibid. pp. 82–83.

tain both women and men. Every noun, pronoun and participle used to refer to them in all the Scriptures is in the masculine gender. Normally, throughout the Bible, men are chosen for such a rugged and hazardous prophetic-evangelistic ministry as is described for the 144,000.

The following reference to the 144,000 also has all the indications of being literal, "These are the ones who have not been defiled with women, for they have kept themselves chaste." (Revelation 14:4a) Although normally there is nothing wrong with having a wife, there are some special ministries where God calls a person to be celibate and totally set apart to his mission (see 1 Corinthians 7:1–7).

Second, I find totally unsupportable the interpretation of the 144,000 being unconverted until the second coming of the Lord Jesus. At the very beginning of the Tribulation, the Bible says, " 'Do not harm the earth or the sea or the trees, until we have *sealed* the *bond-servants* of our God on their foreheads.' And I heard the number of those who were *sealed,* one hundred and forty-four thousand *sealed* from every tribe of the sons of Israel." (Revelation 7:3–4)

The term "to seal" (*sphragizo* in Greek) is used throughout the New Testament to refer to the Holy Spirit's presence in a believer in the sense of a sign of God's ownership. This word was used of the imprint made by a signet ring. In those days every person of means had a distinctive symbol in his signet ring. Whenever a person would purchase something, he would press the ring with his seal into wax or clay and attach it to the purchase. That became the sign of his ownership.

Sphragizo is used in Ephesians 1:13 and 14 in the same sense. The Holy Spirit is God's seal within the believer. It is God's pledge that He has purchased us and will bring us to our heavenly home. God's seal upon the 144,000 signifies the same thing.

Gundry's contention that it is to protect them as unbelievers from God's wrath and the Antichrist's persecution doesn't compute. Why would God have to protect chosen ones from His own wrath? And how could they resist the awesome deceptions of the Antichrist, reject his number on pain of death as unbelievers? Unbelievers would not have the motive nor the power source for sustaining such decisions. There will perhaps be some Israelites saved when they see the Messiah coming, but it surely will not be the 144,000 nor the majority of others who are already saved.

Gundry runs into his greatest obstacle in seeking to explain the judgment of the Gentiles at the end of the Tribulation which is predicted in Matthew 25:31–46. This passage presents such formidable problems to the post-Tribulation system that Gundry just seeks to explain it away and wrench it all the way over to the end of the Millennium. I have just shown why the Lord's separating of the believing sheep from the unbelieving goats wouldn't be possible if the Rapture had just occurred.

I believe it is impossible to move this judgment to the end of the Millennium for the following reasons:

First, the overall context of this passage begins in Matthew 24. Jesus first predicted the general signs that would like birth pangs warn of the approach of the Tribulation's beginning (24:1–8); then, He predicts some major events that will occur during the Tribulation's first half (24:9–14); next He predicts major episodes that break forth during the second half of the Tribulation, including the incident that begins it (24:15–28); next He describes the details of His actual return to earth (24:29–31).

There is a break in the consecutive prophetic narrative

at this point. The Lord steps back and gives a parable to apply how the predicted signs were to be understood. He shows that the generation that would see all the signs coming together simultaneously would be the one that would see them all fulfilled (24:32–35).

The Lord Jesus then gave a historical illustration from Noah's day to show that though we would know the general time of His coming (a generation), we would not know the exact time (a day or an hour). I believe that this illustration also shows how the believer from the Church will be taken out before the judgments of the Tribulation fall (24:36–51).

The Lord gives several parables to illustrate specifically how and on what basis the Jews will be judged at the end of the Tribulation (25:1–30). The specifics of this judgment are given in Ezekiel 20:33–38.

The prophetic consecutive narrative continues in Matthew 25:31–46 for the first time since the description of the Lord's return in 24:29–31. The future historical narrative begins again with, "But *when* the Son of Man *comes in his glory,* and all the angels with Him, *then* He will sit on *his glorious throne.*" (25:31)

So the context shows that this judgment takes place when Christ comes to earth in His glory and takes His seat on His glorious throne, which is the oft-predicted throne of David in Jerusalem. If Gundry were correct, why would the Lord Jesus come to the earth in His glory at the end of the Millennium? He will have already reigned on this glorious throne for a thousand years.

Second, a formidable obstacle to placing this judgment at the end of the Millennium is the conditions that are described as befalling "His brothers." The Lord speaks of hunger, thirst, nakedness, sickness and imprisonment falling upon those who believe in Him. If Gundry's theory were correct and this judgment occurs at the end of the Millennium, it would be impossible to reconcile such conditions with what the Bible promises concerning the Millennial Kingdom.

For instance, it says there will be no sickness:

> "Say to those with palpitating [anxious] hearts, 'Take courage, fear not. Behold your God will come with vengeance . . .' Then the eyes of the blind will be opened, and the ears of the deaf will be unstopped. Then the lame will leap like a deer, the tongue of the dumb will shout for joy . . ." (Isaiah 35:4–6)

> "For the youth will die at the age of one hundred, and the one who does not reach the age of one hundred shall be thought accursed." (Isaiah 65:20)

There will be no want for food, drink, shelter or clothes:

> "And they shall build houses and inhabit them; they shall also plant vineyards and eat their fruit.

> "They shall not build, and another inhabit. They shall not plant, and another eat; for as the lifetime of a tree, so shall be the days of My people, and My chosen ones shall wear out the work of their hands.

> "They shall not labor in vain, or bear children for calamity; for they are the offspring of those blessed by the Lord, and their descendents with them." (Isaiah 65:21–23)

There will be no need for prisons because:

(1) Satan will be bound for a thousand years (Revelation 20:2–3).

(2) "They will not hurt or destroy in all My holy mountain, for the earth will be full of the

knowledge of the Lord as the waters cover the sea." (Isaiah 11:9)

(3) "And the Lord will be king over all the earth . . ." (Zechariah 14:9).

(4) "And He will judge between many peoples and render decisions for mighty distant nations. Then they will hammer their swords into plowshares, and their spears into pruning hooks; Nation will not lift up sword against nation, And never again will they train for war. And each of them will sit under his own vine And under his fig tree, With no one to make *them* afraid, For the mouth of the Lord of hosts has spoken." (Micah 4:3–4)

There is no way to move the judgment of Matthew 25:31–46, with its description of horrible human suffering, over to the end of the Millennium. Those sufferings could not happen in the Millennium. This would directly contradict the many promises of the Millennium conditions quoted above.

THE MID-TRIBULATION ANSWER

Most Mid-Tribulationists would have no problem with their system answering who would populate the Kingdom since according to their view, the Rapture occurs at the middle of the Tribulation and many could be saved afterwards.

There is one exception, however. Relfe paints herself into a corner when she says:

"'. . . until the day that *Noah* entered the *ark*, and the *flood* came, and *destroyed them all.*' This was the first great breakthrough in the study! I had never seen this before, although a long time before I had memorized the Scripture! The *day* representing Christ's coming for the church, *Noah* (representing the believer) entered into the *ark* (representing the place prepared for us), the *flood* (representing the wrath of God) came and destroyed them all (representing a doomed world). *Not one person other than Noah and his family was saved.* The remainder of the world immediately received the wrath of God from which there was no escape . . .

"When this great concept was revealed to me, that whenever Christ comes for His Bride, there would be no one else saved, I was *so shaken* by the false teachings of millions saved after the 'catching away'; the multitudes the 144,000 sealed Jews would win, that I literally detached myself from every teaching, doctrine, or belief I had embraced and as a raft in the ocean, I became free to be blown about by the wind of Heaven, the Holy Spirit of God!"[3]

Relfe's dogmatic statement that not one person will be saved after the Mid-Tribulation Rapture makes it impossible for her to answer, "Who will populate the Kingdom?" According to her view, there will only be unbelievers on earth during the last half of the Tribulation and at the Second Coming. Therefore, there would be no need for separating the sheep and goats. They would all be goats, and thus all cast into everlasting punishment.

Furthermore, there could be no Millennium because there would be no mortal believers, nor any mortals for that matter, left to enter the Kingdom.

Relfe's major premise for establishing her mid-Tribulation view is that the wrath of God only falls upon the second half of the Tribulation, not the first. As I indicated earlier the wrath of God falls on man primarily in the spiritual realm in the first half of the Tribulation, and in the physical realm in the second half. We aren't to believe that God's wrath is expressed only in physical judgments, are we? Indeed, the terrible judgments that God sends upon the world through the unrestrained, deceptive miracles of Satan are far worse because they will send men's souls to hell forever (2 Thessalonians 2:9–13).

God will deliver us from both His wrath in the spiritual and the physical sphere because He will come for us before the Tribulation begins.

My spirit was grieved with some of the statements Relfe made, such as, "And now, Brothers and Sisters in Christ, some of the things I have written in prior chapters, I honestly confessed were 'prudent assessments.' I must now make a radical departure and commend to you that which is contained in this chapter relevant to the overall structure of Daniel's Seventieth Week is Divine Revelation! The same Holy Ghost who moved Holy men of old to 'write the things that shall be hereafter' moved on me divinely revealing to me what it was He originally spoke to them!

". . . Finally brethren, I am aware that the hour has come; and that God has indeed 'brought me to the Kingdom for just such a time as this' and to this very chapter in which I boldly confess that I come to you in the role of a New Testament 'Prophet.'"[4]

There is no question but what Mrs. Relfe is sincere. But to claim that the Lord appeared to her and told her that her mid-Tribulation view was correct is treading onto dangerous ground. All I can say is that we all need to "try the spirits to see whether they are from God." (1 John 4:1)

[4]Ibid. pp. 185–186.

THE PRE-TRIBULATION ANSWER

The pre-Tribulation view has no problem answering who will populate the Kingdom. Nor does it have a problem harmonizing the judgments at the end of the Tribulation.

(1) The Lord will Rapture the Church believers before the beginning of Daniel's Seventieth Week.

(2) The Antichrist will be revealed and will take over the ten-nation confederacy of Europe.

(3) He will sign a covenant with the leader of Israel, the False Prophet, which begins Daniel's Seventieth Week.

(4) Around this same time, God will send the two prophets (Moses and Elijah), and will seal the 144,000 evangelists.

(5) They will have a great harvest of souls, although most will be martyred (Revelation 7:9–17). Incidentally, God says these martyrs are killed during "the great Tribulation," which is the second half of Daniel's final week (Revelation 7:14). (This also disproves Relfe's contention that no one will be saved during the "Great Tribulation.")

(6) The Lord returns to earth and judges the Jewish and Gentile survivors separately.

(7) The believers of both groups go into the Kingdom, and the unbelievers to eternal punishment.

PTL

As I close this chapter, my soul praises the Lord for His grace that has given us a sure hope for the living and not the dead. Believers from the Church will enter the Millennial Kingdom, but in immortal bodies as priests and corulers with the Lord Jesus. And dear brothers and sisters, that's grace!

ELEVEN

THE RESURRECTIONS
IN REVIEW

There are two categories of resurrection in the Bible. One is only for believers who have died, and is called "the resurrection of life" (John 5:29). The other category of resurrection is for all unbelievers of all dispensations, and is called "the resurrection of damnation" (John 5:29, KJV).

There is a strong disagreement between pre- and post-Tribulationists concerning the resurrection of life, or as it is also called, "the first resurrection" (Revelation 20:4–6). The disagreement concerns whether the first resurrection occurs only at the end of the Tribulation (which is the post-Tribulation view), or whether it takes place in several stages at different points of history (the view of pre-Tribulationists and some mid-Tribulationists).

If the post-Tribulationists could prove that there is only one phase to the resurrection of life, and that it occurs at the Second Coming, then they could make a strong case against pre- and mid-Tribulationism. The reason is because there is a resurrection and a translation of saints at the Rapture. If the Rapture is separated by seven years from the Second Coming, as pre-Tribulationists contend, then there has to be at least one more phase in order to resurrect the Old Testament and Tribulation saints. Daniel 12:1–3 clearly places the resurrection of Old Testament saints at the end of the Tribulation. And Revelation 20:1–5 definitely places the resurrection of Tribulation saints **after** the Lord Jesus comes to earth, judges the Antichrist, binds Satan and judges the living survivors.

All seem to agree about "the resurrection of damnation" which raises only unbelievers from the dead in bodies of corruption. This resurrection takes place at the end of time when all unbelievers from every dispensation will be raised to stand judgment at the Great White Throne (Revelation 20:11–15).

The First Resurrection—Several Stages

Paul flatly states that the first resurrection has at least three stages:

Stage one was the resurrection of the Lord Jesus the Messiah. Paul says, "But now Christ has been raised from the dead, the first fruits of those who are asleep." (1 Corinthians 15:20)

Stage two will be the resurrection of at least the believers of the present economy of grace. Paul says again, "But each in his own order: Christ the first fruits, after that *those who are Christ's at His coming* . . ." (1 Corinthians 15:23).

Stage three will be at the end of the Millennium when time ends and eternity begins. It is at that point that death is abolished. Believers who are alive at the end of the Kingdom economy will be translated from mortal to immortal. This is all implied by the statement, "The last enemy that will be abolished is death." (1 Corinthians 15:26)

Gundry disagrees with this, of course. But he does make some interesting statements: "The first resurrection does in fact take place in phases. But only *two* phases of the resurrection can be determined from clear and specific chronological notations . . . *In principle we should not consider a pretribulational phase of the first resurrection impossible,* but we need scriptural evidence."[1] (Emphasis mine.)

I deeply appreciate this honest statement. Now let's look at some Scriptural evidence. As stated above, there are at least three stages, not just two, indicated in 1 Corinthians Chapter 15.

The Different Battalions of Resurrection

The apostle Paul uses an extremely important term in relation to the stages of resurrection. He says again, "But each in his *order* . . ." (1 Corinthians 15:23a). *"Order"* is the translation of the Greek word *tagma* which was primarily a military term. It was most frequently used to designate a division or battalion of soldiers. The best available Greek New Testament lexicon says about this term, "Of a number of persons who belong together and are therefore arranged together; *division; group.* A military term for bodies of troops in various numbers such as divisions or battalions of soldiers . . . in 1 Corinthians 15:23f the gift of life is given to various ones in turn, and at various times. One view is that in this connection Paul distinguishes three groups: Christ, who already possesses life, the Christians, who will receive it at His second coming, and the rest of humanity, who will receive it when death, the last of God's enemies, is destroyed."[2]

[1]Robert H. Gundry, *The Church and the Tribulation,* p. 148.
[2]F. W. Gingrich and Frederick Danker, *A Greek-English Lexicon of the New Testament,* p. 802.

Paul paints a word picture which describes army divisions on parade passing by a reviewing stand at different intervals in time. Even so, the believers are to be resurrected, but each one in **his own division.** The very term, *tagma*, implies a number of phases.

Precedents for Many Phases

There are some very unusual incidences of resurrection which at the very least establish a precedent for having more than two phases within the "resurrection of life."

The *first case* occurred shortly after the Lord Jesus was raised from the dead. The Word of God says, "And the tombs were opened; and *many* bodies of the saints who had fallen asleep *were raised;* and coming out of the tombs after His [Jesus'] resurrection they entered the holy city and appeared to many." (Matthew 27:52–53) This verse definitely indicates that a token number of saints who had recently died were resurrected at the time of Jesus' resurrection.

This group very much resembles the wave sheaf offering that was part of the first fruits of the Divinely ordained schedule within Israel's harvest season. When the first of the grain was harvested, they celebrated the feast of the first fruits (Exodus 23:16). Concerning this, God said to Moses, "Speak to the sons of Israel, and say to them, 'When you enter the land which I am going to give to you and reap its harvest, then you shall bring in the sheaf of the first fruits of your harvest to the priest. And he shall wave the sheaf before the Lord for you to be accepted . . .'" (Leviticus 23:10–11).

The priest waved this bundle of grain tied together from the first fruits (the wave sheaf) before the Lord inside the holy place of the tabernacle of worship. This demonstrated both Israel's thankfulness and their faith in God for a full and bountiful harvest to come.

I believe that this was a beautiful expression of the resurrection. The fact that Jesus is called "the first fruits of those who sleep" certainly authorizes the analogy. For Jesus is both the first fruits and our great High Priest. He took the wave sheaf of believers resurrected with Him and waved them before the Lord in the heavenly tabernacle. He thus expressed faith for us of a certain and bountiful harvest in the future. Just as the wave sheaf was only accepted with a sacrificed lamb, so the Lord Jesus, our Lamb, made the wave sheaf of man's resurrection acceptable. This wave sheaf was a guarantee of our resurrection.

Israel's harvest had many phases. The first fruits and wave sheaf was first. The main harvest was next. Then there was another phase at the end of the harvest called "the Feast of the Ingathering" (Exodus 23:16). Afterwards, the *gleanings* were harvested by the alien and needy in Israel (Leviticus 23:22). The following chart illustrates how Israel's harvest could be a type of the various stages of the first resurrection.

The *second case* that sets a precedent is the future resurrection of the two Old Testament prophets who are sent back to prophesy in Jerusalem for the first three and one-half years of the Tribulation. In the middle of the Tribulation, when unlimited authority is given to the Antichrist (Revelation 13:5–8), he will kill the two prophets (Revelation 11:4–10). Their dead bodies will be exposed to the world in the streets of Jerusalem for three and one-half days. Then, the Scripture says, "And after the three days and a half the breath of life from God came into them, and they stood on their feet; and great fear fell upon those who were beholding them. And they heard a loud noise from heaven saying to them, 'Come up here.' And they went up into heaven in the cloud, and their enemies beheld them." (Revelation 11:11–12)

**ORDER OF RESURRECTION
PRE-TRIBULATION RAPTURE**

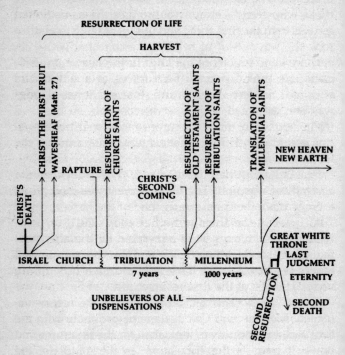

The whole world will probably see this by satellite television. We now have the technical ability to fulfill what is predicted, "And those from the peoples and tribes and tongues and nations will *look* at their dead bodies for three days and a half, and will not permit their dead bodies to be laid in a tomb." (Revelation 11:9)

Gundry objects to this scenario. He makes a big point of the fact that the Scriptures nowhere mention a resurrection of the Church prior to the Tribulation. But then the Scriptures nowhere specifically mention the resurrection of the Church at the middle or the end of the Tribulation either.

The resurrection of the Tribulation saints is mentioned as occurring *after* the second coming (Revelation 20:1–6).

There is no way to escape the chronology of the Tribulation saints' resurrection. According to 20:4, it occurs after the Lord Jesus returns and sets up thrones of judgment on earth.

That does not fit with Gundry's post-Tribulational chronology either. His sequence of events requires the Church to be resurrected just **before** the second coming. So like it or not, there is still a gap of time between the Church's resurrection and that of the Tribulation saints even in the post-Tribulational scheme.

All premillennialists, whether pre-, mid-, or post-Tribulationist, have a bit of a problem with exactly how the saints of the Millennial Kingdom get from mortal bodies to immortal ones. This is so because the Scripture says, "The rest of the dead did not come to life until the thousand years were completed. This is the first resurrection. Blessed and holy is the one who has part in the first resurrection; over these the second death has no power, but they will be priests of God and of Christ and will reign with Him for a thousand years." (Revelation 20:5–6)

These verses seem to indicate that the first resurrection, the one of life, will end with the resurrection of the saints at the end of the Tribulation. In view of this, what happens to the mortal believers at the end of the Millennium?

One good explanation is that only unbelievers who are a menace to society will die. The initial believing parents who start the Millennial Kingdom will have some children who will not believe. This is why it is predicted that the Messiah Jesus will rule the nations with a rod of iron. Isaiah's prophecy supports the theory that only un-believers will die, ". . . the one who does not reach the age of one hundred shall be *thought* accursed" (Isaiah 65:20b). The accursed one who dies would be the un-believer who disrupts society.

Another statement indicates that believers will live through the entire thousand years. Isaiah said not only that a person would be a child at one hundred years of age, but he also predicted that the Kingdom saints' days would be as the lifetime of a tree (Isaiah 65:22). I know of some trees that are more than two thousand years old.

If this explanation is correct, and I think that it is, then the only resurrection that would need to take place at the end of the Millennium is the one of damnation. The millennial saints would be translated directly into im-mortality when death is abolished. (1 Corinthians 15:26)

CONCLUSIONS

We have seen how the first resurrection must have more than one phase. Even if the post-Tribulationists could prove the Rapture occurs at the beginning of Christ's return to earth (which they cannot), they still couldn't answer the problem of the resurrection of Trib-ulation saints which occurs after Christ has returned and judged the earth (Revelation 19:19–20:6).

Relfe, who I found to be a very unorthodox mid-Trib-ulationist, arrogantly paints herself into another theo-logical corner, "Now, in an attempt to clarify a few other classic errors being propagated, let me summarize some of my findings: The pre-Tribulation Theory has *no resur-rection*! The first resurrection of Revelation 20:4–6 is the only resurrection for the just, for the only coming of Christ for the church. (His coming back to the earth is *with all* the saints.) (Zechariah 14:5). Many have manufactured aberrations of the scripture teaching first fruits, gleanings, and harvesting resurrections. Hear therefore, what the scriptures say . . . ," and so on and so forth.[3]

Relfe's statement and following argument in her book are a bit hard to follow, but the essence is this: There is only one resurrection of the just. There are no phases or successive stages within it. The one resurrection of the just occurs at the last trumpet which she identifies as the end of the Tribulation.

This argument truly startled me because Relfe said that the Lord appeared to her on different occasions and told her that He was coming in the middle of the Tribulation. Yet, the clear meaning of the above argument is *a post-Tribulation* Rapture. Because if there is only one phase of the resurrection of the just, then the resurrection that precedes the translation of the Rapture couldn't take place in mid-Tribulation.

I believe that there are several stages to the resurrection . . . and one of them is about to happen!

[3]Mary Stewart Relfe, *When Your Money Fails*, p. 200.

TWELVE

THE PROPHETIC BOOKS UNSEALED

*"But as for you, Daniel, **conceal** these words and **seal up** the book **until the end time;** many will go back and forth, and knowledge will increase.*

*"As for me, I heard but could not understand; so I said, 'My lord, what will be the outcome of these events?' And he said, 'Go your way, Daniel, for these words are **concealed** and **sealed up until the end time.** Many will be purged, purified and refined; but the wicked will act wickedly, and none of the wicked will understand, but those who have insight [who are wise] **will understand.'"** (Daniel 12:4, 8–10)*

Frankly, I have become a bit bored with those *nouveau* post-Tribulationists who give the impression that if you were truly an intellectual and *macho Christian*, you would charge headlong with them into the Tribulation.

And I am amazed that some of the older post-Tribulationists like Alexander Reese, George Ladd and Robert

Gundry spend an inordinate amount of time and energy trying to prove the recent origins of the pre-Tribulation view. Ladd devotes almost a third of his book to this point.[1] Some never tire of tracing the whole original concept of the pre-Tribulation Rapture back to 1830 and a young Scottish girl named Margaret Macdonald, to another Scotsman, Edward Irving, and an Englishman named John Darby.

More will be said about this in a moment, but my main point here is that even if this could all be proven, so what?

The Roman Catholic Church used the same kind of method of reasoning against Martin Luther, John Calvin and the other theologians of the Reformation. They brought up more than a thousand years of Church tradition and institutional Bible interpretation against the reformers' *new* doctrine of justification by faith alone. The Church also quoted a majority of the so-called Church fathers from the second through the fifth centuries who believed in salvation by faith *plus* works. But did that disprove what the Scriptures said? Didn't this rather show that traditional interpretation can sometimes miss a truth that is nevertheless contained in the Scriptures?

Another surprising method of attack used by many post-Tribulationists against the pre-Tribulation position is to list a number of impressive theologians who hold the post-Tribulation view. There is no question that there have been and still are godly, scholarly and effective men of God who hold this view. But does that really prove anything? Can't pre-Tribulationists make their own list of adherents which is at least as impressive? What are we going to say: My godly scholars are more godly and scholarly than yours? Such arguments prove nothing.

[1] George Eldon Ladd, *The Blessed Hope*.

The real issue of eschatology (prophecy of last days) is that God through Daniel clearly forewarned that the book of prophecy would be "concealed and sealed" until the time of fulfillment began to draw near. So what in fact has happened in the historical development of theology should be no surprise. Although every other doctrine of the Bible was progressively and systematically defined, eschatology was the last.

A SHORT HISTORY OF PROPHETIC INTERPRETATION

The first century Church held an undefined faith in the 'any moment' possibility of Christ's return, called the doctrine of imminence. It also believed in a literal thousand-year reign of Christ on earth after the Second Advent, called premillennialism.

Prophecy's Dark Ages

The influential early Church leader, Augustine (A.D.. 354–430) dealt the doctrine of prophecy the most damaging blow of anyone in history. He plunged the study of prophecy into darkness for almost 1,400 years by systematically teaching that prophecy could not be interpreted literally.

Augustine held to a literal, grammatical and historical interpretation of every other field of Bible doctrine, but taught that prophecy must be interpreted allegorically. He did this in order to be able to sustain his views of the Church, which he set forth in a profound book called *The City of God*. This book dominated the thinking of the Church for hundreds of years afterward.

Augustine taught that the Church had taken Israel's place, and had been given the promises and covenants which (in this view) Israel had forfeited by rejecting

Christ. He taught that the Church is the Kingdom of God in an allegorical sense, and that there would be no literal future 1,000-year earthly kingdom over which Christ would reign. (Amillennialism began here.) He taught that the Church should rule the world even in a political sense (as the Millennial Kingdom will rule in the future).

Augustine's Influence

Augustine's views became the foundation upon which the Roman Catholic Church was built. It still holds most of his views.

Augustine's teachings also became the philosophical basis for "Christian" anti-Semitism. He taught that Jews had no more purpose in God's plan; that they would never be reborn as a nation; that the covenants were no longer valid to them; that they were spiritual castaways with no future hope, Christ-killers who had no more place in God's plan and imposters. (All this, as strange as it may sound, was the result of a method of interpreting prophetic passages in an allegorical sense. Let me emphasize again, no one who interprets prophecy literally, as Jesus Himself and the apostles interpreted Old Testament prophecies in the New Testament, could ever fall into Satan's anti-Semitic trap.)

The Period of Prophetic Ferment

When the Reformers broke away from the Roman Church in the early sixteenth century, they retained Augustine's allegorical, amillennial view of prophecy.

For the next 250 years, reformed theologians began to reexamine all areas of systematic theology. It was during this period, when Protestants were dividing into many denominations with divergent views about amillennialism, that a new view, postmillennialism, emerged.

This view taught that the Church would eventually convert the whole world through the preaching of the Gospel. This would usher in the golden age promised for the Millennial Kingdom. They believed the Church would rule the world for a thousand years. Christ would then return and take the Church into eternity. Liberals at this time even accepted Darwin's theory of evolution, with all its optimism, as God's method of ushering in the "golden age." More conservative post- and amillennarian theologians recognized this as a departure from the faith and attempted to combat the theory. This was one of the reasons for the rise of the many prophetic conferences of the last century. Augustine's nonliteral interpretation of prophecy was called into question. Premillennialism emerged, claiming to return to the early Church's prophetic view and method of prophetic interpretation.[2]

From the time of Augustine until the early nineteenth century, the traditional church's interpretation of prophecy did not allow for the possibility of a literal 1,000-year Kingdom, a literal Tribulation, *or* a Rapture that was distinguished from the Second Advent. In their view, the Church was already in the "Tribulation," so it stands to reason that they would hold to a post-Tribulation coming of Christ.

The return to a literal, grammatical, historical interpretation of prophecy during the early nineteenth century called for a thorough redefining of systematic eschatology for the first time in history. It was in this larger historical context that the whole controversy concerning the Rapture began. To say that the controversy started with the single vision of a fifteen-year-old Scottish girl is patently ridiculous.

Because there has been so much made of this girl's vision, I am going to quote it in its entirety.

[2]Walvoord, *The Blessed Hope and the Tribulation*, pp. 14; 15.

The following is Margaret Macdonald's account of her vision which was received in 1830. This is taken from Robert Norton's publication, *Memoirs of James and George Macdonald, of Port-Glasgow* (1840).

"It was first the awful state of the land that was pressed upon me. I saw the blindness and infatuation of the people to be very great. I felt the cry of Liberty just to be the hiss of the serpent, to drown them in perdition. It was just 'no God.' I repeated the words, Now there is distress of nations, with perplexity, the seas and the waves roaring, men's hearts failing them for fear—now look out for the sign of the Son of man. Here I was made to stop and cry out, O it is not known what the sign of the Son of man is; the people of God think they are waiting, but they know not what it is. I felt this needed to be revealed, and that there was great darkness and error about it; but suddenly what it was burst upon me with a glorious light. I saw it was just the Lord himself descending from Heaven with a shout, just the glorified man, even Jesus; but that all must, as Stephen was, be filled with the Holy Ghost, that they might look up, and see the brightness of the Father's glory. I saw the error to be, that men think that it will be something seen by the natural eye; but 'tis spiritual discernment that is needed, the eye of God in his people. Many passages were revealed, in a light in which I had not before seen them. I repeated, 'Now is the kingdom of Heaven like unto ten virgins, who went forth to meet the Bridegroom, five wise and five foolish; they that were foolish took their lamps, but took no oil with them, but they that were wise took oil in their vessels with their lamps.' 'But be ye not unwise, but understanding what the will of the Lord is; and be not drunk with wine wherein is excess, but be filled with the Spirit.' This was the oil the wise virgins took in their vessels—this is the light to be kept burning—the light of God—that we may discern that which cometh not with observation to the natural eye. Only those who have the light of God within them will see the sign of his appearance. No need to follow them who say, see here, or see there, for his day shall be as the lightning to those in whom the living Christ is. 'Tis Christ in us that will lift us up—he is the light—'tis only those that are alive in him that will be caught up to meet him in the air. I saw that we must be in the Spirit, that we might see spiritual things. John was in the Spirit, when he saw a throne set in Heaven.—But I saw that the glory of the ministration of the Spirit had not been known. I repeated frequently, but the spiritual temple must and shall be reared, and the fulness of Christ be poured into his body, and then shall we be caught up to meet him. Oh none will be counted worthy of this calling but his body, which is the church, and which must be a candlestick all of gold. I often said, Oh the glorious inbreaking of God which is now about to burst on this earth; Oh the glorious temple which is now about to be reared, the bride adorned for her husband; and Oh what a holy, holy bride she must be, to be prepared for such a glorious bridegroom. I said, Now shall the people of God have to do with realities—now shall the glorious mystery of God in our nature be known—now shall it be known what it is for man to be glorified. I felt that the revelation of Jesus Christ had yet to be opened up—it is not knowledge about God that it contains, but it is an entering into God—I saw that there was a glorious breaking in of God to be. I felt as Elijah, surrounded with chariots of fire. I saw as it were, the spiritual temple reared, and the Head Stone brought forth with shoutings of grace, grace, unto it. It was a glorious light above the brightness of the sun, that shown round about me. I felt that those who were filled with the Spirit could see spiritual things, and feel walking in the midst of them, while those who had not the Spirit could see nothing—so that two shall be in one bed, the one taken and other left, because the one has the light of God within while the other cannot see the Kingdom of Heaven. I saw the people of God in an awfully dangerous situation, surrounded by nets and entanglements, about to be tried, and many about to be deceived and fall. Now will **the wicked** be revealed, with all power and signs and lying wonders, so that if it were possible the very elect will be deceived.—This is the fiery trial which is to try us.—It will be for the purging and purifying of the real members of the body of Jesus; but Oh it will be a fiery trial. Every soul will be shaken to the very centre. The enemy will try to shake in every thing we have believed—but the trial of real faith will be found to honour and praise and glory. Nothing but what is of God will stand. The stony-ground hearers will be made manifest—the love of many will wax cold. I frequently said that night, and often since, now shall the awful sight of a false Christ be seen on this earth, and nothing but the living Christ in us can detect this awful attempt of the enemy to deceive—for it is with all deceivableness of unrighteousness he will work— he will have a counterpart for every part of God's truth, and an imitation for every work of the Spirit. The Spirit must and will be poured out on the Church, that she may be purified and filled with God—and just in proportion as the Spirit of God works, so will he—when our Lord anoints men with power, so will he. This is particularly the nature of the trial, through which those are to pass who will be counted worthy to stand before the Son of man. There

will be outward trial too, but 'tis principally
temptation. It is brought on by the outpouring of the
Spirit, and will just increase in proportion as the Spirit
is poured out. The trial of the Church is from
Antichrist. It is by being filled with the Spirit that we
shall be kept. I frequently said, Oh be filled with the
Spirit—have the light of God in you, that you may
detect satan—be full of eyes within—be clay in the
hands of the potter—submit to be filled, filled with
God. This will build the temple. It is not by might nor
by power, but by my Spirit, saith the Lord. This will
fit us to enter into the marriage supper of the Lamb. I
saw it to be the will of God that all should be filled.
But what hindered the real life of God from being
received by his people, was their turning from Jesus,
who is the way to the Father. They were not entering
in by the door. For he is faithful who hath said, by me
if any man enter in he shall find pasture. They were
passing the cross, through which every drop of the
Spirit of God flows to us. All power that comes not
through the blood of Christ is not of God. When I say,
they are looking from the cross, I feel that there is
much in it—they turn from the blood of the Lamb, by
which we overcome, and in which our robes are
washed and made white. There are low views of
God's holiness, and a ceasing to condemn sin in the
flesh, and a looking from him who humbled himself,
and made himself of no reputation. Oh! It is needed,
much needed at present, a leading back to the cross. I
saw that night, and often since, that there will be an
outpouring of the Spirit on the body, such as has not
been, a baptism of fire, that all the dross may be put
away. Oh there must and will be such an indwelling of
the living God as has not been—the servants of God
sealed in their foreheads—great conformity to Jesus—
just the bride made comely, by his comeliness put

upon her. This is what we are at present made to pray much for, that speedily we may all be made ready to meet our Lord in the air—and it will be. Jesus wants his bride. His desire is toward us. He that shall come, will come, and will not tarry. Amen and Amen. Even so come Lord Jesus."

Some Observations

How anyone with a straight face can say that this vision is the origin of the whole pre-Tribulation view is beyond me. The following are a few observations on what it teaches:

(1) She definitely teaches *a partial Rapture*. The spiritual Christians are to be removed and the unspiritual remain to go through fiery trials.

(2) She taught that even the spiritual ones would be on earth during the Antichrist's (The Wicked One) period of terrible deceptions. This means that the "spiritual Christians" would at least go through half of the Tribulation.

(3) She equates "the sign of the Son of man" from Matthew 24:30 (which is referring to the Second Advent) with the Rapture statement of 1 Thessalonians 4:16, "The Lord Himself will descend from heaven with a shout." She says they occur at the same time. Even Dave Mac-Pherson acknowledges this.[3] In spite of what others may say, this makes her view of the Rapture post-Tribulational.

The Snow Job

MacPherson and others have sought to disprove pre-Tribulationism by tracing it to this vision. But the very

[3] *The Incredible Cover-Up* by Omega Publications, p. 154.

evidence MacPherson quotes proves the exact opposite of what he claims it teaches.

Furthermore, to say that John Darby, who was adamantly against the charismatic gifts, got his insight into prophecy from Margaret Macdonald is incredible and unprovable. Margaret Macdonald herself doesn't seem to have made much of her vision. In fact, there's very little recorded about it.[4]

It is possible that Darby was not aware of it, for he never mentions it, though he does write concerning her.[5] But even if he had been aware of it, it really makes no difference, for her views are not only different but contradictory to what Darby believed. To portray Darby as a plagiarist, eager to take all the glory, is to slander a brother in the Lord with no evidence. There's also no reason to believe that a careful scholar like Darby would allow himself to be influenced by the vision of a young, unschooled girl, since he didn't believe in her gift to begin with.

From all we can gather of the times, John Darby was a Biblical scholar who was simply a part of the wave of new interest in prophecy. The return to literal interpretation of prophecy led him and others to begin to redefine prophecy, and to arrange it into a cohesive system.

So What?

The most important factor in this whole controversy is, "What does the Bible say?" I totally agree with Ladd when he said, "Let it be at once emphasized that we are

[4]I'd like to say that although I don't agree with the authenticity of her vision, records show her to be a beautiful sister in the Lord, filled with love and compassion for others.

[5]In Darby's book, *The Irrationalism of Infidelity* (1853) he speaks of Margaret Macdonald and her two brothers, disputing the authenticity of their gift of tongues.

not turning to the church fathers to find authority for either pre- or post-Tribulationism. The one authority is the Word of God, and we are not confined in the strait-jacket of tradition."[6] All I can say is "amen" to that statement.

As I stated at the beginning of this study, my purpose for writing this book was not to cling blindly to a system of prophetic interpretation, but rather to objectively and honestly investigate what the whole Bible says.

In closing this book I can say in all good conscience that I believe the Scriptures teach a pre-Tribulational coming of the Lord Jesus Christ for His Church.

No matter which view one holds on the Rapture questions, there are some difficult problems that have to be reconciled within the system. I believe that the pre-Tribulation system answers all the Scriptures on the subject in the most consistent and harmonious way.

On the other hand, the post-Tribulation system has to allegorize some major portions of the Scripture, such as Matthew 25:31–46 and the question of who will populate the Kingdom, in order to make their system work.

Second, the major assumption of many of the post-Tribulationists' arguments is that if they can punch holes in the pre-Trib system, it somehow establishes their own.

What is said about the post-Tribulationists also applies to the Mid-Tribulation view.

ON A PERSONAL NOTE

I have never been more thankful to God for the personal hope of the Lord's return for the believer before the coming world holocaust. I had unwittingly begun to take this wonderful truth for granted.

[6]Ladd, op. cit. p. 19.

It breaks my heart as I daily pore over world events and see how rapidly the world as we know it is moving toward a catastrophic end.

—Experts say that we are headed for a global economic collapse. Third world countries keep piling up massive debts. They can't even pay interest, much less principal on their loans.

—Many jobs lost in the latest recession will never be restored—experts speak of a whole generation being unemployable because of the painful change from the industrial age to a new technical age of uncertain destiny.

—The Arab-Israeli conflict continues to smolder with the constant threat of igniting the fuse of Armageddon.

—The Soviet Union, already the mightiest military power in history, continues to move in all parts of the globe and wear down the will of the free world to resist.

—Nuclear weapons capable of destroying all life on earth continue to be produced at the rate of approximately six warheads per week.

—"Star Wars" type technology rapidly moves toward lasers and deathrays of unimaginable lethality.

—China, with more than one-fourth of the world's population, continues to prepare for war.

—Global weather patterns continue to change— storms of unusual force strike in new places.

—Lawlessness is rampant

  • murders continue to increase—no city is safe;

  • gang rapes occur while average citizens look on and cheer;

- jails are filled to overcapacity with criminals of all kinds;

- drugs are virtually a staple of the modern society;

- family units are almost nonexistent;

- bizarre murders with no motive are commonplace.

—Famines continue to expand over large sections of the world's population.

—Volcanoes, long dormant, explode.

—Earthquakes continue to increase in frequency and severity.

To the untrained eye, this may sound like unrelated bad news. But to the student of prophecy, it all fits into a precise pattern that was forecast long ago. This pattern clearly shows us that the Lord's coming for the Church is very near.

The hope of the Rapture is a very practical force in my life at this point in history. It motivates me to gain a combat knowledge of the Bible in order to be able to face the perilous times that precede the Tribulation. It motivates me to win as many to Christ as possible before it's too late. I want to take as many with me as I can. Although I grieve over the lost world that is headed toward catastrophe, the hope of the Rapture keeps me from despair in the midst of ever-worsening world conditions.

The one who knows that Jesus Christ is in his heart and has the sure hope of the Lord's coming for him before the Tribulation is the only one who can face today's news and honestly be optimistic.

My prayer is that this book has helped you to have a certain and sure hope of the Lord's "any moment" return to take you to His Father's house.

I'll see you at His feet!

HAL LINDSEY

ABOUT THE AUTHOR

HAL LINDSEY, named *the bestselling author of the decade* by the New York Times, was born in Houston, Texas. His first book, *The Late Great Planet Earth*, published in 1970, became the bestselling non-fiction book of the decade, selling more than 18 million copies worldwide. He is one of the few authors to have three books on the New York Times bestseller list at the same time.

Mr. Lindsey was educated at the University of Houston. After serving in the U.S. Coast Guard during the Korean War, Mr. Lindsey graduated from Dallas Theological Seminary where he majored in the New Testament and early Greek literature. After completing seminary, Mr. Lindsey served for eight years on the staff of Campus Crusade for Christ, speaking to tens of thousands of students on major university campuses throughout the United States.

Mr. Lindsey currently has an extensive ministry. He is senior pastor of the Palos Verdes Community Church, has a weekly radio talk show heard in over 200 cities, and a regular television show on Trinity Broadcasting Network.

Hal Lindsey has an extensive collection of messages on tape. He has taught many books of the Bible in verse by verse series, as well as prophetic lectures on current world events and issues. If you would be interested in receiving a tape catalogue, please write to the address listed below.

Hal Lindsey Tapes
P.O. Box 4000
Palos Verdes, CA 90274

BANTAM
SHOP-AT-HOME
C·A·T·A·L·O·G

Special Offer
Buy a Bantam Book
for only 50¢.

Now you can have Bantam's catalog filled with hundreds of titles plus take advantage of our unique and exciting bonus book offer. A special offer which gives you the opportunity to purchase a Bantam book for only 50¢. Here's how!

By ordering any five books at the regular price per order, you can also choose any other single book listed (up to a $4.95 value) for just 50¢. Some restrictions do apply, but for further details why not send for Bantam's catalog of titles today!

Just send us your name and address and we will send you a catalog!

RUROUNI KENSHIN

VOYAGE TO
THE MOON WORLD

VOYAGE TO
THE MOON WORLD

Original Concept by
NOBUHIRO WATSUKI

Written by
KAORU SHIZUKA

Translated by
**Cindy H. Yamauchi and Mark Giambruno,
REGION FREE**

VIZ Media
San Francisco

RUROUNI KENSHIN -MEIJI KENKAKU ROMANTAN- MAKI NO ICHI
© 1996 by Nobuhiro Watsuki, Kaoru Shizuka
All rights reserved.
First published in Japan in 1996 by SHUEISHA Inc., Tokyo.
English translation rights in the United States of America and
Canada arranged by SHUEISHA Inc.

Illustrations by Nobuhiro Watsuki
Cover design by Amy Martin

Published by
VIZ Media, LLC
295 Bay Street
San Francisco, CA 94133

www.viz.com

Library of Congress Cataloging-in-Publication Data

Watsuki, Nobuhiro.
[Rurôni kenshin. English]
Rurouni kenshin : voyage to the moon world / Kaoru Shizuka ;
original concept by Nobuhiro Watsuki ; translated by Cindy H.
Yamauchi and Mark Giambruno.
p. cm.
Includes bibliographical references and index.
ISBN-13: 978-1-4215-0604-3 (pbk. : alk. paper)
ISBN-10: 1-4215-0604-1 (pbk. : alk. paper)
I. Shizuka, Kaoru, 1958- . II. Yamauchi, Cindy H. III. Giambruno,
Mark, 1957- .
IV. Title. V. Title: Voyage to the moon world.
PZ49.31W38713 2006
[Fic]--dc22
                                                    2006011834

Printed in Canada

First printing, October 2006

CONTENTS

CHARACTERS

A patriot of the Meiji Restoration era, he was once feared as the assassin Hitokiri Battôsai. No longer a killer, he now lives his life as a *rurouni*, a wanderer.

HIMURA KENSHIN

Instructor at the Kamiya dojo. A tomboy who is quick with her hands and her words, she is also a woman with a kind heart.

KAMIYA KAORU

Currently the only pupil of the Kamiya dojo. He is a very self-assured and often rude boy.

MYÔJIN YAHIKO

A cadet in the former Sekihô Army. He abandoned his life as a fight merchant and became a comrade of the Kamiya dojo group.

SAGARA SANOSUKE

One of the daughters of the owner of a popular Asakusa beef-pot restaurant called Akabeko. She maintains a close relationship with Kaoru and the others.

SEKIHARA TAE

Although born to a samurai family, this quiet girl works as a waitress at the Akabeko.

SANJÔ TSUBAME

Voyage to
the Moon World

KATSU KAISHÛ Excelling as a vassal during the end of the Shogunate era, he was also appointed to an important position in the New Government.

ÔKUMA DAIGORO A student studying under Kaishû.

KATSU ITSUKO Kaishû's third daughter.

ÔKUBO TETSUMA A former student at the Katsu residence, he currently works for the Ministry of Home Affairs.

A Gift as a Lure

Sekihara Tae's arrival was met with sincere welcome by the trio at the Kamiya Kasshin-ryû dojo, and with particular pleasure by the two young men, Himura Kenshin and Myôjin Yahiko. Tae was accompanied by a student in his late teens, who she explained was a regular at Akabeko, the restaurant where she worked. Never one to visit empty-handed, she'd also brought a gift of high-quality beef prepared at her restaurant.

Oh, good...this one is spared from eating Kaoru-dono's dinner, Kenshin thought. Yahiko must have been thinking the same thing, for the two looked at each other and smiled happily.

The beef-pot restaurants—with their hanging signs extolling "Beef for Good Health" brushed boldly in red ink—made their appearance in Tokyo Prefecture in the second year of Meiji (1869). However, there are many variations on the possible origin of beef-pot restaurants in Japan. Some say it was in Osaka in the fourth year of Ansei (1857), during the final era of the Shogunate government. Yet others say a bar in Yokohama called Ise Kuma started the practice in the second year of Bunkyû (1862). It is also said a restaurant that opened for business near the British Legation in Takanawa in June of the third year of Keio (1867) could have been the first. Whatever the case, back in those days, the Japanese were not as aware as Westerners of the good flavor of beef. Eventually, between the Japanese love of new trends and the New Government's encouragement of meat consumption, the public became familiar with the good taste of beef, and beef-pot restaurants such as Nakagawa-ya of Shibarogetsu-cho, Torikin of Kagurazaka, Nakazome of Kakigara-cho, and Iseshige of Kodenma-cho opened for business one after another.

By the spring of the eleventh year of Meiji, there were more than five hundred beef-pot restaurants in Tokyo Prefecture. When it came to taste, Akabeko was acknowledged to be top-notch. The key product served at beef-pot restaurants—beef-pot—came in two grades: premium and standard. To put it simply, the premium dish was what is known today as *sukiyaki*, and the standard fare was stewed beef. Called *yakinabe*, the beef was stewed in a greased pot with seasonings and large pieces of green onion, and then the boiling-hot contents were eaten with a side dish of beaten raw egg. So delicious...

Seeing Yahiko drooling dreamily before him, Kenshin noticed that his own chin was moist. Kamiya Kaoru, owner and instructor of the dojo, focused her suspicious gaze on the sorry state of the two young men. "Hey, you two. Are you paying close attention to Tae-san's story?"

Kenshin fumbled for a response, but Yahiko, though startled, quickly recovered. "We heard it. Basically, that student over there wants us to search for his lost book," he replied bluntly. Even though the student looked five or six years older, as far as Yahiko was concerned, he in no way looked as strong. The student had a very slight build, his glasses had thick, heavy-looking lenses, and he appeared fragile in every way.

"Yes, that's right. It's considered to be very valuable, and if Ôkuma-san has lost it, he said he would be kicked out of his sensei's house. Right, Ôkuma-san? Isn't that so?"

Urged on by the worry marring Tae's beautiful brow, Daigoro Ôkuma barely managed to mumble "yes" in a feeble voice.

"Hmph. Just because he lost one lousy book, that's no reason to kick someone out. Right, Kaoru?" As usual, Yahiko's addressing her without an honorific got on Kaoru's nerves, but she held back her feelings and asked Tae to continue with her tale.

This sounds like it's going to be a bit complicated, Kenshin thought as he listened to Tae.

Tae's story went something like this: The previous

afternoon, while Daigoro was engrossed in reading, the sensei who provided his housing asked him to run an errand. So, with the partially read book tucked in the front of his kimono, he went to Ueno to take care of business. His destination was the Tendai Buddhist sect at Kan-eiji temple, where he was to deliver a box of *les biscuits* handed to him by his sensei. The Fugetsudo bakery of Ryogoku Wakamatsu-cho had begun selling *les biscuits* in July of the previous year, and they had quickly gained popularity as domestically baked Western-style sweets.

"Please inform your sensei that we have indeed received it." With these formal words of confirmation, the cloth *furoshiki* wrapping was returned to Daigoro, and he headed back home.

If Daigoro had gone straight home, it is likely that nothing would have happened. But at about that time he started to get hungry, and thinking of the rather plain meal waiting for him at home, Daigoro made an unplanned visit to the Akabeko restaurant.

Akabeko was overflowing with customers eating dinner, and Tae and the other servers were busily tending to their work. After a while, space in a corner booth became available, and when the beef-pot was finally served Daigoro enjoyed his meal in bliss. When he was finished eating, Daigoro casually looked around and noticed Tae and the others still bustling about. As a regular customer, he felt that perhaps he should help out a bit. Daigoro removed the book he'd borrowed from his sensei from inside the front of his kimono, wrapped it in the furoshiki, and placed it next to the seat cushion with extra care.

Thinking it would be good to get a bit of exercise after the meal, he helped carry meat and vegetables for about fifteen minutes, but a big surprise awaited him when he prepared to leave. He returned to his seat after using the restroom, only to find that the book and furoshiki had vanished. The color drained from Daigoro's face as he frantically searched the area. But the book and furoshiki were nowhere to be found.

Disconcerted, Daigoro explained to Tae and the other servers what had happened, and asked everyone to search the restaurant. At the end of the story, neither the valuable book nor the furoshiki cloth were found.

"Hmmm. You must be really bothered by this." Kaoru glanced at the downcast Daigoro, who looked like he was about to cry at any moment, then turned to face Tae.

"Ôkuma-san is a regular at our restaurant, and this incident happened while he was helping us out..." Tae murmured in a low voice, seemingly at a loss.

"Hmph. So, it's all this student's fault for wandering off. He's just suffering the consequences, if you ask me." In Yahiko's eyes, everything was clear-cut, with no allowances for objections or foolishness. "Why don't you just apologize, and if your sensei still says he wants to kick you out, I say just *leave*. If you don't mind this beat-up ol' dojo, you can stay here with me."

Kaoru, who was seated next to Yahiko, had been trying to be tolerant as she listened to him speak, but when he called her place a "beat-up ol' dojo," she finally snapped. "What did you say, Yahiko? Say it again! What about my dojo?"

"No...uhhh...I mean..." Considering how Kaoru could get when she was angry, even Yahiko couldn't be impudent all the time. After all, Kaoru had total control over the necessities of Yahiko's life.

"You keep your mouth shut, Yahiko!" Kaoru's commanding words ended that conversation.

"If I lose that book, I can't go on living..." For the first time, Daigoro managed something like a full sentence. As might be expected from a man of his slight build, he had a high, weak-sounding voice, very different from the impression one might get from his powerful-sounding name.

"You're Ôkuma-san, right? So, what exactly is that valuable book all about?"

"It's a book written by a Frenchman named Jules Verne, and translated, the title is *From the Earth to the Moon*. Although it's in the form of a novel, it contains legitimate science."

Upon hearing the title *From the Earth to the Moon*, those present all looked at each other. Nothing was said at first, probably because no one knew what kind of question

16

should be asked.

"Uh, this one would like to know...when you say 'moon,' are you referring to *the* moon?" a bewildered Kenshin finally asked, as if to speak for everyone.

"That is correct. The story is about humans traveling to the moon."

"So, what is *From the Earth to the Moon* about?"

"Well, y-you see..." Daigoro went on, with a twinkle in his eye. "Three humans and two dogs are placed inside a hollow cannonball, and it is shot through a cannon aimed toward the moon. The cannon is called the *Columbiad*, and there are two Americans and one Frenchman inside the cannonball."

"Th-then, how long does it take to reach the moon?"

"Well, according to the calculations of a place called the Cambridge Observatory, if a cannonball could be fired at a speed of 11,000 meters per second, the moon could be reached in 97 hours, 13 minutes, and 20 seconds."

Yahiko, who had been quietly listening to the conversation between Kenshin and Daigoro, suddenly burst out laughing. "Gimme a break. That's just for kids! It's so stupid."

"Behave yourself, Yahiko!" Kaoru glared in disapproval, but this time, Yahiko was not about to retreat.

"But isn't it true? All this talk about living and dying just because he's lost a stupid book full of crap is just way too much. You know, I'd be better off listening to a fairy tale about Moon Princess Kaguya."

"Th-that's so mean... You make it sound so terrible. But tell me, what is so stupid and full of crap about it?" Daigoro glared sharply at Yahiko.

"The moon! We're talking about the moon! Traveling to such a far away place, in 97..."

"Ninety-seven hours, 13 minutes, and 20 seconds. That's a little over 4 days, 1 hour, and 13 minutes."

"Whatever it is, there's no way you could get there in such a short time. C'mon, it takes four or five days to get from Tokyo to Kyoto, even if you hurry. And I've never heard of the moon being closer than Kyoto."

"Oh, no. It's not... What I'm talking about is the latest, most advanced style of barrel, 900 feet long and made of cast iron. This *Columbiad* cannon would use 40,000 pounds of guncotton, so the projectile speed would be brought up to 11,000 meters per second upon firing."

In her mind, Kaoru tried to imagine herself, Kenshin, and Yahiko placed inside a cannonball. But instead of envisioning the cannonball flying up in the air, she could only conjure the image of the trio burning to death. It just didn't seem very realistic.

Sensei Katsu Kaishû

To Kaoru's right, the endless procession of questions and answers between Yahiko and Daigoro continued.

"So tell me, when is this departure to the moon going to happen?"

"December 1st, 10:46 p.m. No, to be exact, 10:46 p.m. and 35 seconds."

"December 1st of what year of Meiji?"

"Um, that's...well... In the beginning of the book, it says the late 1860s..."

"See, I told ya! It's all nonsense. The 1860s passed by a long time ago. This is the 11th year of Meji, 1878! I've never read anything in the newspapers about someone traveling to the moon in any part of the world. That book's total nonsense..."

Having had the inconsistencies in the story of *From the*

Earth to the Moon pointed out to him, Daigoro had no choice but to fall silent. Looking down, his fragile body sagging, Daigoro was a pitiful sight. But Yahiko's attack was still not over.

"Science, you say? Hmph. The world has no time for that nonsense. Hey, you must've heard about it, too—that rumor about ghostly sightings, right smack in the middle of Tokyo, in broad daylight!"

Daigoro was confused and didn't know how to reply.

"Listen, you stop that now, Yahiko!" Kaoru scolded loudly. But Yahiko, on a roll, refused to stop.

"Shut up, ugly! I bet you're really scared, too!"

"What did you just say? You pointy-eyed shrimp!"

"Say that again!"

As quick with their fists as with their tongues, the pair narrowly avoided getting into a scuffle, thanks to Tae chiming in to say she had also heard that rumor.

"I've heard that it could be the vengeful ghost of a monk who hanged himself during the Revolution," said Tae.

It was true that around this time, there was talk of a strange voice heard at the Homei-in temple of Kanda Myôjinshita. As a matter of fact, there were more than a few people who heard this voice and were uncertain of whether it belonged to a man or a woman. Talking about ghostly voices in this modern era might seem ridiculous, but because of the incident, a soba place near Homei-in called Kagetsu-an was almost driven out of business due to the sudden drop in customer traffic in the area.

A Buddhist monk at the Homei-in temple had hanged himself in the main hall when government decrees were issued to separate the Shinto and Buddhist religions. As a result of the Meiji government's movement to favor Shintoism, including the abolishment of Buddhism and removal of Buddhist imagery, many despairing monks throughout the country committed suicide due to hardship and oppression. Even ancient temples suffered—Nara's Kofukuji temple had to auction off their five-tiered pagoda. Such tragedies occurred numerous times during the first ten years of Meiji, and many Buddhist altar trappings and temple treasures were sold off.

In contrast to the commotion in his surroundings, Daigoro's depressed state of mind was perhaps akin to the disappointment the monks had felt. Kaoru and Tae wanted to offer something comforting, but not knowing what to say at a time like this, they were silent. Kenshin placed his hand lightly on Daigoro's shoulder and said with a smile, "The moon is far indeed. But Daigoro-dono, wouldn't it be great to go there someday?"

"Yes." With a look of relief, Daigoro nodded firmly. "In the future, I'd like to be a scientist. For that reason, I don't want to be expelled from my sensei's house."

"We haven't asked you about your sensei, have we? So, who is this sensei, and where does he live?"

Daigoro replied in a barely audible voice, "He is the former Councilor and Lord High Admiral, Katsu Yasuyoshi-sama."

His title, Kaishû, was better known than his newly assumed name, Yasuyoshi, which was derived from rearranging the characters of the position he formerly held with the Shogunate government, Protector of Awa Province.

"When you say Katsu, do you mean Katsu Kaishû, who surrendered Edo Castle?" Yahiko spoke the name with mixed emotions. Yahiko's father had been a low-ranking vassal of the Shogunate government who received an annual stipend of 30-koku 2-nin buchi, a small salary equal to that of a police detective of the time. He had been a regimental soldier in the Shogi-tai, who died in combat at their base in the mountains of Ueno, where they were resisting the imperial troops who were following the tide that led to the overthrow of the government.

Wasn't Katsu Kaishû the very man who acted as a representative of the Shogunate government, allowing imperial troops to enter the city without resistance? As far as Yahiko was concerned, the man was a traitor who might well have been the cause of his father's death in battle, which later contributed to his mother's illness and eventual death.

The name weighed heavily on Kenshin as well, for Katsu Kaishû used to aid the Ishin Shishi during the final era of the Shogunate government, when Kenshin was known as Hitokiri Battôsai.

A dark, complex mood settled upon the group, but Tae helped to turn things around. "In the beginning, I thought about asking Sanosuke-san to help search for the book, since he's behind in paying his tab at the restaurant. However, when I went to visit him at the Gorotsuki row houses on the edge of town, he was out somewhere. So, I decided to ask Kaoru-san, even though I was sure it would be troublesome for her. But then I remembered that she has *two* reliable swordsmen at her place."

Yahiko felt better when he heard Tae say "*two* swordsmen." Recently, he had been getting rather sick of doing frequent chores for Kaoru on top of his *kenjutsu* sword training. Beef-pot was included in the deal, so regardless of the issues, it seemed like a good idea to pitch in and help.

"Hmmm. Katsu Kaishû is your sensei, then." Kenshin crossed his arms over his chest. "So, Daigoro-dono, do you have any idea, any kind of clue as to when the book disappeared within that fifteen minute period?"

"Yes. Right before I went to the restroom, I glanced toward the seat. The furoshiki cloth was there for sure."

Then Daigoro murmured in a low voice, "Most likely, it was while I was taking care of business."

"It was probably stolen, then." Kenshin now looked concerned. "Tae-dono, at the time were there any unfamiliar customers at the restaurant? Was there anyone besides your regulars?"

Tae tried very hard to recall the details. Suddenly, she remembered something. "Now that you mention it, there were two customers I'd never seen before. One of them was a gentleman in Western-style clothing, fair-skinned, with a moustache. The other man..." She glanced at the sword lying to the right of Kenshin. "Although the law prohibits it, the other man wore a sword on his hip. An unusually long sword, with a red hilt. He was a ruddy-faced man with a large build, almost like a sumo wrestler. The left side of his face was badly pockmarked from his cheek to his chin, and he had mean-looking eyes."

"Did those two come to the restaurant before or after Daigoro-dono?"

"It was after. Their seats were far apart, though."

Daigoro must have been followed, Kenshin thought. *So, their target was the book in Daigoro's possession?* While he turned these thoughts over in his mind, a revelation struck Kenshin, but he chose not to mention it. In a quiet voice, he said, "In any case, first and foremost, we should pay a visit to Katsu-sensei."

"Then, you're saying you'll help us out?"

Kenshin watched as a look of joy swept across Tae's face. Next, he glanced at Daigoro sitting beside her, who still seemed to be depressed. Kenshin asked the question that had been bothering him. "Katsu-san...er, Katsu-sensei has already been notified of this, yes?"

"Yes."

"And what did sensei tell you?"

"At first, he yelled, 'You stupid fool!' quite vehemently. After that, when I mentioned the name Akabeko, it turned out that he knew the place and said that restaurant's beef-pot was delicious, and it looked to me as if his anger had subsided a bit. Then he said 'Ôkuma, go find it, even if it kills you. Otherwise, I won't let you back in the house, and I will drag you down to the police if need be...'"

"Anything more than that?"

"Yes, he said to settle the matter by the day after tomorrow, and that he can't wait any longer than that."

"Is that so..." Kenshin now felt like helping Daigoro out. It wasn't because he had found out that Daigoro's sensei was Katsu Kaishû. Leading the life of a rurouni, Kenshin saw some of himself in Daigoro, who dreamed of the moon.

Daigoro-dono must be wandering the endless trail to the moon. The thought moved Kenshin's heart. "All right, then," said Kenshin as he stood up.

Kaoru quickly asked where he was going, and Kenshin smiled. He was not rushing off—he'd felt his hunger become unbearable as he'd listened to Tae and Daigoro's story, and was ready to alleviate the problem. "This one will have to eat first, which is fortunate, since this one would like a taste of that beef while Tae-san is still here."

Once he decided to help Daigoro, Kenshin quickly sprang into action. His mouth stuffed with beef, he instructed Daigoro, Kaoru, and Yahiko to make the rounds of used booksellers, bookstores, newspaper agencies, and publishers.

According to Daigoro, the science adventure novel by

Jules Verne had been printed in the French newspaper *Journal des Débats* as a series entitled, "De la Terre à la Lune," and was compiled as a book later that year. The year was 1865, the first year of Keio, in the final era of the Shogunate government.

Jules Verne spent the next five years expanding on the story in *From the Earth to the Moon,* and finally published the sequel *Around the Moon,* which detailed the moon journey itself. That was in 1870, the third year of Meiji, and of course the story hadn't been translated into Japanese yet, so there were very few people who knew about Verne's work.

Katsu Kaishû said that his eldest son, Koroku—who was studying abroad at the Annapolis Naval Academy in the United States—had brought the book home with him last December as a gift. Katsu liked its unconventional content, and had treasured it ever since.

"All because I insisted on borrowing a treasured book that sensei received from the young master..." Daigoro said in a troubled manner, as the thick lenses of his glasses fogged up, obscuring the slightly droopy eyes in his long, tanned, almost horse-like face. Because he felt so remorseful, he hardly touched Tae's beef-pot at all.

Not wanting to see Daigoro in such a state, Kenshin replied, "Daigoro-dono, it's not good for you to go hungry. It has been a while since this one has enjoyed such a delicious dinner and it mustn't go to waste."

Kaoru, who was seated beside him, caught his slip of the tongue with her sharp ears. "Kenshin, what do you mean, you haven't had such a delicious dinner in a while? Are you saying the dinner I cook for you every night doesn't taste good?"

Cornered, Kenshin nervously replied, "N-no, of course that isn't the case. But, because a professional charges money, it naturally has to taste better, you see..." Despite his weak excuse, Kaoru appeared calm, but Kenshin knew her anger was bubbling just below the surface. Had Tae not been there, Kaoru might have thrown everything she could lay her hands on at Kenshin. Although gentle affection shone in the dark depths of Kaoru's eyes and her every movement was exquisite, she was quick with her hands and words, and her strong-minded attitude was not to be underestimated.

Kenshin was ready to retreat, but instead he cleared his throat loudly as if to recover his dignity, looked toward Daigoro and said, "If those two customers intended to steal the book from the very beginning, their motive can be easily pinpointed. If they wanted *From the Earth to the Moon*, a precious book not yet introduced in Japan, their next course of action is limited, whether they want to sell it at a high price or translate and publish it on their own. If possible, we should notify the police. It would be helpful if they would check with all the newspaper agencies, publishers, and bookstores in the city."

"But sensei told me not to take the matter to the police."

"Hmmm…"

As Kenshin stopped to ponder this, Daigoro suddenly shifted where he knelt, bringing his knees together and straightening his posture. "I beg you. Please give me your assistance." He bowed his head deeply. His slim figure seemed even smaller and skinnier than before. Seeing his appearance, no one present had the heart to deny him assistance.

For and Against
the Moon Voyage

The time was a little past eight o'clock. The night was lit by light leaking from the houses lining the street. Kenshin hurried as he followed the map Daigoro had drawn for him. As if to race him, two rickshaws passed Kenshin and disappeared.

We will make inquiries at the publishers and bookstores tomorrow, but there is something this one needs to be certain of tonight, Kenshin thought.

The sudden visit from the peculiar guest and his unusual story had aroused Kenshin's curiosity somewhat, but there was something about the story that felt strange, like the awkward feeling of the rarely-worn *haori* jacket on his shoulders, and he just couldn't get it off his mind. Was it because of that outrageous tale of the moon voyage?

He hadn't wanted to wear the haori jacket at all. But he was going to visit the former Councilor and Lord High Admiral Katsu Kaishû, and Kaoru insisted that going in his casual wear would be impolite, so she lent him her late father's kimono. The awkward feeling that came from his unfamiliar wardrobe couldn't be helped. Kenshin smiled with a touch of bitterness, but it didn't take long for the smile to disappear from his face.

He felt a presence after he'd walked about two *cho* from the Kamiya dojo. He casually looked over his shoulder, but there was no indication of anyone approaching.

Kenshin picked up his pace and pushed on for another three cho or so, then ran swiftly to hide in an alley. He pressed his left thumb against the guard of his *sakabatô*, releasing it from the sheath. The blade on his sword was reversed, making a cutting or killing blow impossible in a typical swordfight. Kenshin was aware of this, but nevertheless he was on guard, meaning the presence he felt behind him posed a threat.

He probably followed this one all the way from the dojo. It takes an extraordinary ability to go unnoticed for more than two cho. Kenshin held his breath and waited for movement behind him. He no longer felt the presence, and relaxed his guard, but moments later the dark silhouette of a large man slowly crossed the entrance to the alley and walked on. Kenshin could clearly make out the man's two swords in the darkness, and one of them was long, with a red hilt. Kenshin held his breath again. Suddenly, the man returned, and once again slowly passed in front of the mouth of the alley. Kenshin emerged into the main street and slid his sword silently from the sheath.

Kenshin's attack seemed to slash through the air at the very moment that the man began to turn around, but the blow was deflected with a heavy thud. The enormous shadowed figure ran off without a sound, crossed the nearby bridge, and disappeared into the darkness on the opposite shore. Despite his bulk, the opponent's agility was formidable. Kenshin's wrists and palms were still numb from his blow being deflected. Kenshin sheathed his sakabatô, and the numbness lingered as he massaged his hand.

This is indeed interesting... The prowler must have been a member of the gang that stole the furoshiki-wrapped book from Daigoro, and must have followed Daigoro to the dojo earlier. Kenshin knew that the prowler was probably trying to find out who Kenshin was—this new player who had left Daigoro behind after nightfall—and where he was going. And the prowler wouldn't forget that this new enemy possessed formidable skill with a sword. Kenshin started walking slowly down the dark street. He felt that he was now involved in a baffling struggle, whether he liked it or not.

It was getting foggy and the night air was warm and damp. The lights hanging from the eaves of the merchants' houses looked blurred in the fog.

One hour later, Kenshin arrived at Katsu Kaishû's residence in Akasaka, Hikawa-cho Yon-banchi. When he announced his name and the purpose of his visit before the main entrance, a woman came through a small, low side gate. She was a beauty—petite with a slender waist, twinkling eyes and slightly stern features. Combined, they displayed the typical charm of a young woman, making her all the more attractive in the eyes of men. The elegance of her fine upbringing could be seen in her dress and deportment.

About the same age as Tae-san, perhaps? Kenshin's guess was a good one, but as she briskly led him forward, he did make the mistake of assuming she was a maid in Katsu's household. He would later discover that the woman was Katsu's third daughter, Itsuko.

She guided Kenshin through a long, dimly lit hall, turning first left, then right, then through a *tatami* mat-lined hallway before finally ushering him into a room far in the back. On the way, they passed a small man who appeared to be a servant. The man, in his fifties and wearing shabby clothes, bowed his already lowered head as he passed Kenshin.

In the eight tatami-mat room, a lamp burned brightly, prepared to welcome a guest. A freestanding armrest was positioned a short distance from the lamp. The master of the house must sit there. An imported clock on a stand had been placed in the alcove. But the room looked quite dreary otherwise, with disorderly piles of books stacked everywhere.

"Please wait here for a moment," Kenshin's guide Itsuko said in a brisk tone, then politely closed the sliding *fusuma* door and left.

The fusuma door facing the hallway opened and Itsuko returned, this time carrying a tea set. Itsuko politely offered some tea to Kenshin, then placed the set by the master's seat and quietly left the room.

Silence fell over the room; a silence that was absolute. *Surely, Daigoro's studies would progress very well in this kind of environment*, Kenshin thought, nodding to himself. Suddenly, breaking the silence, the loud laughter of a man echoed throughout the house. The laughter was distant, but it sounded youthful and candid. It was followed by a dignified cough, and it appeared that the source of the laughter was approaching.

Hmmm...could it be...?

The fusuma door on the opposite side of the hallway opened, and the source of the laughter and cough made his appearance. He wasn't a very tall man, but looked dignified in his haori jacket decorated with a family crest. He probably stood less than five *shaku*, one *sun*, about 4 feet 11 inches. The man was in his mid-fifties, and the beard on his chin looked rather sparse.

As this one expected! Kenshin, while on his knees in a deep bow, saw with his keen eyes that the man they had passed earlier—the one who looked like a servant—was indeed the master of the house, Katsu Kaishû.

"I am Katsu Yasuyoshi. I am told this midnight visit concerns Ôkuma Daigoro, but what could this be about?" In a crisp Edo dialect, Kaishû urged Kenshin on as he took hold of the cup in front of him and sipped some tea. His tone was breezy, but the eyes underneath their aging lids had a fierce glow, and were piercingly sharp as he gazed at Kenshin.

Kenshin maintained his silence, and Kaishû spoke again.

"Oh, don't be so darn serious. Himura Kenshin-san, is it?"

"Yes," Kenshin replied, still in the same position.

"Himura-san, I've heard that our Ôkuma is in your care. So, what's going on at this hour...?"

"Katsu-sensei, it is this one that needs to ask a question. What is the purpose of luring this one to meet with you?" Kenshin said in a quiet but somewhat accusatory tone.

Kaishû stirred his small body to shift his knees toward Kenshin. Then suddenly, he laughed out loud. "Ha, ha, ha, just as I expected...I have to say, I'm still a pretty good judge of people."

Kenshin waited silently for Kaishû to continue.

"Yes indeed, you guessed right. I just knew from the very beginning that you were going to visit me tonight." Kaishû offered some tea to Kenshin as he continued. "You know, that beef-pot restaurant Akabeko has been my favorite place for some time. That fool Ôkuma may not remember, but I was the one who took him there the first time. You saw right through it, but I often go there alone, incognito, to eat the 'standard fare.' Some time ago, I spotted you and your comrades by chance, while you were there for a meal. I've heard you're a regular at the place. You see, while I may look like this now, I used to be a swordsman. I was a pupil of Shimada Toranosuke-sensei of Jiki Shinkage-ryû before the Revolution. I even have the certificate of proficiency. Used to earn my living that way, too. But even so, when I took one look at you, a shiver ran up my spine. You look like him—the man who used to personally guard me in the days at the end of the Shogunate era. Okada Izô was his name—a good man—but everyone used to fear him, and called him Hitokiri Izô." Kaishû smiled as he said this, and leaned on the nearby armrest.

Kenshin's eyebrow twitched slightly at the word hitokiri, but he otherwise remained expressionless as he listened to Kaishû.

"Say, I reckon you're pretty good at this," Kaishû said, patting his right arm lightly with his left palm, a gesture that suggested Kenshin was a skilled swordsman. "You're good, but you kind of smell like Izô. Well, to tell you the truth, I was wondering until a moment ago whether I should ask you or not. But Itsuko, who greeted you—by the way she's my third daughter—that girl said you looked like a good-natured person. When she told me that out in the hallway, I couldn't help laughing out loud. But I think I'll trust the intuition of Ôkuma, who relies on you, and my daughter, who says you're good. Himura-san, would you please help me?"

Kenshin was taken aback to see Kaishû bow his head meekly. *How should this one reply? And if this one is given details about the kind of help needed, involvement may become unavoidable.* Such were the concerns in the back of his mind. "Katsu-sensei, this one only meant to lend a helping hand to Ôkuma-dono, to look for his lost book. As for the other matter, uh…"

"I heard, Himura-san. My request may seem irrelevant, but in the end, it's not entirely unrelated to what Ôkuma lost." Kaishû smiled bitterly.

"Is that book called *From the Earth to the Moon* so very important to you, sensei?"

"Hmm… It is indeed a very interesting book, but I don't believe in the content at all. Did Ôkuma tell you what's in that book?"

"Yes, just the outline."

"It would probably fool a woman or a child, but those who have studied science even a little bit can easily tell right off that it's bogus. You see, Himura-san…"

Kaishû was talkative. He went on for some time, attacking Jules Verne's *From the Earth to the Moon.* "Placing three people in a cannonball and firing it from a cannon with a big bang... Realistically, this is impossible in the first place. Nine times out of ten, chances are the people inside wouldn't survive the shock of the discharge. Besides, a cannon powerful enough to reach the moon doesn't exist," Kaishû said. "You're probably too young to remember, but there was the Armstrong cannon that demonstrated its power during the Revolution at the end of Shogunate era. Yeah, it's the cannon that's fired to signal the noon hour on the Imperial Palace grounds. It's the most powerful cannon in the world, but its range is at best four to five thousand meters. At the time, the twenty-four pound cannon in Japan said to have the longest range was limited to 2,800 meters. Just look at what's described in that book: 86,410 *lieue!* That's 86,410 ri, close to 340,000 kilometers! If you could even reach that neutral point where the earth's gravity and the moon's gravity are evenly balanced... If you could make it to that point—which, if I'm not mistaken, is 9/10 of the distance between the two—the cannonball will become weightless and fall to the surface due only to the moon's pull. It's an outrageous story to begin with."

Oro...

"Let's just say there were a fantastic cannon that could shoot cannonballs far, far away. Don't tell me there's a metal that can withstand the kind of shock produced when fired." Here, Kaishû cited an old Chinese proverb about self-contradiction, in which a merchant hypes his "unstoppable spears" and "impenetrable shields" until someone asks what would happen if they were used against each other. This was unsurprising from a man who spent his youth during the end of the Shogunate era as a swordsman, aspired to learn the Dutch language, studied in the Nagasaki Naval Academy, and then became one of the first Japanese to travel to the United States. His theory was flawless, as expected from a crafty old badger.

The Hidden Secret

"Then, why is Katsu-sensei so obsessed with that book?" Kenshin's doubts were understandable.

Kaishû frowned as if he were being put on the spot. "What I've learned through study is limited to steamships and steam locomotives. I can't imagine anything beyond that. However, that fool Ôkuma has the nerve to say that in the near future, people will fly through the sky like birds. He believes from the bottom of his heart that someday, people will be able to go to the moon, so far away. Himura-san, if possible, I'd like to have him live that dream for the rest of his life."

Kenshin felt that he had glimpsed the true Katsu Kaishû, a man who made clever use of praise and criticism. However, those words had barely left Kaishû's mouth when he nonchalantly contradicted his previous remarks.

"Anyway, *From the Earth to the Moon* really doesn't matter at all."

Kaishû's next words surprised Kenshin even more.

"What I'm asking for and expecting from your skills isn't about the book, it's about the furoshiki cloth that was stolen along with it."

"F-furoshiki cloth, you say?"

"Yes, indeed. That furoshiki isn't any old furoshiki. There's a little secret to that fabric. If that secret is revealed, my head will be lopped off." Having said so much in a single breath, Kaishû moistened his throat with some tea and continued. "Right now, the government suspects me of furnishing war funds to Saigô's army during the Seinan War. As a result, I'm being interrogated almost every week."

"To Saigô's army?" Kenshin held his breath in response and glanced at Kaishû.

Kaishû shook his head quietly and said, "I wished I could've helped Saigô. But the time wasn't right for that." As he said this, he slowly closed his eyes. He looked as though he were reminiscing about the events of a year ago. "Many dissatisfied former samurai joined Saigô's army during the Seinan War. But, Himura-san, have you ever heard a rumor that former Shogunate *bakushin* retainers participated as well?"

Once again, Kenshin looked at Kaishû's face in surprise. Seeing that, Kaishû "The Badger" nodded slowly.

"The Tokugawa is still undecided concerning the

punishment of the 15th Shogun, Lord Yoshinobu. That gentleman is not a court noble, a samurai, or a commoner. He has been left without any social status at all. I want the 15th Shogun, who saved the citizens of Edo from war, to make peace with the government as soon as possible. During the Revolution, I sacrificed many people. To make amends for that... This is the only work I haven't finished in the era of Meiji. Himura-san, for me, the Revolution isn't over yet."

Listening to Kaishû's story, Kenshin was finally seeing the real heart of the situation. When the Meiji era began, Kaishû managed to help former *hatamoto* and bakushin Shogunate retainers seek employment, and raised money for their living expenses to prevent them from rioting, all the while planning to restore the rights of Tokugawa Yoshinobu. The flow of the Tokugawa clan's hidden funds was about to be exposed to the public eye.

"The enemy is probably Beni Aoi, a group of degenerate former hatamoto who hate me. Right about now, I'm sure they're going to the trouble of picking apart *From the Earth to the Moon*, looking for coded messages and signs to Saigô's army."

According to Kaishû, the associates that made up Beni Aoi consisted of discontented former hatamoto whose lives were ruined by the Revolution. While their motto was "Revive the Tokugawa Government," they lurked in the darkness and used their money to hire thugs to dig up scandals, while secretly conspiring to overthrow powerful government officials.

"Their information network should not be taken lightly. As a matter of fact, they have their eyes on my—the Tokugawa's—hidden money. Moreover, I've heard that blood-thirsty assassins are among those they've hired with their lavishly spent funds."

Kenshin remained silent.

Kaishû glanced away a moment, but turned his eyes back to Kenshin, his gaze noticeably sharper. "How about it, Himura-san?" Kaishû asked Kenshin again. "Will you help me? I'm not asking you because I want to save my life. If the Tokugawa's hidden money is found and confiscated by the government, then surely some former bakushin will plan a rebellion to show their discontent. If that happens, it'll be impossible to bring the 15th Shogun back into society."

Kenshin was hesitant to make a decision. He understood Kaishû's concerns very well, and the fine fellow of small stature before him had explained almost too thoroughly why his help was needed. That said, he was hesitant because it seemed as though the true nature of the enemy he would have to fight, the Beni Aoi, was totally unknown, indistinct, and shrouded in dark mystery. They had a gloomy air about them that was almost eerie. A mere rurouni meddling with such affairs couldn't make much difference. He couldn't help but feel that Kaishû, perhaps driven by urgency, was giving him too much credit.

Kenshin's personal feelings also caused him to hesitate. Once Kenshin had abandoned his past as the assassin Hitokiri Battôsai, he had wandered the city streets as a private citizen, and though he felt a hint of loneliness, he also felt the relief of being free from any weight on his shoulders. Any direction the wind blew, wherever fancy took him, the easy day-to-day life of a rurouni was carefree, except for a small desire to at least protect those who crossed his path. But he was now a guest at the Kamiya dojo, and he had ties to people like Kaoru, Myôjin Yahiko, and Sagara Sanosuke. There was joy, but in some corner of his mind, he could not deny that at times he felt it as a burden.

Furthermore, if he became further involved in Kaishû's scheme, he could end up bearing a heavier burden. Responding to Kaishû's request would mean that very soon he'd be drawn into the vortex of a bloody conflict, man-to-man and power-to-power. It already had the smell of blood about it. Depending on the circumstances, it meant the possibility of reviving Hitokiri Battôsai, which he'd desperately tried to keep trapped within himself. But Kenshin, without mentioning a word of what was going through his mind, simply stated his concerns about Kaishû's request. "Katsu-sensei, this one regrets to say that this one is not fit to handle such an important duty. In the first place, this one doubts sensei knows anything about this rurouni."

"Yes, that's certainly true." Kaishû's attitude was soft in every way, gently but deliberately persuasive. "But,

Himura-san, that's really not the point here. We all have a thing or two in our pasts that we don't want to talk about. I've got them, too. What about you? Isn't that why you're a rurouni?"

Kenshin kept silent.

"I've seen you, and now we've met and talked. That's good enough for me."

In the end, Kenshin gave his consent. It could be said that Kenshin gave into the man's persistence, but he was dealing with the awe-inspiring Katsu Kaishû. The man's persuasive bearing was surely a factor.

Kenshin replied that he intended to serve diligently, but politely requested that Kaishû not expect too much.

Kaishû appeared relieved at last, but he was a man of tough character and continued to press Kenshin. "You know, I'm going to be interrogated by the police again the day after tomorrow. It's like that saying, poke a bush, and a snake comes out—the police don't know anything at all about the Tokugawa's hidden money, but with those suspicious guys hanging around me, I can't say they won't find out about it by chance. It's a secret route that's taken eleven years to establish, but depending on the situation, everything would have to be concealed. It's too bad, but if that happens, I'll have to dismiss Ôkuma. That guy doesn't know anything, but the fact remains that he was used as a connection." This practically amounted to setting a deadline of the day after tomorrow. Kaishû clapped his hands and called for a family member. Again, it was Itsuko who appeared.

"Himura-san, I'm awfully tired tonight. I'm going to excuse myself to get some rest. Please, feel free to stay awhile." As Kaishû said this, he blinked his eyes and massaged his brows gently with his fingertips. The piteous signs of weakness were prominent on his stern face. The weekly police interrogations were probably becoming a huge psychological burden.

Eventually, Kaishû stood up and was about to leave the room when he turned and spoke to Itsuko, who was properly seated in the corner of the tatami mat-lined room. "Hey, Himura-san is single and isn't promised to any woman." Kaishû's words were unexpected, and Kenshin's dumbfounded eyes met those of Itsuko.

"Oh, Father…" Itsuko's cheeks immediately began to blush crimson. For a moment, her slender body seemed to glow with dazzling femininity.

Kenshin may or may not have noticed it as he said to Itsuko, "Then, this one will also take leave."

It appeared that Itsuko had been preparing a late-night meal, but Kenshin declined apologetically and left Katsu's residence.

The First Assassin

By the time Kenshin was on his way home, it was already past nine thirty. A thin, hazy moon had risen into the sky. For a time, the silhouettes of people carrying paper lanterns moved about, but by ten, the pedestrian traffic had ceased entirely. Kenshin took a different route from the one he had used when heading to Katsu's residence.

Kenshin had good night vision, and in addition, he carried a paper lantern given to him by Itsuko in his right hand. He certainly wouldn't be making any wrong turns, but Kenshin looked as though he preferred to walk in deserted areas. Before long, he was far from the houses that dotted the area. He came to a gently sloping street lying between fields that stretched out on both sides. There was silence in every direction, and save for the hazy moon in the sky, darkness dominated. About two cho ahead, in

51

the downtown area, the street intersected another street lined with rows of merchants.

The unfamiliar call of a bird greeted Kenshin after he'd walked less than one cho at a rather slow pace. There was a long call, *hew-ee, hew-roo-roo, hew-roo-roo*. Then, as if to respond to it, two short calls, *kwi-kwi*, echoed across the dark landscape. Kenshin quietly released his sword from its sheath. He felt someone move swiftly behind him. Then, another movement. "Surrounded, it seems," Kenshin murmured to himself as he blew out the flame inside the paper lantern. At some point, the birdcalls had stopped.

There was an aura of death drifting over the silent, colorless earth. Some woods were faintly visible in the darkness ahead, about a half cho away. As Kenshin eyed the distance, he pushed his slightly drawn sword a little below his waist, then bent over forward and started running at full speed. Just then, *shuriken* came flying out of the darkness. With what could only be described as animal intuition and instinct, Kenshin dodged the shuriken that assailed him as he continued to head for the woods.

When he had almost reached the trees, Kenshin saw before him what appeared to be darkness overlapping the darkness. He instantly dropped to one knee in a defensive crouch, only to discover the dark silhouette of a man as enormous as a cliff waiting for him. The man had drawn a long sword—almost the size of a short spear—and taken up a ready position, with his sword angled toward Kenshin.

With deadly precision he slid the point of his sword down until it was clearly aimed at Kenshin's neck. A beast's fierceness emanated from the man, and Kenshin felt it press in on him.

"I was only testing you earlier. However, I won't go easy on you this time. His High Excellency has granted me permission. If you wish to live, let's hear what you discussed in your secret meeting with Katsu Kaishû, and the secret of that book. Otherwise—" In the darkness, the giant bared his teeth and smiled.

"Do you belong to Beni Aoi?"

In response to Kenshin's question, the man showed his teeth a little, as if he were trying to smile, but the words that left his mouth were curt and dry. "Indeed, we are a group of loyal samurai who have risen to overthrow the corrupt New Government and restore the Tokugawa Shogunate."

Kenshin kept a careful eye in all four directions as he continued to speak to the giant before him. "Challenging the New Government's troops won't bring you victory, for they were not defeated even when Saigô Takamori was involved."

"Stop your ranting! If we have the war funds, we can assemble soldiers and weapons. If they cannot be arranged for domestically, we can bring them from overseas. In order to do that, we need the Tokugawa's hidden funds—the funds that Katsu must possess. You! What do you know of them?" The giant of a man raised his voice for an instant.

But Kenshin didn't say a word. The man allowed his battle *chi* to flow into the long sword he held ready.

Such formidable chi. Kenshin clenched his teeth and tried to counter the giant's overwhelming chi, but for some reason changed his mind and stopped, then appeared to relax his muscles, letting his eyes close halfway and his mouth open slightly.

An obscure, elusive color began to wrap around Kenshin's face, spreading to his entire body. It appeared that he was neither blocking the enemy's chi nor absorbing it, but instead turning himself into a kind of nothingness, increasing his transparency in an attempt to let the enemy's chi pass through him.

"Hmm, you've dodged my battle chi..." said the gloomy voice of the gigantic man in the darkness. With that, a tremendous amount of menacing energy radiated from the point of the sword he held poised in a low, ready position. "To find such a skilled swordsman in the Meiji era..." The dark, gigantic man muttered toward Kenshin, who stayed hidden in the darkness. The giant casually filled his long sword with silent fighting energy.

Astonishment ran through Kenshin's body like an electric shock. The surge of chi from his giant opponent's sword increased. It certainly resembled the mastery of *musô-ken*, a secret technique mentioned in every book about sword-fighting techniques.

Kenshin did his best to maintain his state of nothingness

and emptiness. He was unable to think of a way to counter this intense chi at the moment, except to hide human emotions deep inside his heart. Kenshin kept his sword slightly drawn, and from a low-profile position that bordered on crawling on the ground, he peered into the darkness to observe his opponent.

There are two ways to emit chi. Inner chi is generated within the body and stored to release all at once, while outer chi is absorbed into the body, circulated, and then released. Kenshin tried to figure out which of the two types of chi his opponent possessed. Creating a void in his heart and maintaining a state of nothingness wouldn't exhaust Kenshin's energy, but he hoped his opponent's enormous energy would eventually wane and require replenishment. *That's the case with inner chi, at least…*

The use of outer chi was the technique spreading through the country of China on the neighboring continent, which in many cases was about mastering the absorption of outer chi, and those who perfected it were able to use chi almost continuously.

In the darkness, the huge man continued to emit his chi.

This can't be good.

Just as Kenshin was pondering whether he should bring his chi back into his body in order to emit a sudden burst of power and use the distraction to move forward and attack, it happened.

The eyes of the gigantic man, which glowed abnormally in the dark, seemed to dim. The opponent's chi must have been the inner kind. Perhaps his energy was becoming depleted.

Kenshin enacted a quick series of controlled rolls, ending each roll with his right knee solidly placed on the ground in his ready position, and approached the enemy head on from the left, slashing the gigantic man's shoulder in a single stroke with his sakabatô. For a second, the opponent's enormous body sagged. But the movement was deceptive, and the sharp point of the giant's sword flashed through the air, aiming for Kenshin with a blow from above. Kenshin didn't jump back, but instead parried the opponent's sword point with the guard of his blade, as if challenging him to close combat. Kenshin then returned the blows twice, then three times in a continuous attack.

The giant opponent endured the persistent assaults, but seemed bewildered by Kenshin's attack. Kenshin seemed to be acting with total disregard for his own defense as he launched furious counter-attacks. But moving forward to attack leaves a spot unguarded. If an opponent takes advantage of that spot, there is no doubt that any swordsman will be endangered.

Kenshin stared cautiously into his opponent's eyes. The giant's half-open eyes glowed in the dark with a tinge of evil, waiting to take advantage of a chance to attack. While staring at each other, the power of the man's chi seemed to put pressure on Kenshin's chest. Moving in small steps from left to right, Kenshin attacked with a blinding speed.

The two swords made a metallic sound, and sparks flew as they clashed in midair. The pair passed by each other, came to a stop, then turned around and locked their swords again. The gigantic man was clearly a formidable enemy. He persistently challenged and counterattacked. However, Kenshin had not yet used his special *Hiten Mitsurugi-ryû* moves. That could mean he was still ahead in the game. As a matter of fact, Kenshin was gradually gaining ground.

Kenshin's single downward stroke from an overhead position, delivered as he stepped forward, was quicker than the giant's interception with his long sword. Like a shooting star, Kenshin's sword point drew a circle in the dark and precisely struck the shoulder of the gigantic man. For the first time, the giant leapt backward of his own volition. His body still facing Kenshin, he quietly retreated until two ken stretched between them. One had to admit the giant's moves showed amazing skill. The large, dark body entered the ready position again, but a hint of desperation tainted the chi at the point of his sword.

Let this next stroke determine the winner, Kenshin thought as he paused to adjust his timing. Having made up his mind, he felt ready to display his Hiten Mitsurugi-ryû move. From a lower overhead position, Kenshin tipped the point of his sword to the side and leapt sharply upwards.

"Ah...!" The gigantic man was taken by surprise. Kenshin had leapt high in the air and was hovering over him like a hawk taking aim at its prey. Then, with all his might, Kenshin delivered a single blow to the large, dark body of his opponent—*Ryûtsuisen*, the secret Dragon Hammer Strike. The ground shook with a dull thud as the gigantic man collapsed. If Kenshin's sword had been normal, the man would have been cut completely in half.

Eventually, the killer energy surrounding Kenshin dissipated, and silence returned as if nothing had happened. Kenshin cautiously checked his surroundings, then re-lit the lantern he had thrown aside and examined the giant's possessions. A coin purse and a hand towel bearing the dyed logo of a soba place in Kanda Myojin-shita called Kagetsu An were inside the front of the man's kimono.

Unexpected Visitors

"Kenshin, how long are you going to sleep?"

Kenshin threw off the bedding in surprise when Kaoru's voice from above awoke him. He instantly remembered that after defeating the assassin, he had returned around dawn and had gone to sleep right there in the dojo, using his arms as a pillow. Kaoru was probably the one who had placed the bed covers over him; the fact that her eyes were a bit red seemed proof of that. No doubt this stouthearted girl hadn't slept a wink while she waited for Kenshin's return.

"Much appreciated," Kenshin thanked her as he scratched his head.

"Breakfast is ready. Although it's already noon." Kaoru did her best to act distant, but every move of her body was filled with kindness toward Kenshin.

Kenshin stepped out to the yard, and as he washed

his face and rinsed his mouth, his hunger after spending a long night out caught up with him. Kenshin headed for breakfast.

He nodded slightly in greeting and after announcing he was ready to eat, Kenshin happily wolfed down the breakfast Kaoru had prepared—the same cooking that Yahiko so severely criticized. "By the way, where are Ôkuma-dono and Yahiko?" Kenshin asked as he lifted a portion from a side dish to his mouth.

"They went out together a while ago. They're going to visit all the newspaper agencies, publishers, and used bookstores. I'd better get going, too."

"Is that so..." Kenshin seemed to be lost in thought for a moment, but quickly said, "Kaoru-dono," and looked at her quietly.

"Seconds?"

"No...um...uhhh..."

"Oh, please...what is it then?"

Kenshin told Kaoru the details of his discussion with Katsu Kaishû, and a summary of the incident that occurred on the way back.

"So, that's what happened." Kaoru stared at Kenshin, her pale chin buried in her collar, giving her a look of innocence. Then Kaoru frowned and said, "So it really wasn't *From the Earth to the Moon*, but the furoshiki cloth that Katsu-sensei wanted. Then, it's a waste for Ôkuma-san and Yahiko to visit the publishers and such."

"No, that may not be the case."

"Huh?"

"The Beni Aoi is probably keeping an eye on this dojo. The gang is most likely following Ôkuma-dono and Yahiko as we speak. The enemy is spying on us to try to discover where the hidden money is located. They believe *From the Earth to the Moon* is the key to cracking the code. It may be safer for Yahiko and Ôkuma-dono to continue their rounds of the bookstores. In the meantime, this one will—"

"What should I do?"

"Please, stay here."

"No way! That's not..." Kaoru's beautiful face pouted. "I want to go with you to find the hideout of the Beni Aoi group, or whatever it's called."

"But...there are skilled assassins among them..."

"I'll be all right, I'm an instructor of Kamiya Kasshin-ryû. I won't be a hindrance."

"Well, that is surely the case, but..." Kenshin fumbled as he tried to convince Kaoru to change her mind, but he was losing to Kaoru's eagerness. To Kenshin, Kaoru was by far a more challenging opponent than the gigantic man the previous night. While Kenshin looked helplessly about and Kaoru prepared to leave, a voice outside announced that a visitor had arrived. Kenshin had heard that voice last night. There was no mistake—it belonged to Katsu Itsuko. A cold shiver ran down his spine.

"Just a moment!" Kaoru hurried to the entrance hallway,

then stood transfixed for a moment when she encountered an unfamiliar couple in Western clothes. The man was in his thirties and had a lean, handsome face. His hair was cropped short and slicked back fashionably. His tall physique looked fine in a suit, and the Inverness cape worn over his clothes looked quite modern. The way he had his left hand inside his pants pocket and held a cigar between the fingers of his right hand looked a bit affected to Kaoru, but even so he was attractive and had an air of keen intelligence. Kaoru's attention, however, was more focused on the woman in Western clothes standing next to him. She wore her semi-formal dress in a very stylish way, and had a crimson ribbon tied in her hair, which was braided and looped in the Margaret style. Kaoru had never met or spoken to them before, but being a person of determination and intelligence, Kaoru's intuition was strong. "Um, excuse me, but are you Itsuko-sama, from Katsu-sensei's place?"

The woman smiled in response to Kaoru's question. If Kaoru were asked to describe a young lady raised in a privileged environment, Katsu Itsuko was certainly the type that would come to mind, even though Kaoru was unfamiliar with such women. Kaoru wanted to ask why they'd taken the trouble to visit a place like this, but as if reading her mind, the tall man spoke.

"Ôjo-sama has come to see a swordsman named Himura Kenshin, who visited her residence last night. My name is Ôkubo Tetsuma, the Katsu family's former pupil, now working for the Ministry of Home Affairs. I am accompanying ojô-sama as her guide, and also as her bodyguard. You'd do well to remember me."

There was more than a hint of arrogance in the man's tone. That said, if people knew who Tetsuma was, they probably would've thought it understandable, given that he was the head of the Ôkubo family. The family had been the Shogunate's hatamoto retainers until the end of the Shogunate era, rating an annual salary in the range of 3000 koku, almost a hundred times that of a low-ranking vassal like Yahiko's father. Ôkubo had managed to avoid the turmoil of the Revolution and become a high official in the Ministry of Home Affairs, which enjoyed the highest authority and privileges within the New Government.

The man's tone got on Kaoru's nerves, however.

"Well, thank you for your introduction." As she pondered what to say next, Kenshin showed up wearing a happy smile on his face. He appeared to be in a good mood, his stomach full after the late breakfast.

"Well, hello there, Itsuko-dono. Apologies for visiting so late last night."

Itsuko smiled and gave a small curtsy at Kenshin's carefree words. Tetsuma, standing beside her, felt as though he'd glimpsed Itsuko's absolute trust in Kenshin, and inwardly he wasn't very happy about it. Kaoru's inner heart wasn't exactly calm either.

"Let's not stand around the entrance hall. Please, come

inside. Right, Kaoru-dono?" Urged on by Kenshin, Kaoru had no choice but to guide the two guests inside. Kaoru nodded her head and led the way, inviting the couple into the receiving room.

The four sat around the low table. Itsuko and Tetsuma were seated in places of honor, with Kenshin and Kaoru facing them. They exchanged greetings once again, and Kaoru left her seat to prepare tea and sweets. As if she had been waiting for that, Itsuko spoke to Kenshin in a reserved manner. "That lovely lady…is she Himura-sama's wife? Or perhaps your fiancée?" She spoke in a low voice, but it still reached Kaoru as she stepped into the hallway.

"No, that is not the case. This one is a mere rurouni. Kaoru-dono is the owner of this dojo, and this one is but an idle guest." When Kenshin's voice reached the departing Kaoru's ears, she let out a small sigh of disappointment and continued walking to the kitchen.

"Is that so?" Itsuko said with a twinkle in her eye, which caused a shadow to flit across Tetsuma's face as he sat beside her.

"Red hair with a large cross-shaped scar on his left cheek—I imagined how amazing such a swordsman might appear, but with such a short and thin build, your physique looks unexpectedly delicate," Testuma muttered, with a suspicious look at Kenshin.

Itsuko was quick to apologize. "Ôkubo-san, what a thing to say. Himura-san, I'm sorry…"

"Ah, this one doesn't mind. Really, there's nothing to apologize for."

Last night, when Kenshin saw Itsuko for the first time, he thought she strongly resembled Kaoru. But now that they were face to face and he was able to see her and talk to her again, he realized she was very different from Kaoru in both features and temperament. Kaoru could not stand being alone, and her personality was lively by nature. This girl's body seemed filled with determination, but Itsuko was much like her beautiful, balanced appearance—she seemed to have a quiet, introverted personality.

"You took the trouble to come to us about Ôkuma, so I told my father that even though the book may be precious, which is more important: a single book, or Ôkuma's future? As you may know, my father is an eccentric person, and he just kept smiling..." When Itsuko had realized the conversation with her father wasn't going anywhere, she had decided to bring Ôkuma back on her own.

Judging from the way Itsuko is talking, she must be unaware of the facts regarding last night's incident, Kenshin thought.

"But ojô-sama," said Tetsuma, "for you to go about on your own is out of the question. A suspicious gang is following sensei around. It is fortunate that I happened to run into you, but for a young lady of the Katsu family to come to a place like this..."

Right at that moment, Kaoru entered the receiving room, carrying tea and sweets. *Sorry for having a "place like this!"*

Kaoru barely swallowed the words before they came out of her mouth.

A moment later, Kenshin asked, "Ôkubo-dono, is the suspicious gang you mentioned truly Beni Aoi, or members of the police force, acting under the orders of the Ministry of Home Affairs?" One side of Tetsuma's face twitched as he glared at Kenshin, who had asked the question with a firm look on his face. Tetsuma's expression revealed that he knew of the existence of the Beni Aoi.

"Himura-san, what is this Beni Aoi?" A strong shadow of suspicion fell over Itsuko's eyes.

Kenshin simply replied that it was thought to be an association of aggressive former Shogunate retainers. Then, as if to ask for confirmation, Kenshin said, "Isn't that so, Ôkubo-dono?"

A thin smile appeared on Tetsuma's face. "Quite so. Those foolish men...in this era of culture and progress, they seriously believe in their dream of reviving the Tokugawa family. I've heard their leader is referred to as the High Excellency. Katsu-sensei has been blamed as a villain who sold out the Tokugawa. That probably makes it easier for him to be the target of such unenlightened people. Well, as long as I'm with the police force of the Ministry of Home Affairs, I'll definitely get on their tails and round up the whole gang." Tetsuma imagined the defeated Beni Aoi before him, and cast a cruel, scornful eye upon the lot.

Fencing Match: Japan vs. the Western World

"By the way Himura-kun, I've been training in Western-style fencing since my teens. I've earned the masters certificate, too. How about it? It's been a long time, and I feel like having a match against Japanese swordplay. Could you give me a lesson on the moves?" Tetsuma urged Kenshin, his face pale and expressionless. His narrow, almond-shaped eyes pierced Kenshin's own. But Kenshin was not one to fall for such an obvious challenge.

"This one is just a guest here. Teaching sword skills wouldn't be appropriate."

"I see you still wear your sword, even though the law prohibits carrying them. Apparently, you are very attached to it. Surely, you must have fine skills. And I would like to have the honor of seeing them."

"No, this one's sword skills are not worth showing to others...ha, ha, haha..."

"Are you trying to laugh this off?" Tetsuma appeared to be losing his patience. His complexion grew livid, his gaze sharper, and a hint of sarcasm entered his tone.

A cold shiver ran through Kaoru's spine as she sat beside Kenshin. Despite that, she firmly stated, "Our dojo's style is Kamiya Kasshin-ryû. I lack experience, but as the instructor, I will take on this match, if you wish."

Tetsuma, who appeared to be thinking about withdrawing from a bout against a woman, replied, "Oh, that's interesting. Let us have a match then." Tetsuma removed his jacket and pulled an odd-looking sword from the leather case he had brought with him.

"You should stop, Ôkubo-san." Surprised by the way things were unfolding, Itsuko tried to stop Tetsuma, but he was not one to withdraw easily.

Looks like I have no choice but to fight, Kaoru decided. She glanced quickly at Kenshin, but he was reaching for some sweets on the table, seemingly unaware of the situation.

Kenshin, you fool! Kaoru shouted in her mind as she went to another room to change into her training gear. Upon returning, she led everyone to the dojo.

Inside the dojo, the light from the sun rising high in the sky poured through the vertical bars of the *musha-mado* windows. Tetsuma's sword sparkled in the sunlight. For those unfamiliar with it, it must have been a strange sight. It was a saber-style fencing sword.

Kaoru was so amazed by the sword, it left her momentarily speechless.

Such a beautiful girl, Tetsuma had time to think as they stood face to face. Of course, he'd thought so from the moment he saw her in the entrance hall. Even in her unfeminine training outfit, her balanced features, lean and slender appearance, and dark, clear eyes were especially captivating. Tetsuma swallowed.

"This is used for training. The sword point is capped with rubber, but serious injury is possible if it hits the wrong spot." As Tetsuma spoke, he glanced toward Kenshin, who was standing over to the right side of the dojo. Kenshin was having a conversation with Itsuko.

"Let us begin." The formal words to begin a match spoken, Kaoru pointed her bamboo *shinai* at her opponent's left shoulder, then fixed her eye on Tetsuma's moves. She suppressed her intense fighting spirit and her anxiety about the mysterious sword by maintaining a state of nothingness.

Tetsuma's ready position looked strange to Kaoru, who was only familiar with Japanese sword fighting. The sword in his left hand was thrust forward, and the other hand was raised behind his back, with the elbow slightly bent. It appeared that he maintained his physical balance that way. His stance was different as well. His rear foot was arched up so that only the very tips of his toes rested on the floor.

The pair stood still for a minute or two. Suddenly, Tetsuma's whole body spread out like a bird, and the next moment, his body slid across the dojo floor. His posture resembled a leopard stalking its prey. His ready position wasn't the only thing odd about his movements. The point of his thin, sharp sword quivered in an up-and-down motion, much like the tail feathers of a wagtail. Even though the point of his sword was moving, Tetsuma's oblique stance, with the sword in one hand, was not off-balance at all. He drew closer in a straight, magnificent run, as fast as the wind.

With her eyes wide open, Kaoru waited. As Tetsuma rushed in with his uniquely long, thin sword, Kaoru shortened the distance between them by half a step and engaged him. The dull sound of the bamboo sword and the Western sword colliding echoed through the dojo. The silence was broken, and now the two swords clashed together in midair without pause. At times they rubbed and struck against each other with intense vigor, and the sounds of shinai and saber colliding continued.

Once the pair was engaged in the swordfight, it was obvious that Tetsuma was much taller than Kaoru. It was almost puzzling, trying to figure out where in his tall, slender body all that strength could be stored. Tetsuma's movements were light, and although the point of his sword precisely struck Kaoru's arms and shoulders, it was capped with a rubber tip, and did not puncture her skin. That said, each stroke hit with a substantial force, and when the same spot was repeatedly struck, Kaoru's skin turned from red to blue, and the pain became quite intense. Moreover, Kaoru's shinai was in danger of being knocked away by Tetsuma's Western sword.

"Ta-ha!" Tetsuma let out a strange cry and pressed forward with force. Tetsuma seemed to have decided that Kaoru's defenses were nearly at their limit. Kaoru retreated back with an agile move. The distance between the pair increased slightly. Tetsuma decided to put an end to the match.

He's coming!

At the moment Kaoru predicted this, Kenshin's voice rang out sharply. "Kaoru-dono, move forward!"

As if in time with the voice, Tetsuma made his move. Instead of shuffling his feet forward, he made a diving move to thrust his sword at Kaoru's abdomen. But instead of turning away, Kaoru moved forward as Kenshin's voice had instructed. It was a snap decision; if it weren't for her unwavering trust in Kenshin, she couldn't have done it. Kaoru narrowly dodged Tetsuma's killer stroke, then swung her shinai down onto Tetsuma's left shoulder. The dry sound of the bamboo striking echoed through the dojo, and Tetsuma dropped his strange-looking sword.

Kaoru drew in a deep breath, and Itsuko flashed a smile. But Kenshin again called out to her in a stern voice. "Kaoru-dono, *zanshin!* Don't drop your guard!"

Then it happened. His weapon dropped due to the painful blow, Tetsuma quickly seized the sword with his right hand while still kneeling, then delivered a fast, keen stroke. The killer sword almost delivered a painful blow to Kaoru's thigh, but by maintaining her position through zanshin, she leapt out of the way and shifted position for her next strike.

"Ei!" With a piercing cry, her shinai struck a direct blow to Tetsuma's forehead. Tetsuma fell to the dojo floor with a ground-shaking thud.

Kaoru had treated the match like an extreme life-or-death struggle. While she was catching her breath, Kenshin broke into a smile and applauded to celebrate her victory. "My, you have improved your skills, Kaoru-dono."

"Fool..." Kaoru whispered back to him. She bowed in front of the shrine, then retreated to another room to change. If Itsuko weren't there, she could've jumped into Kenshin's arms and cried. It would have been a great ending to her victorious match, but when it came to Kenshin, the timing never seemed right.

Kenshin quietly picked up the sword that Tetsuma had dropped. He removed the rubber cap from the sword tip and appeared to examine something, then replaced the cap again and discreetly placed the sword inside the leather case.

Meanwhile, Ôkuma Daigoro and Yahiko were roaming

around downtown on tired legs. Yahiko happened to spot a diner with "liquor and meals" written large on a rusty red paper lantern. For some time, Yahiko had been feeling faint from hunger, so he nodded his head toward the paper lantern.

"Even if we return to the dojo now, all that's waiting for us is Kaoru's crummy dinner. Why don't we stay out, eat something a little better here, and then move on to Ginza?" Without waiting for Daigoro to reply, Yahiko entered the restaurant and ordered bowls of rice and a few other side dishes, one after another. Finally, he started to relax.

Daigoro wore a navy *kasuri* kimono with striped *hakama* pants made with fabric from the Kokura region. While he had the appearance of a fine student, his presence was barely noticed, as usual.

"C'mon, cheer up." Yahiko could be rude, but he was actually a kindhearted boy by nature. He tried in vain to comfort Daigoro—who was feeling disheartened because there had been no sign of the lost book—but his efforts only depressed Daigoro further. "Hang in there, try to be a man."

"I'm not from a samurai family like you, Myôjin-kun."

"Stupid fool, this is the era of culture and progress, and coming from a samurai family doesn't have anything to do with being a man. You can't expect to make your moon trip like that." Yahiko mentioned the moon voyage without giving it much thought, but Daigoro seemed to become even more nervous. Yahiko's sharp eyes noted the change, and decided that this would be a good chance to ask for more details about *From the Earth to the Moon*, which he had been curious about since yesterday.

"Inside the cannonball, there are machines named 'Reiset' and 'Regnault,' with two months worth of chlorate of potash stored inside. These machines maintain a temperature of over four hundred degrees Celsius, and by converting eighteen pounds of chlorate of potash into chlorine of potassium, the seven pounds of oxygen necessary for three people to survive for one day are produced. Along with that, the carbonic acid produced by breathing is absorbed by a supply of caustic potash." Such was the explanation to Yahiko's question about how people would breathe inside the cannonball.

While they were talking, the bowls of rice and side dishes they had ordered arrived. When Daigoro saw this, he said with a twinkle in his eye, "Myôjin-kun, a meal in space begins with three pieces of bouillon."

"B-bouillon?"

Daigoro eagerly tried to explain to Yahiko, but his expression showed that Yahiko had no idea what Daigoro was talking about. "Bouillon is a tablet made from beef extract. When you pour hot water on it, the tablet dissolves, softens, and spreads."

"I-is that supposed to be good?"

"I don't know, but it sure sounded good the way it was

described in that book."

In addition, Daigoro discussed how the observatory first calculated the speed of the *Columbiad* cannon by showing Yahiko this algebraic expression:

$$1/2 \ (v2(v\text{-}square) - v02)(v\text{-}zero\text{-}square)) \ =$$
$$gr \ [r/x - 1 + m/m1 \ (r/d - x - r/d - r)]$$

"...and so, it's calculated by taking into account the distance from the center of the earth to the center of the moon, the earth's radius and mass, and the moon's mass as well. It's called integral calculus, and this..."

Yahiko stared with blank eyes, and was dumbfounded by the difficult vocabulary and numbers he was hearing. Finally, he found it unbearable. "W-wait! I understand...no, I don't understand the details, but now I think I understand a little of the dream you're after," Yahiko said, thrusting his chopsticks with his right hand to interrupt Daigoro. "I want to be strong, like Kenshin. I want to be the number one swordsman in Japan! In the world! Ôkuma, you become the number one scientist in Japan, in the world! Then, you take me to the moon." As he said this, Yahiko reached across the dinner table and seized Daigoro's shoulders. His body was small, but he had strength, and Daigoro's eyes filled with tears from having his shoulders gripped so firmly.

"H-hey, did that hurt?"

Daigoro shook his head in response to the worried-looking Yahiko, and simply replied that he was happy, then slowly ate his bowl of rice.

"Hmph, you fool. Don't worry me like that." Nervously, Yahiko wolfed down his bowl of rice as well.

The Second Assassin

Even after the match, Itsuko engaged in small talk as an excuse to linger at the Kamiya dojo. As a topic of conversation, she offered the news that the imported *chocolat* she brought as a gift would be manufactured domestically by the end of the year.

Kenshin whispered something into Kaoru's ear and asked her to leave quietly via the backdoor. Then, along with a sour-looking Tetsuma, wholeheartedly took on the role of listener and laughed merrily at Itsuko's observations about modern culture and progress. Meanwhile, Kaoru hurried to Akabeko to fetch Tae.

Is Ôkubo Tetsuma one of the men who stole Ôkuma Daigoro's book? Kenshin speculated.

When Kaoru returned, out of breath, she had Tae sneak a look at Tetsuma from the adjoining room. Unfortunately,

Tae took one look and said, "He's not the one." She was sure he was not the man she had seen earlier. Besides, he had no moustache.

"Oh...?" Kaoru replied in disappointment, but Tae continued observing the occupants of the adjoining room.

"But later that day, I think he was the one who sat where Ôkuma-san had been earlier."

"Really?" Kaoru gasped as she looked at Tae. Tae said nothing, but the sparkle in her eyes was confirmation enough.

"Pardon me, but I need to speak to Kenshin for a moment." Kenshin excused himself and followed Kaoru to the kitchen, where she told him about Tae's testimony.

"Is that so...?" Kenshin was lost in thought, and didn't appear ready to take any action.

After a while, Tetsuma got up from his seat, hoping to urge Itsuko to leave. It was already past three o'clock, but as luck would have it, there was a two-seat rickshaw waiting for customers out on the street. The back of the rickshaw was decorated with a lacquered image of Ushiwaka-maru and Benkei fighting in the snow, a modern display of poetic charm.

"We must excuse ourselves now. Uh, Himura-san, please tell Ôkuma that he may return to the residence at any time." With Tetsuma and a reluctant Itsuko on board, the rickshaw left the Kamiya dojo behind. The noise of the rickshaw's iron wheels echoed in the street and lingered in the ears of Kenshin, Kaoru, and Tae as they saw the pair off.

A little past seven that same day, Nakajima Torazô, one of Katsu's senior students, burst into the Kamiya dojo, his face pale.

"Itsuko ojô-sama is in serious t-trouble!" He must have run the whole way, for Torazô fell to his knees in the entrance hall and gasped for breath, air whistling through his parched throat. Once his breathing calmed down a bit, Torazô explained that around six o'clock, just as they were getting anxious about Itsuko's late return, a neighbor's child delivered a letter from an unknown sender. "Here is the letter. As soon as sensei reads it, he said to take it to Himura-san."

Anger surged through Kenshin's entire body as he read the letter. The note demanded that Katsu reveal every secret of the Tokugawa's hidden money before reporting to the police questioning regarding the Seinan War, at 10 a.m. tomorrow. It ordered the recipient to come to the Ueno Tosho-gu temple precinct at 8 a.m. "Do as we say, or we will kill Itsuko." The letter was signed "Aoi" in deep red. Kenshin's face grew pale, as did Kaoru's, Yahiko's, and Daigoro's.

"Nakajima-dono, didn't Ôkubo Tetsuma accompany Itsuko-san?"

Torazô seemed bewildered by Kenshin's sudden

question.

"He said that he got out of the vehicle first, near the house."

"Nakajima-san, I..." Daigoro didn't know the whole story behind the incident, and already seemed distracted. But this was no time for passive pondering.

"Kaoru-dono, this one happens to know where to look. If this one does not return in about an hour, please tell Katsu-sensei to send the police to Homei-in of Kanda Myojinshita. Homei-in is that haunted temple near Kagetsu-an." With those words, Kenshin left the dojo, his sakabatô at his waist.

The Beni Aoi's leader, called the High Excellency, was probably Ôkubo Tetsuma. Kenshin had been fully aware of it, but allowed Itsuko to leave with him, assuming that Tetsuma wouldn't do anything foolish to reveal his identity. But Kenshin had failed to realize how urgent the situation really was.

After Kenshin had defeated his mysterious attacker, he had visited Kagetsu-an—the name of the soba place dyed on the man's hand towel—but hadn't spotted anything unusual there. Kenshin had briefly inspected the area and was about to go back when he noticed that Kagetsu-an was near Homei-in Temple, the place that Yahiko had mentioned earlier. It was the same place where ghostly voices were rumored to be heard.

The stories said that a head monk hanged himself in the

temple during the upheaval of the anti-Buddhist movement, and that his vengeful ghost lingered as a curse on Homei-in. No one, not even the people in the neighborhood, came near the abandoned temple anymore. But in the pre-dawn light, Kenshin had seen the shadow of someone inside the temple.

The Beni Aoi has taken Itsuko-dono hostage to get the Tokugawa family's hidden money before the police do. Not only that, Kenshin thought, *but Ôkubo Tetsuma was once a pupil at Katsu's house, so he must have run errands for Katsu-sensei, just like Daigoro. Unlike Daigoro, Tetsuma is ambitious as well as clever, and likely became suspicious about those errands.*

Sakabatô secure at his side, Kenshin ran like the wind through the dark streets, arriving quickly at Homei-in temple. As if on cue, rain began to drizzle down. The layout of the temple was still fresh in Kenshin's mind, and he quietly proceeded to the back entrance and slipped onto the grounds through a gap in the slanted, rotting gate. No trace of light disturbed the temple office or the monks' living quarters, and the main wing was dark and devoid of any human presence. But the slightest trace of what appeared to be lamplight leaked from the corner of the crumbling main wing.

This is indeed the place.

Kenshin approached the main wing. There was no doubt the Beni Aoi were there, swords at the ready, holding their breaths and waiting like hungry wolves. Suddenly, he felt a cold shiver on his skin. *This is a place of death*, he thought. But Kenshin had no reason to hesitate.

He approached, paying close attention to his surroundings. But the darkness was absolute in the narrow corridor of the temple grounds that stretched along both sides of the main wing, and Kenshin could feel no hidden presence.

Heh, so they're permitting this one to pass through unharmed. Trying not to laugh, Kenshin proceeded down the connecting corridor. But again, he found no one. There were a few small rooms next to each other, and Kenshin examined each and every one cautiously until he noticed a faint, flickering light in front of what seemed to be a main room. *Is the enemy near the light source, waiting with Itsuko?*

Before Kenshin could take a step forward, the large fusuma door in front of him slid open unexpectedly, and two shadows leapt toward him. They were about to cry out, but in one fast and continuous motion, Kenshin twisted his body, drew his sakabatô, and struck them down in a single blow. Kenshin caught the two before they could fall to the floor and make a noise, and slowly laid them down on the floor. Such a display of skill was to be expected from the ancient kenjutsu Hiten Mitsurugi-ryû, which originated in the Sengoku era and focused on sword battles against multiple opponents. He glanced around again before entering the room the pair had emerged from. Kenshin noticed a flicker of light leaking out of the gap between the fusuma doors that connected this room to the next, and quietly crept toward it.

The hall visible through a tear in the paper panel of the fusuma door was in utter disorder, and Itsuko was laying on top of a straw mat spread haphazardly in the corner, bound hand and foot, her mouth gagged. About ten men were sitting in a circle in front of the alcove, picking at snacks and taking turns drinking from a single bottle of saké. The men wore lewd smiles on their sweaty cheeks and whispered to each other. But Ôkubo Tetsuma was not among them.

Silently, Kenshin moistened the hilt of his sakabatô with spit, then placed his hand on the fusuma door to open it. Just then, a man crashed through the ceiling above him and came swooping down. "As to be expected from Himura Kenshin—no, Hitokiri Battôsai, the strongest Ishin Shishi at the end of Shogunate era. How did you find this place?" The man glared at Kenshin with a bold smile. He appeared close to forty, his tanned features were lightly carved with wrinkles, and a neatly groomed moustache adorned his face. An extraordinary physical power seemed to lurk under his black clothing.

"And you are…?"

"Ha, ha, ha, ha! I'm the one they call the High Excellency, the leader of the Beni Aoi. How could you men be so careless?" The man calling himself High Excellency clucked his tongue and began to whirl the pilgrim's staff in his hand like a windmill. "Die, Battôsai!"

The men inside the hall panicked at their leader's cry, forming a ring with Itsuko as their shield. With enemies to the front and rear, Kenshin was indeed in a "place of death." He slowly shifted his feet forward. His left thumb pushed against the guard to unsheathe the sword a little, then he held the sword close to his waist. His right hand hung down, slightly away from his side. Again, Kenshin shifted his feet slowly toward the leader.

The man calling himself the High Excellency held his staff above his head, but wavered as he retreated a bit. Kenshin stepped forward, and without warning the man swung the staff down on Kenshin's shoulder. With blinding speed, the man withdrew the staff and switched to a backhand grip before thrusting the staff toward the pit of Kenshin's stomach. Kenshin's right hand seemed to casually deflect the High Excellency's extended staff, but in a skillful stroke of his sheathed sword, he parried the blow too quickly for the eye to see. Starting with more distance between them this time, the High Excellency pretended to edge forward, then struck head-on. Kenshin didn't try to dodge. He stepped forward and raised his hands. The High Excellency's staff changed course at lightning speed, aiming for Kenshin's throat. Kenshin's body spun like a top and drew close to the High Excellency, forcefully deflecting the pilgrim's staff. Although Kenshin's sheathed sword struck his shoulder, the High Excellency managed to leap backward. The High

Excellency drew his staff into an overhead defense as Kenshin drew near.

Although normally gentle—and even silly at times—Kenshin seemed like a different person at that moment. There was a fierce expression on his face, as if he had transformed into a sword-wielding demon. It was unthinkable that anyone could emerge the victor against a man with such an expression, a man whose very appearance proclaimed the countless life-or-death battles he had won.

His mind sharply focused, Kenshin let his right arm hang slightly away from his side, like a bird preparing to take flight. His entire body looked relaxed, but his left hand was still poised by the hilt of his sakabatô. The hidden change within him was difficult to gauge but his strange posture overwhelmed the High Excellency. His attack was blocked, and before he knew it, the High Excellency was cornered in front of a small room. Without a sound, Kenshin closed in. For the first time, his right hand moved—a fast, sweeping motion. His sakabatô glinted twice, three times as if to deliver the final blow. The High Excellency desperately shifted his staff into a vertical position, but he was unable to block Kenshin's secret sword move, *Ryûsôsen*. The sakabatô roared as it cut through the air, knocking the High Excellency completely to the ground, staff and all. Kenshin twirled around. There was nothing the Beni Aoi could do in the face of the terrifying intimidation radiating from Kenshin's entire body.

The Final Assassin

The Beni Aoi began trembling, and none of them were able to look Kenshin in the eye. Their overwhelming fear sapped their fighting spirit, and made them feel they had been forced into a life-or-death situation. This swordsman had defeated the High Excellency as well as the gigantic man who came before him. He was no one to mess with; he was the one known as Hitokiri Battôsai, the strongest of the Ishin Shishi at the end of Shogunate era.

We'll all be killed. The members of Beni Aoi didn't know that Kenshin had forbidden his sakabatô to take human lives. The men's bodies were slick with sweat from the tension, and just like a mouse cornered by a cat, they recklessly challenged Kenshin.

We have Kaishû's daughter.

"D-don't move, Hitokiri Battôsai!" one of the men yelled

out, the blade of his *wakizashi* short sword pressed against Itsuko's neck. Itsuko, with her hands and feet tied and her mouth firmly gagged, had passed out from terror some time earlier. The nine remaining Beni Aoi formed a semicircle with Itsuko in the center, and surrounded Kenshin. "Don't try anything, or we'll kill this girl."

One of the men told him to hand over his sword. Retreating half a step, Kenshin sheathed his sakabatô and removed it from his waist, sheath and all, acting as though he were going to hand it over to the man in front of him. Grasping the end of the sheath, Kenshin held out his arm, presenting it hilt-first to the man. There was a look of relief on the man's face. The distance between them widened slightly, and the man grabbed for the hilt. Kenshin threw himself to one side, diving to the ground in a break-fall position. While on his back, he used his hand to knock the man off his feet. With the sound of a rotting tree falling, the man collapsed onto the wooden floor, the sakabatô still in hand.

Kenshin retrieved his sakabatô with remarkable swiftness while the men surrounding him remained stunned by what had just happened. Kenshin rolled forward once and struck a single, quick blow against the man who was holding the wakizashi to Itsuko's throat, then rose to his feet. The silence of Kenshin's movements made the action even more terrifying. Every man stood still in shock, and a chill ran down their spines. Kenshin straightened his sakabatô. Itsuko was lying unconscious behind him, with a wall behind her, so there was no need to take precautions against enemies appearing from that direction.

"Are you still going to fight?" In response to Kenshin's words, two men came forward. Both swung their wakizashi overhead and attacked without a moment's hesitation.

It is not always advantageous to fight with a long sword when battling indoors. It can lead to unpredictable mistakes, depending on where one is during an attack. The pair from Beni Aoi knew that. Their method of attack, continuous waves from the front and back, left and right, gave the impression that they were used to doing this.

Kenshin remained unfazed by the pair's alternating sword attacks as he ducked and slipped between them, accurately deflecting their swords. These enemies had swift movements that required caution. By the time Kenshin turned around after checking up on the few men in front of him, the pair was already on him again. A wakizashi slid toward his shoulders, then another came roaring from an overhead angle.

Kenshin barely deflected the attack of the first wakizashi. The point of his sakabatô made it up in time to engage with the second wakizashi, and he had enough time to dodge them and shift his weight onto his waist in order to swing his sword down in a single diagonal stroke.

The first man let out a terrible cry as he tried to ram Kenshin. Kenshin dodged gracefully, which made the man lose his balance and pitch forward until he collided headfirst into the body of the High Excellency, lying on the floor.

"You enemy of the Tokugawa...Hitokiri Battôsai, go to hell!" The man with the second wakizashi spewed a curse as he rushed forward to attack. His attack was reckless, but because he was cornered, the sharpness of his skills could not be dismissed.

Confined by the indoor setting, Kenshin faced the man with extra caution. When an opportunity arose, Kenshin stepped forward, attempting to deliver a single stroke of his sakabatô to his opponent's torso. The man barely dodged Kenshin's sword.

The man's eyes were as narrow as a piece of thread, and they glowed maliciously. His swordplay was comparable to the High Excellency and the giant from the previous night. He was probably one of the key swordsmen in Beni Aoi.

Kenshin relentlessly deflected the opponent's attacks, then unexpectedly withdrew his sword. Drawn in by the feint, the opponent swung his short sword overhead and brought it down with killing force. It was an intense blow, but at the last moment Kenshin ducked and delivered a stroke that ripped into the man's side at an angle. The Beni Aoi fell silently sideways onto the wooden floor.

As Kenshin straightened, another enemy stepped in from the side and attacked. The sword he had in his hand was a typical *katana*, but like the pair before him, he was a violent opponent. Completely ignoring Kenshin's ready position, the man brandished his sword overhead and recklessly attacked. Kenshin dodged left and right as he waited for the right moment, then sent his opponent's sword reeling away. Kenshin's sakabatô flashed toward the man's right arm as he tried to hurriedly retrieve his sword. The man shrieked loudly, grabbed his damaged arm, and retreated backwards, then fell to his knees with a thud and collapsed in a sitting position.

Like the others, the fourth man's identity was unknown, but his swordplay was keen. Moreover, he was rather large, although not as gigantic as the man from the previous night. Kenshin's opponent controlled his sword with ease, and displayed an agility not commonly seen in such a large man. The sword came roaring down toward Kenshin's head. Kenshin stretched out and deflected the sword. Next, he took a wide step forward with his right foot and struck a forceful blow to the man's right side. But the man did not retreat. He shrugged off the blow and came charging forward.

Itsuko was lying on the floor a few steps behind them. If Kenshin were pushed back any farther, she might be trampled. Kenshin slid his feet to the side. Following Kenshin's movement, his opponent moved swiftly to the side as well. Their swords did not part, their bodies were in contact, and the battle had turned into dangerous close combat. The man pushed with his long sword, transmitting a persistent strength that seemed to grip Kenshin's sakabatô. Short and slender, Kenshin was pushed a half step back by the bigger man's strength. His opponent seemed two or three times larger than Kenshin as their bodies moved closer. If Kenshin were to disengage his sword and counterattack, he risked Itsuko getting hurt. Kenshin did his best to keep the tension off his arms, and endured it by concentrating his strength in his abdomen.

Swordplay isn't about strength.

Just as Kenshin clucked his tongue, the man doubled the force of his attack. An enormous weight, like a huge boulder, bore down on Kenshin, and he countered it with all his might. Although not enough to push the man back, Kenshin's efforts momentarily held the force of their strengths in balance. At that moment, Kenshin leapt to the side. The man swung his sword down as he stepped forward, and the naked blade grazed Kenshin's shoulder. But as Kenshin leapt past, his sakabatô struck the man's midsection, landing a crushing blow to his opponent's ribs.

Two more to go.

"I'll take Itsuko-dono back now." Ôkubo Tetsuma's familiar voice called out from the darkness behind Kenshin, adding that he had seen the Hiten Mitsurugi-ryû techniques. Kenshin's terrifying glare had been fixed on the last two standing Beni Aoi, but now he turned toward the voice. The surrounding shadows obscured all but the dark outline of the other man.

"I had a bad feeling. So I came running, and just look what we have here." Even in the darkness, Kenshin could sense Tetsuma's smile. Kenshin tried to respond, but Tetsuma's sudden yell cut off any words he might have spoken.

"Beni Aoi, you are under arrest! Surrender, or I will punish you with my own hands!" Tetsuma slipped past Kenshin as the echoes of his words died, brandishing his Western-style sword as he strode into the main room. There was a flash of blade and the sound of a sword ripping through the air, and the remaining Beni Aoi collapsed like broken dolls.

"S-spare me!" the last man screamed.

But Tetsuma's sword did not stop there. He turned mercilessly on the rest of the Beni Aoi, who lay scattered across the floor, defeated by Kenshin's sakabatô. But as Tetsuma's sword arched down, Kenshin stepped in to block the blow, and stood before his fallen enemies, protecting them.

"Ôkubo-dono, people will die from even the lightest prick from the point of that sword. That blade of yours should be pointed at this one, not at your comrades." An indescribable rage filled Kenshin, and for an instant the eyes that glared at Ôkuba Tetsuma were the eyes of the killer, Hitokiri Battôsai.

"So you knew about the deadly poison on the point of my sword, and my true identity..."

"Why, Ôkubo-dono? Katsu-sensei was your teacher..." Kenshin resisted the urge to slice Ôkuba in two and rid the world of such foul vermin. Instead, he concentrated on calmly drawing out answers from Tetsuma, allowing his anger to cool off by focusing on his task.

"Many sacrifices were necessary to accomplish the Revolution. But this is still not a world where everyone can live happily. Until it is, the Revolution is incomplete. I want to bring about a second Revolution, but to do that I need money and power."

"So the restoration of eighty thousand Shogunate retainers was all a lie?"

"Slogans are better when they are clearly defined. Ha, ha, ha! I don't care about the Tokugawa family."

Kenshin said nothing, and his silence encouraged Tetsuma to continue.

"How about it, Himura-kun? Why don't we join forces? With your sword skills and my wits, we could conquer the world."

Kenshin remained silent, his cold stare locked on Tetsuma.

"Fine. If that's not possible, then…" His mind made up, Tetsuma slowly raised his Western sword. Kenshin followed suit, bringing up his guard. But he was surprised by Tetsuma's stance. Across the room, Tetsuma was coldly balanced with his sword in his right hand, the opposite of the time when he had a match with Kamiya Kaoru. His left hand was raised behind him, elbow slightly bent.

"You see, I'm not left handed." Tetsuma smiled, the point

of his sword slightly raised. In this unique stance, with his Western sword thrust forward from his side, Tetsuma appeared divided by the faint glow of the narrow blade. His smile quietly disappeared.

He must be gathering his battle chi. An eerie pressure, like the thin blade of a sword, closed in on Kenshin. Tetsuma's sword point was dipped in poison. A mere scratch would be lethal. Kenshin shrugged off the pressure and edged a half-step forward, then another half step. Tetsuma moved his feet lightly to the left and right, retreating backwards. Although Tetsuma's retreat seemed casual, his sword never wavered from its shoulder-high position. A chill spread through Kenshin, as if he had been splashed with cold water. Once again, he was reminded that this opponent was no average swordsman.

Ôkuba must be defeated without his sword touching this one.

Kenshin's hands gripped his sword and tried to close the distance between them. But he could make no headway and the gap seemed to be getting wider. This Western style of body movement seemed to allow the length of Tetsuma's stride to vary widely, and Kenshin, who had no experience with this type of combat, found it difficult to gauge the distance between them.

The Western sword thrust forward in the dim light from the paper lantern. Kenshin slowly edged his toes toward the sharply glowing sword point. He must avoid impatience. The slightest touch could mean his life. Kenshin loosened his grip slightly, then moved his feet forward. Tetsuma, who Kenshin thought would retreat again, did not move. When the distance between them shrank to approximately two ken, Tetsuma pointed the tip of his sword down, leaving him slightly open on his right side.

Hmmm!

Kenshin forced himself to ignore the bait. Tetsuma was obviously trying to lure Kenshin into attacking first. If he were to fall for it...

Kenshin concentrated his strength in his toes, then kicked off the floor. As he ran, Kenshin raised his sakabatô over his head. Kenshin struck out with his sword, not at Tetsuma, but against the Western sword pointing eerily toward the ground. Instantly, the Western sword sprang upward like a whip. The two swords met in midair and bright sparks flew. Tetsuma's sword slid upward, then tried to reel away Kenshin's sakabatô. The force of Kenshin's downward blow prevented that, but his sakabatô still came close to being torn from his grasp. Kenshin could not allow the tip of the Western sword entangled with his to touch him. The two men leapt past each other. Kenshin recovered quickly and readied himself for another exchange.

Tetsuma held his ground as well, returning to his unique ready position.

Maintaining his pose, he nimbly moved his feet to shorten the distance between them. Impressively, his upper body did not sway despite the quick movement of his feet.

Tetsuma's graceful advance came to a dead stop, but it was just a brief pause before Tetsuma rushed into combat range. He thrust his sword forward, then changed course to try to sideswipe Kenshin's leg. All it would take to finish this battle was a single wound, even on a hand or foot.

Tetsuma's sword swung toward Kenshin with a terrifying sound like rushing wind. Kenshin narrowly dodged the blow by leaping up, then swinging his sword toward his opponent's angled shoulder. After parrying, Kenshin plunged down low enough to scrape the ground as the two opponents passed each other, then struck out from his reversed position, aiming at Tetsuma's torso. The tip of his sword nearly reached Tetsuma's abdomen.

Tetsuma shifted back into his sideways ready position as if the attack had never happened. But suddenly, his knees buckled and his body slowly began to tip over. He fell to the dark ground with a thud. Kenshin straightened his legs and stared at Tetsuma's body.

"So, this is it..." Tetsuma's trembling voice faded into a whisper, and he slid the length of his Western sword across his neck.

"Ôkubo-dono, the book and furoshiki cloth..." Tetsuma pointed at his inner pocket.

He's not an evil man.

When Tetsuma issued his challenge at the Kamiya dojo, the tip of his Western sword had already been dipped in poison. But the tip that would bring certain death in a single strike had been covered with a rubber cap, and never once had Tetsuma removed it. To Kenshin, the choice was similar to his own use of the sakabatô, but they had taken different paths to get to their decisions.

Kenshin's lone figure emerged from the temple, leaving the rest to the police officers who would soon come running. The rain had ceased, and a thin, blurry moon shone softly in the night sky.

A trip to the moon... Although many feelings have been left unresolved, at least Daigoro's dreams have been protected, Kenshin thought. Moreover, Itsuko was still unconscious and hadn't had to witness Kenshin's terrifying battles and expressions.

But most importantly, Ôkubo Tetsuma's participation proved that the suspicion pointed at Katsu Kaishû was a result of Tetsuma's conspiracy. Katsu's innocence was very welcome news to those planning to aid the eighty thousand former Shogunate retainers.

The leader of the Beni Aoi, who called himself the High Excellency, turned out to be a disgruntled high-level official in the Meiji Government, and the entire incident was covered up.

Ôkuma Daigoro happily returned to his position as a student in Katsu's home. There was a rumor that he later traveled overseas, but what happened to him after that is not known for certain. One theory states that Inoue Tsutomu, the translator of the Japanese edition of *From the Earth to the Moon*, published in September of the 19th year of Meiji (1886), was in fact Ôkuma Daigoro. But although some people hold to these outrageous claims, the truth remains unknown.

Sanosuke and
the Nishiki-e

TSUKIOKA TSUNAN

A former cadet in the Sekihô Army. Currently a popular *nishiki-e* (color woodblock print) artist.

POLICE CHIEF

In charge of the Tokyo Prefecture police force, and one of the few who knows about Kenshin's past.

UJIKI

A former assistant inspector with the Police Sword Corps. A master of Satsuma *Jigen-ryû*.

Early Afternoon

The afternoon sunlight poured into the alley of the Gorotuski row house, where Sagara Sanosuke was lost in thought as he rested in the doorway. The wife of a clumsy carpenter living in the far side of the row house called out to him as she walked by.

"What's the matter with you, young fellow? Basking in the sun so early in the day? Hmph. How can you afford such luxury?"

"Wh-what?" replied Sanosuke, standing up out of reflex.

This sharp-tongued woman's husband was a very hard worker. He left the house early in the morning and worked until sundown to earn his money. While the husband seemed to be always covered in sawdust, his wife couldn't be called much of a hard worker. Even in this impoverished back-alley tenement, there were wives who worked hard, and wives who didn't. After they sent their husbands off to work, some wives worked at home after quickly tidying up, and others lounged around all day next to the well. When they tired of that, they would visit other people's homes and chat over tea until the sun went down. Chatting wasn't necessarily a bad thing, but even viewed in a favorable light, the clumsy carpenter's wife belonged to the latter group— those who didn't work. She was well equipped with thick lips that wouldn't wear out from all the talking, healthy jaws, and large eyes and ears that displayed her love for gossiping.

Although Sanosuke had been dozing earlier using his arm as a pillow, the high-pitched laughter of the wives standing beside the well and the endless crying of babies had interrupted his short nap.

Darn it, don't lump me together with you lot.

He wanted a word with her, but the wife had turned her stout back to him and was striding energetically into her own house. Soon the wife's loud, high-pitched voice was heard scolding her child, who had probably made some careless mistake.

With an inward sigh, Sanosuke's thoughts shifted. Maybe he did deserve sarcasm from a row house wife. Back when he was a fight merchant in West Tokyo's underground society, he used to make a living picking fights and scuffling in the public streets. Charging a fee to fight was part of his daily life, and people called him Kenka-ya Zanza because of the way he brandished his powerful *zanbatô*, a huge sword designed to cut a horse out from under its rider. When he was fighting, Sanosuke was able to forget everything. His body and soul were free to concentrate on the battle in front of him. But when the fight was over, he was overcome by melancholy and helplessness.

Captured by strange, inexplicable thoughts, Sanosuke was overtaken by loneliness, accompanied by a sorrowful lethargy that was a bleak contrast to his gallant appearance.

I know I gotta do something about it. Although he thought about it, he had drifted day after day, accomplishing nothing. *Hmph. Gotta say, the whole process of thinking is a real drag.*

The rurouni, Himura Kenshin, had turned the fighter around—a fighter who had lost his way, and couldn't escape the strange place in which he found himself. The strength of Hitokiri Battôsai, that legendary man of unparalleled skills who had sided with the Ishin Shishi at the end of the Shogunate era, was extraordinary. Sanosuke had picked a fight with him and had been critically injured. His prized zanbatô was broken in two, and the sturdy body he was so proud of was bruised all over. He lost a lot of blood, and ultimately he ended up in a hospital for three months. It was the first time he had ever been defeated in a fight, but

BORN FIRST SON OF A FARMER IN SHINSHŪ ON THE FIRST YEAR OF MANEN. RUNS AWAY FROM HOME TO JOIN THE "SEKIHŌ ARMY" AT AGE 9. REVERES SAGARA SŌZŌ AS A MASTER, BUT SŌZŌ IS EXECUTED AFTER BEING UNJUSTLY ACCUSED OF LEADING AN ILLEGITIMATE REVOLUTIONARY ARMY. THE SEKIHŌ ARMY CRUMBLES.

SAGARA SANOSUKE (19)

AFTER THAT, HE BECOMES A "FIGHT MERCHANT" UNDER THE NAME ZANZA, PASSING HIS DAYS IN MEANINGLESS COMBAT. HAVING LOST TO HIMURA KENSHIN IN HEATED BATTLE...

...SANOSUKE BEGINS FREQUENTING THE KAMIYA DOJO. CURRENTLY LIVING A CAREER-FREE LIFE AT HIS OWN PACE.

NISHIKI PAINTINGS...?

being totally crushed left him feeling strangely refreshed. After that, he gave up being a fight merchant and became Sagara Sanosuke, a guy who just liked to fight. However, now he had too much time to himself and felt somehow out of place.

Oh, well. Maybe I'll go to Akabeko.

Out of habit, he glanced at the wicket gate, but no one came to hire him to fight anymore. Sanosuke kicked the sagging door and began to walk.

It was already past lunch, but Akabeko was bustling as usual.

"Welcome!" The server's cheerful and lively voice greeted his arrival, and the conversations of satisfied customers mingled with the tempting smell of beef-pot as he proceeded to the back of the spacious restaurant. Sanosuke climbed into one of the booths and sat down, then requested one order of standard beef-pot from Sekihara Tae, whose head was wrapped in a hand towel.

It seemed as though a long time passed between when he ordered his food and when he finished his meal, but it was actually less than thirty minutes. In the meantime, the late lunch crowd had dispersed and the restaurant was gradually shifting to dinner preparations. Tae came out of the back and poured him another cup of tea, then placed a small teapot on the table.

"Um, Sanosuke-san, I have a favor to ask," Tae said as

she looked restlessly around the restaurant, apparently a bit nervous. A suspicious look crossed Sanosuke's face as she continued in a low voice, "If you don't mind, could you please buy a nishiki-e for me?"

"A nishiki-e?"

Nishiki-e are colored *ukiyo-e* woodblock prints, also known as Edo-e. Portraits of actors and landscapes were popular themes back in the Edo era, but by the Meiji era, various subjects were being painted, and before long nishiki-e were established as one of Tokyo's specialties. Around the time of the eleventh year of Meiji, artwork of heroes, warriors, and handsome swordsmen from the end of the Shogunate era and the Seinan War were selling like hotcakes. According to the newspapers at the time, Taiso Yoshitoshi, Utagawa Kunisada, Kuniteru, Hiroshige III, Yoshimori, Shosai Ikkei, and such were counted as "Modern Painting Experts."

"Yes, there will be a new arrival today at the picture book shop, but it's by a popular artist and will sell out right away. I'd like to go buy one, but I really can't sneak away from work."

"So, you want me to go buy it for you. "

"Yes, if you don't mind." Tae gazed at Sanosuke intently. Her eyes were indescribably fetching, and for a moment Sanosuke got nervous. Being relied on wasn't a bad feeling, but running errands?

I must really look idle, Sanosuke thought to himself.

"Why don't you ask Yahiko or someone else, instead?" Sanosuke suddenly recalled that Myôjin Yahiko worked as a day laborer at Akabeko, performing miscellaneous chores. It was bad timing.

"Hey, I'm working too, stupid!"

Yahiko appeared unexpectedly, holding a broom and a dustpan, his kimono sleeves pulled up out of his way with a cord. Yahiko grumbled under his breath and walked off toward the back. Sanosuke watched him exit, then rubbed the side of his face with his hand and resigned himself to accept the errand.

"Fine. So what exactly do you want?"

"*Swordsman Iba Hachirô* by Tsukioka Tsunan."

Although the artist's name was unfamiliar, even Sanosuke had heard of Iba Hachirô from the Shogunate's commando unit, known to be most handsome swordsman of the end of the Shogunate era.

According to the Iba family biography, Hachirô was the alias of Hidesato, who had been blessed with a fair and handsome appearance. The biography went on to exclaim that Hachirô had been an avid reader and author, and that his poetry should be committed to memory.

Hachirô was born in the first year of Koka (1844) as a legitimate son of Iba Gunbei (Hidenari), a gokenin Shogunate vassal receiving a stipend of 100-pyo. Hachiro's father was the eighth master instructor of the *Shingyoto-ryû* dojo in Shitaya Izumibashi Dori, and he was trained in kenjutsu from a very young age. Eventually, he was promoted to the kenjutsu department of Kobusho Martial Arts School for the Shogunate retainers, operated by the Shogunate government. He once guarded the 14th Shogun, Tokugawa Iemochi, on a journey to the capital city, Kyoto.

He was promoted from an Edo Castle guard to the position of okuzume, essentially a personal bodyguard for the Shogun. Hachirô was placed in a commando unit after the military reform and reorganization, and fought bravely in the Battle of Toba and Fushimi. His performance made Nozu Shichizaemon (Shizuo), from the opposing Satsuma clan, sigh in praise, "Iba Hachirô, as might be expected from a Shogunate army." But those who fought for the Shogunate were at a disadvantage, and the defeated Shogunate army made the decision to retreat to Edo. Hachirô opposed this while shedding tears of anger, and it was said he moved the entire assembly. Although he did return once to Edo, Hachirô protested in favor of total defiance and clashed with the imperial army over the Hakone Gateway. On the afternoon of May 26th, in the fourth year of Keio (the first year of Meiji, 1868), he was critically injured near Yumoto Sanmai-bashi when his left arm was partially severed during the battle of Hakone Yamazaki. Even then, Hachirô's fighting spirit did not waver, and swearing by his honor and pride as a member of the Shogunate's direct retainers, he continued with total defiance by crossing to Ezo (Hokkaido). According to historical records, on May 12th in the second year of Meiji, he is said to have died from an illness as a result of his wounds. He was twenty-six years old.

Sanosuke was once a cadet soldier in the Sekihô Army, and though he was on the opposing side, he did not dislike the way Iba Hachirô had lived his life. Probably because of this, he teased Tae freely. "Pretty shallow tastes for someone like you."

Sanjô Tsubame called out to Sanosuke as he was leaving the restaurant. She obviously wanted to ask something, but the quiet girl could not bring herself to say it. Her slightly tense, pale face was trying to convey something to Sanosuke, and at last he realized that Tsubame must want a nishiki-e of Iba Hachirô as well.

"Okay, so I need to get two prints of Tsukioka Tsunan's *Iba Hachirô*, right?" said Sanosuke as he left the Akabeko beef-pot restaurant.

Reunion of Two Men

As Sanosuke stood at the storefront, looking at the display of nishiki-e, someone called from behind. "Sano?" When Sanosuke turned around, he saw Kenshin and Kaoru standing there.

"Oh, you guys..."

Sanosuke greeted Kenshin and Kaoru with a broad smile, but their faces held suspicion. It was understandable. To them, he was out of place, like a drunkard in front of a candy shop. But they were also brimming with curiosity. They tried persistently to find out what he was buying at the bookstore, as well as why and for whom. But once the situation was explained, it wasn't really interesting after all. Sanosuke purchased two nishiki-e of Tsukioka Tsunan's *Iba Hachirô* as he heard Kenshin and Kaoru sigh in disappointment behind him.

"You're lucky, sir. Those are the last two." The owner of the picture book shop spoke proudly about how good business was, thanks to the popularity of Tsukioka Tsunan's artwork. But to Sanosuke, the lecture was not as important as the price that he was being asked to pay. "That will be ten sen total."

Sanosuke was totally broke, without a single sen in his pocket. He never paid his bill at Akabeko and took that kind of lifestyle for granted. "Oh, I don't have any money." Sanosuke took advantage of Kaoru's presence and had her pay the ten sen. His business done, Sanosuke casually browsed the pictures in the store with Kenshin and Kaoru until his eyes stopped on one particular piece of artwork.

"Is this...?" There was no mistake. It was labeled *Sekihô Army First Unit, Sagara Sôzô*. There he was, Captain Sagara, the man Sanosuke would never stop respecting, and would never dream of forgetting. In the picture, Sagara Sôzô was holding an unsheathed sword in his hand, and behind him were two young boys. Kenshin frowned sternly, and Kaoru's beautiful face was suddenly marked by tension.

This isn't good.

They knew all too well the story of how Sanosuke became a fight merchant.

Four years older than Iba Hachirô, Sagara Sôzô was born in the eleventh year of Tenpô (1840) and originally went by the name Kojima Shirô. He excelled in Japanese literature and military science, and established a private school before becoming actively involved in the stormy state of affairs at the end of the Shogunate era.

After many twists and turns of fate, Sôzô befriended Saigô Takamori of the Satsuma clan, and was put in charge of creating public disorder in Edo, a strategy employed by the imperialists seeking to overthrow the Tokugawa government. After the Battle of Toba and Fushimi, he organized the Sekihô Army as a vanguard for the imperial army's Eastern Expedition Troops and became Captain of the First Unit.

On his departure to the war front, Sôzô was authorized to promise the reduction of the land taxes by half as a measure to secure his troops' safety in rural areas. In other words, wherever the army advanced, they won over the locals with his guarantee and got them to side with the imperial army, at the same time procuring funds and acquiring weapons and food. Later, the New Government abandoned the ideals of the Revolution due to financial difficulties, and withdrew the earlier commitment to reduce land taxes. In desperation, they declared the Sekihô Army—which had already produced excellent results in attracting popular sentiment—to be a "false army." When they refused orders to return to the capital, the government arrested every regimental soldier of the First Unit at Shinano no Kuni Shimo Suwa. Eight officers were beheaded, including Sôzô, and the rest were exiled. Sôzô was said to be twenty-nine years old when he was lead to his execution.

"The days when the weak are oppressed and must meekly accept their misfortunes are over, and there will come an era where there is no upper or lower, and there will be equality among the four social classes." As a young cadet soldier, Sagara Sanosuke had heard Sôzô say repeatedly, "We, the Sekihô Army, are the pioneers, and the arrival of a new era depends on our performance. Whether it happens in a year, or ten years, is up to us."

Sanosuke was enthralled by Sôzô, so much so that he asked if he could take the captain's last name for his own when the time came for all social classes to stand equal. But Sagara Sôzô and the Sekihô Army were obliterated, all for the convenience of the New Government.

The sight of the execution grounds where the eight heads, including Sôzô's, were displayed broke Sanosuke's heart. In remembrance of what had been done, Sanosuke channeled all his dark emotions into the symbol he now wore on his back—*aku*, the kanji character for evil. It is not an exaggeration to say those feelings and strong will determined the direction of Sanosuke's life thereafter.

On behalf of the captain, there's something I need to say.

The New Government built the Meiji era on the sacrifices of the Sekihô Army. If nothing else, I will remind them of that.

Certainly, the Sekihô Army could be accused of being aggressive. There were times when they committed outrageous acts for the sake of causing a disturbance in

Edo city. But unlike the Satsuma and Chôshû clans, they were forced to accept unpleasant roles because they had neither the support of the clans nor the social background to create that support.

Their drive to give their best was fueled by a burning desire to build a new Japan, and could not be written off as a half-hearted attempt by a false imperial army. But the people did not care to notice such facts.

Even a one-inch insect has half an inch of soul. It doesn't matter if people are going to forget the Sekihô Army. But I can't throw away my half-inch of life. This had been Sanosuke's philosophy until today. The people around him had advised him many times to stop thinking about revenge. Every time he heard that, his desire for vengeance grew stronger.

"Where is he?" Sanosuke asked the store owner as he looked up from the nishiki-e.

"Huh?"

The response of the shop owner, who had no idea what was going on, filled Sanosuke with an emotion so intense it could not be described, but most closely resembled pure fury.

"Where is this Tsunan guy? Tell me!" he bellowed, hurling his words at the man.

"Th-the row house slum in the next city! But he doesn't like people. Even if you go there, I doubt you'll be able to see him," the owner replied with a pale face.

As the owner stammered out his answer, Sanosuke gasped

for air. An overwhelming, unfamiliar emotion flooded his body. Sanosuke gave into the dizziness, entrusting himself to his disconnected mind. Eventually, he calmed down, and slowly began to walk.

"Of course he'll see me. There's no reason for him not to."

"Sano…" Kenshin gazed imploringly at Sanosuke's back. Sanosuke did not respond. His jaw was locked tight in the effort to suppress the violent emotions that threatened to erupt from the depths of his heart. About an hour later, Sanosuke stood under the overhanging roof of the row house and announced his arrival.

"Tsukioka-san… Tsukioka-san, are you there? Tsukioka-san…" Sanosuke carefully controlled himself and was very patient as he called out, but there was no response from inside. He felt the blood rush to his head the moment he realized he should've just pounded on the door sooner.

"I know you're in there, Tsukioka Katsuhiro—former Sekihô Army cadet!" He used his fist, a fighter's specialty, as well as his voice to batter the door. The door finally opened in response to the terrible sound, and a man appeared. He had a cloth tied around his forehead, perhaps to keep back his overgrown hair. He had a noble, high-bridged nose, thin, firm lips, deep eye sockets and chiseled cheeks, as if his flesh had been carved. His skin was an earthen, wasted color, as though he spent many long years without exposure to the sunlight.

"Just as I thought," Sanosuke said, as if to make sure. Sagara Sôzô's nishiki-e was still clutched in his hand. "So, it was you who drew this."

"Sanosuke, how did you...?" Tsunan stared into space for a moment, then looked at Sanosuke. Something wasn't quite right. The shock of seeing something so unexpected seemed to be storming his mind.

"I could tell right away, for I can see you and me as we were long ago, standing beside the captain."

"I see... Yes, you're right." Tsunan's face broke into a smile. Indescribable emotions were exchanged across the doorway.

They disappeared into the back. Watching over this scene, Kenshin and Kaoru gave a sigh of relief as they finally understood what was going on. Tsukioka Tsunan was a survivor of the Sekihô Army just like Sanosuke.

Kenshin urged Kaoru, "Let's go home, Kaoru-dono."

"He's Sanosuke's old friend. Aren't you going to introduce yourself?"

"Sanosuke was followed because he didn't seem to be his usual self, but there was nothing to it. Moreover..." Kenshin smiled at Kaoru as he paused. "Moreover, as can be seen from what aku means to him, the Sekihô Army is a special memory for Sano. Outsiders are unnecessary in a place of memories." As he said this, Kenshin turned in the bright afternoon light, and Kaoru thought she felt something that could only be understood by the minds of men.

The Grenades

Kenshin walked a few steps, then stopped in his tracks. He felt someone, somewhere was watching them. There were a few people in the alley by the row house, but none of them were the watcher. Kenshin slowly turned around, as though talking to Kaoru, and casually looked over the surroundings. He noticed a man standing alone under the eaves of the row house, dressed in fashionable Western-style clothes. *Hmm, has this one met him...?* Kenshin's memory wasn't clear.

The man looked about thirty years old and had a thin face. Something about his eyes and the way he was standing made Kenshin shiver. The man stared without blinking at Kenshin with no hint of emotion. His legs were set comfortably apart and his left hand was hidden, probably concealing a weapon. It could have been a sword or a staff, or even a pistol. His stance signaled that he was prepared to use any one of those weapons at a moment's notice.

Is he keeping an eye on Tsukioka Tsunan? Instinctively, Kenshin knew that was the case. Kenshin casually placed a hand on Kaoru's shoulder while discreetly resting his other hand on the hilt of his sakabatô. Kenshin tried to shift Kaoru to the opposite side of his body to shield her, but Kaoru didn't quite understand his intentions. She was already panicking about his hand on her shoulder.

"K-Kenshin, what are you doing?" She whispered nervously, but Kenshin had no time for explanations. The man might have had a pistol, and if he pulled it, Kenshin would have to counter by drawing his sakabatô.

The man looked familiar, but Kenshin still couldn't remember who he was. Regardless, the man was watching Tsunan, and although Kenshin didn't know much about Tsunan, his instincts told him that the watcher was dangerous. At the very least, this man wasn't someone Kenshin wanted to have around.

The man smirked at Kenshin, then turned and walked briskly away. Soon, he was far in the distance, and all that remained were Kaoru's confused emotions.

"Kenshin…" Kaoru said, gazing intently at him.

"Oro…?!"

After inviting Sanosuke inside, Tsunan closed and locked the shoji door then lit the paper lamp with a flint. Even though imported kerosene lamps were slowly gaining popularity in Tokyo Prefecture, not everyone welcomed them. In one amusing incident, dim paper lamps were suddenly replaced with kerosene ones in a school dormitory, but instead of welcoming the improvement, the students complained that they were too bright! But kerosene lamps were convenient tools, and their eventual popularity was inevitable.

Kaika Shinsaku Dodoitsu (A Song of Progress and Invention) even celebrated the development with the lyrics "Gaslamps outdoors, lamps indoors / People on wheels in Misujimachi."

Ordinary citizens were establishing a modern lifestyle, but Tsunan seemed to have rejected these new conveniences, choosing to live as if it were still the Edo period.

"It's been a long time," Tsunan finally said. A cold bottle of saké had quickly dissolved the distance between them.

"An artist. Thinking back, you were always skilled with your hands, and you mixed gunpowder and handled complicated cannons with no problem at all," Sanosuke happily reminisced. But Tsunan had no interest in talking about old times. He looked worried and depressed as he sipped his saké.

"What do you do now?" Tsunan asked curtly.

"Nothing much." Sanosuke lowered the saké cup from his lips. His eyes were already growing red. "Well, I'm having a good time, in my own way."

"Is that so?" Tsunan replied. "So, you've been having a

good time, huh? Not one good thing has happened for me in the past ten years. Until I saw you, I can't remember smiling, not even once."

Not knowing what to say, Sanosuke took another drink.

"I've spent ten years cursing the men who dishonored Captain Sagara and the Sekihô Army."

"Tsunan…" Sanosuke raised his hand, interrupting. Gloom filled the room, and a chill ran down Sanosuke's spine. Tsunan was not one to lie or exaggerate. For most people, the Sekihô Army was just some incident that had happened back at the end of the Shogunate era. But for the man caught by Sanosuke's gaze, it had been a heavy cross to bear.

Although there was no way to know how Tsunan had spent the past ten years, Sanosuke couldn't help but feel an obligation to his former comrade.

"I feel the same pain you do," Sanosuke replied in a low whisper. He brought the saké cup to his mouth and tossed back a drink. Tsunan watched Sanosuke intently, his jaw clenched. Tsunan's almond-shaped eyes were angled slightly upward, and the bright pupils and firm lips, both expressive of his strong will, gave him something of an evil look. Tsunan hesitated for some time, but at last seemed to make up his mind to speak.

"To tell you the truth…" Tsunan said in a low, depressed voice. "Ha, ha, ha! What a day this day has been." Tsunan changed the subject with a subtle grin. He apparently needed some time to prepare himself before continuing.

Sanosuke allowed the silence to stretch until Tsunan spoke again.

"But, to be reunited with you on the very day that all the arrangements have been made... Perhaps this meeting was guided by the captain, up in heaven."

"Katsu...?" A slip of the tongue caused Sanosuke to call Tsunan by his original name, and his friend's expression turned stern. Sanosuke felt a chill run down his back. *It can't be*, he thought. But Tsunan seemed unconcerned and continued as if to clear the air.

"Sanosuke, why don't we organize the Sekihô Army again?"

"What?" Sanosuke's expression stiffened. As he gulped down the cold saké, he felt uneasiness rise in his throat.

"Let's crush the Revolutionary Government that destroyed the Sekihô Army, and create the new era that Captain Sagara strived for."

"Katsu, what on earth are you planning to do?" Sanosuke's tone was subdued and accusatory, but Tsunan didn't seem to mind.

"You ask what I've planned, but there's only one goal for the Sekihô Army—crush the Meiji Government that stands in our way and establish a new era of true equality between—"

"Don't tell me you were too busy drawing pictures to hear about the Seinan War. Even Saigô Takamori—the

Revolution's greatest hero—and the strong Hayato men of Satsuma who followed him didn't last more than six months," Sanosuke replied bitterly with a glance at Tsunan. Anger stirred inside of him, but Tsunan wasn't riled.

"Saigô took up arms in Kagoshima, on the edge of Japan. It's too far away to stage a march on Tokyo, so in the end, it was all in vain. My target is the center of Japan. An attack here, in Tokyo Prefecture." In a calm, almost brazen manner, Tsunan continued. "First, we attack the Ministry of Home Affairs, where domestic matters are controlled. We'll bring operations to a complete standstill. If I could, I'd crush the Ministries of the Army and the Navy, and the Ministry of Finance at the same time, but I can't handle everything *alone*."

"Alone?" Sanosuke's confusion was evident on his face. He thought the idea was absurd. Tsunan could well be a megalomaniac—in fact, it seemed quite evident that he was. "What can one man do?" Sanosuke scoffed. The plan to overthrow the government didn't surprise him, but he was dumbfounded that this great *coup d'état* was supposed to be executed by just one person. It was insanely reckless.

"Yes, I'm alone. Except for those who may follow in my footsteps, anyway. There's no way I can trust anyone, so I've been moving ahead with this plan on my own." Suddenly, Tsunan stood up and calmly walked toward the closet. "But even if I'm alone, I have these..." he said as he opened the fusuma door. The paper lantern's soft light illuminated the darkness of the closet's interior.

There inside were the results of the knowledge that Tsunan had cultivated while in the Sekihô Army—shelves filled with handmade grenades.

Strange Sanosuke

"These are my creations. I've taken extra precautions for the past ten years so as to avoid detection. What do you think? Surely no one would ever imagine that a mere artist was creating such things." Sanosuke stared in awe as Tsunan continued. "With these, I'll blow up the ministries, one after another, and weaken the country's centralized power. Naturally, disgruntled former samurai families and peasants will take advantage of the situation and begin to riot throughout the country. Weak and exhausted by the Seinan War, the current government will be helpless. All we'll need to do then is wait for it to tumble down like an avalanche."

Tsunan's ten years of isolation had had been spent in service to the plans that obsessed him. He had accomplished all this with no one to consult with or criticize his plan, and was convinced that his lonely uprising could overturn society. Tsunan continued to speak like a man possessed—most likely, he had carried on conversations with himself almost every day while single-handedly preparing this outrageous plan. He believed without a doubt that after the period of mass turmoil was over, an era of true equality among the four social classes would arise, and the honor of the Captain and the Sekihô Army would be restored. Sanosuke didn't interrupt Tsunan, and for the most part played the listener.

"I've already obtained a hand-drawn map showing the interior layout of the Ministry of Home Affairs. The plan will be carried out tomorrow—there will be a new moon and it's a Sunday night, so very few people will be around." Tsunan avoided looking at Sanosuke, focusing on the saké cup in his hand. Almost as an afterthought, his mouth finally formed the words that he really wanted to say. "Sano, since you're having a good time these days, I don't want to force anything on you. As a former Sekihô Army soldier, I will carry out this plan, even if I have to do it alone. But, could you think about it until sundown tomorrow, and let me know your answer?"

A short time later, Sanosuke was on his way home.

It's impossible, he thought to himself. No matter how Sanosuke looked at it, it was unlikely that bombing the ministry offices and sporadic riots could cause the Meiji Government to fall. Even if the plan were carried out, it was glaringly obvious that it would suffer the same failure as the Shinpuren, Hagi, and Akizuki uprisings in the past.

He's blind to the present after spending ten long, lonely years thinking only of avenging the captain and the Sekihô Army. But, still...ten years... Sanosuke envisioned a long, straight path before him. But once tread upon, it was one that would never allow him to turn back...

Sanosuke looked up at the night sky as he walked, trying to pretend that nothing was wrong, even as a dizzy, violent feeling was welling up in the depths of his heart. He couldn't decide if it was rage or sadness. "It's already spring, so why is this cold wind blowing?" Although he spoke of the wind, it might have been his own fate he was lamenting.

Sanosuke felt a fire beginning to blaze inside him. If he left things as they were, he'd not only end up being unable to avenge Captain Sagara, he would lose his former war buddy forever. These feelings urged Sanosuke to make a decision. Of course, there was no way for anyone else to guess what was going on in his mind.

At the Kamiya dojo, Kaoru and Yahiko faced each other, their shinai training swords in the ready position. They both had on their training kimono and hakama, but neither wore masks or hand protectors. Almost an hour had passed since they'd started, and there were no signs that their training would end any time soon.

The morning sun poured in from the high windows designed to bring in the light, making the sweat pouring off their foreheads sparkle. It was just before seven, and the sunlight was growing gradually brighter.

Kenshin observed the training from the raised instructor's seat to the side, arms folded. Actually, he was pretending to observe, but in fact he was dozing off. Just as Kenshin's head started to nod and his body sway, Kaoru's sharp battle cry electrified the atmosphere inside the dojo.

Yahiko responded with a battle cry of his own. Their bodies maneuvered rapidly, and the sound of their swords striking each other rang out. Kaoru's battle cry echoed again throughout the dojo. Yahiko's small body flew backwards, landing hard.

"What happened, Yahiko? Are you giving up already?" Kaoru's voice was only slightly winded, and a frustrated Yahiko tightened the grip on his bamboo shinai and positioned himself once again.

"Hmph! I let the ugly girl who can't get up in the morning beat me on purpose," Yahiko replied, breathing hard. He rushed in to attack a hole in Kaoru's defense that she had purposely left open. As Kenshin had pointed out when praising him for his improvement, Yahiko was very quick with his shinai. But Kaoru moved even faster, sliding her feet lightly and deflecting Yahiko's blow, then striking him on the shoulder as she passed. By the time Yahiko turned around, she had already stepped within striking range of his head. Kaoru silently unleashed her chi as she swung her shinai down, striking Yahiko's head. She did her best to go easy on direct blows, but Yahiko was shorter than Kaoru. Instead of striking his forehead, the single blow landed directly on top of his head. Yahiko blinked a few times at the stars that appeared before him, then collapsed onto his back with a thud.

Kenshin and Kaoru came running, surprised by the loud sound his body made when it hit the floor. Yahiko had passed out with a happy expression on his face, but failed to regain consciousness even after Kaoru slapped his cheeks several times. Concerned, Kenshin grabbed a bucket of water used for cleaning and mercilessly splashed the contents onto Yahiko's face.

"Yahhh!" Yahiko came to right away. To Kenshin and Kaoru's surprise, Yahiko immediately assumed the ready position as he stood up.

"I'm not going down yet." Before them stood the gallant figure of a youthful samurai devoted to the sword.

Yahiko... Kenshin and Kaoru swallowed their words in silent agreement.

Breakfast followed shortly after the training session. After the meal, Sanosuke dropped by while the three were having a lively conversation. He watched their faces as he talked about the harmless aspects of the previous evening's reunion with Tsunan.

"Huh?!" Kaoru suddenly blurted in exaggerated surprise. To back up Kaoru, Kenshin overreacted as well.

"So, Tsukioka Tsunan is Sanosuke's old friend?!"

"Hey, what's with the awkward surprise?" Sanosuke felt there was something strange about the pair's reaction, but he didn't let petty things bother him. "Well, whatever. I want to celebrate our reunion with a party. You think I can use the dojo tonight?"

Kenshin seemed to be deep in thought while he listened to Sanosuke explain his plan, but Kaoru and Yahiko both harbored the same concerns.

"You can use the dojo," Kaoru replied. Then she looked directly at Sanosuke and said, "You say you want to have a party, but where's the money for it going to come from?" Before he could answer, she drew her own conclusions and her expression changed. "So you're planning to sponge off us? Oh no, you don't! Absolutely not!"

Sanosuke hesitated, taken aback by Kaoru's intensity. Finally he replied with a smile, "Don't worry, I'll take care of the money." That said, he got up to leave.

The three stared dumbfounded at Sanosuke's back as he walked away. At that moment, Kenshin was struck by a realization.

"Sano." As if released from a spell, Kenshin called out to stop his friend. "Uhhh...so just how is Tsukioka-dono doing...?"

Sanosuke stopped in his tracks, then turned around and

replied, "He said he was going to complete an unfinished nishiki-e, then deliver it to his publisher Iroha-Ya in the afternoon. He should be here by six this evening."

Sanosuke took half a dozen steps, then remembered something. "Oh yeah. Invite Tae and that young girl, too. They'll probably be happy about it." Sanosuke then left the dojo at a brisk pace, not looking back. He just didn't seem to be himself.

"Strange. He's acting strange, very strange! I wonder if Sanosuke is ill. Is he?!" Call it women's intuition, but Kaoru seemed very suspicious of Sanosuke's unusually commendable behavior.

"P-please relax," Kenshin managed to say as Kaoru pressed against him, grabbed his collar, and shook him.

"It's probably just because it's spring..." Yahiko muttered to himself as though he understood everything. He was unconcerned about Kenshin and Kaoru's worries.

Thirty minutes later, Kenshin disappeared from the Kamiya dojo.

An Unexpected Visit

A small door beside the main gate opened, and the student Kenshin had arranged the meeting through appeared and asked Kenshin to enter before guiding him into the police chief's house. The student led Kenshin to a guest room that looked out onto a spacious garden. After a while, a different student brought tea and sweets. Kenshin felt thirsty when he saw the offerings, and reached for the cup, savoring the hot, aromatic tea.

There was a wooden brazier in the room, but no lit coals inside. The shoji doors that partitioned the room and the yard beyond the open veranda had been left open, but during daytime, the early spring weather didn't feel that cold. Glancing at the garden, Kenshin saw red and white plum blossoms blooming here and there.

"Himura-san, thank you for waiting." The police chief

wore black-rimmed glasses and had clear-cut features and a healthy complexion. He was somewhat nervous as he announced his arrival. He had taken the trouble to change into his uniform, even though it was his day off. The chief had his reasons to be concerned. When Kenshin had first arrived on this surprise visit, he had faced the student gatekeeper and requested a meeting.

"This one has come to visit the police chief at his residence, knowing it may be inconvenient for him because it is his day off. But if this visit were delayed until tomorrow morning at the police station, it could be too late."

The police chief had then appeared, wondering what this could be about. Kenshin made it clear that this was a serious, confidential matter. After a brief introduction, Kenshin sat up straight and broached the subject right away.

"There is something this one would like to know," Kenshin said. "Chief, this one would like to ask candidly, have you heard of any large-scale matters, such as a conspiracy to overthrow the government, for example?"

The chief eyed Kenshin with suspicion through his round, black-rimmed glasses. His classic features had taken on a stern edge. "Well, nothing like that..." The chief minced words, unsure of how to reply.

The chief knew that the Himura Kenshin before him was a legendary swordsman also known by the alias Hitokiri Battôsai, and was a former Ishin Shishi patriot who had sided with the Chôshû. He also knew that after the Revolution, Kenshin refused any government position, and had wandered the country as a rurouni. Not only that, but several times in the past, the police had requested Kenshin's assistance in solving difficult cases. Moreover, Yamagata Aritomo, Minister of the Army and the chief's superior, had told him repeatedly about Kenshin's personality. There was no doubt that the two men were already acquainted, but still, this visit from Kenshin was very sudden, and one couldn't help but feel that his question was just as abrupt.

"What do you mean by that? Himura-san, have you heard something?"

"No, not exactly." As Kenshin said this, a maid working in the residence brought fresh cups of tea and some different sweets. The conversation ground to a halt. To kill time, the chief offered Kenshin the new batch of sweets.

"Would you care for some, Himura-san? These are alphabet sweets. They were first sold around the Motoshiba area in the fifth year of Meiji, and became rather popular at one point. In addition to the twenty-six letters of the English alphabet, some have phrases pressed on them, such as 'Culture and Progress.' I'm hesitant about having everything reflect Western European ways, but I believe 'Culture and Progress' is meaningful to the Japanese people."

Kenshin took the sweets, and glanced at the pond in the garden. The harsh sunlight of the day reflected on the surface of the water, creating small, sparkling circles. After making sure the maid had left, Kenshin spoke once again.

"Chief, although the Seinan War has ended, society is still as turbulent as ever. If this one were the sort of man who harbored growing discontent and dissatisfaction toward the current government, now would probably be the time to do something about it."

Beads of sweat formed on the chief's brow as he listened, head bowed. Although there was no conclusive evidence, this was Hitokiri Battôsai, the lone sword who had devoted himself to overthrowing the Tokugawa government. And his finely honed intuition, backed by experience, had latched onto something. This was not a matter to be laughed off.

Kenshin spoke with unusual eloquence. "One of the people precious to a rurouni like this one has been acting somewhat strangely since last night. This man is not one to be easily shaken by ordinary matters, but the way he acted this morning was not normal. There is something that he cannot confide in this one, his friend. It appears he has become involved in something. Chief, this one is no longer an Ishin Shishi. But if at all possible, this one wants to protect those whose paths cross this one's. This one has no desire to inconvenience the police. However, anything would help. This one needs information, some kind of clue. Otherwise, when something does happen, this one will be at a loss."

"Himura-san..." The chief's downcast face was troubled, and his forehead was now sweating profusely. The chief pulled a handkerchief from his pocket and wiped the perspiration from his brow. His lean, clear-cut features had lost some of their vitality. He took a sip of tea to moisten his throat, then said in a decisive tone, "What I'm going to tell you must be kept a secret from everyone—may I ask that of you?"

"Yes, of course. Now then, is there something you know?"

"No, there's nothing conclusive," the chief said with a sigh, then paused awhile before continuing.

"It's just as you have surmised. The Seinan War has ended, but in this city and all over the country, confusion still plagues our society. The police fight every day to protect the current government and the nation. We fight to realize the still incomplete ideals of the Meiji, which are to improve the lives of the common people a little at a time, making life better than it was under the last government.

"The Seinan War brought anti-government resistance from opposing groups under control. On the other hand, there has been a disturbing movement inside the government that used to be insignificant, but has recently shown rapid expansion. For example, in the Ministry of the Army, a small group of men who are discontent with their rewards from the previous war have secretly begun to meet. We're currently investigating this, but according to unconfirmed information, these men are planning an armed uprising."

Kenshin listened quietly, suppressing his shock. He

could begin to see the world the man before him lived in. The police were the ones being slandered by many people as "agents of national authority." The chief was surrounded by enemies both internal and external, and was battling them every day. That was this man's livelihood.

"It's not that we don't understand their point. During the Seinan War, the rebel army frequently bemoaned, 'If the red hats and cannon hadn't been there...' Frankly, it's true that the imperial army relied on the Imperial Guards with their red hats, as well as the power of their ammunition.

"Assistant Inspector Ujiki and many of the other swordsmen who have troubled you were former sword commandos during the Seinan War. That war is over now, and to balance the national budget the number of temporarily employed imperial officers and soldiers had to be cut back. Select elites remained in the military, and skilled men who were discharged were recruited as police officers.

"But this year, the government disclosed its plan to slash the annual budget for the Ministry of the Army. Although this was unavoidable, many of those discharged—officers and soldiers alike—must be angered by the government's actions."

Kenshin remained silent as he listened to the chief. His shadow of doubt had slowly taken on a well-defined shape.

"Now, then... Narrowing it down to those who present

the most immediate threat of overthrowing the government, I would say there are perhaps two other groups." The chief named a group of thieves and smugglers—formerly from samurai families—who ran their operations out of their own Hisago Inn, located in Asakusa Tajima-cho. He also spoke of a group whose hideout was the Yôzen-in temple in Senju Kita-gumi, where the gekken-kai government-sanctioned kenjutsu tournament was held.

Neither of these triggered a response in the back of Kenshin's mind. Since Tsukioka Tsunan made his living as an artist, there could be a link between him and the group at the thieves' inn. But the other man he'd seen yesterday evening didn't look at all like a thug to him, yet was the type of person who openly displayed his murderous intentions.

He's not the type to fit in with the gekken-kai, thieves, or smugglers. Kenshin's chest tightened with anxiety, wondering what the watcher really did for a living.

A New Suspicion

He may be a police officer, either active or retired... At that moment, a scene flashed unexpectedly into Kenshin's mind. How long ago was it? When he first wandered into the downtown area, he remembered having a run-in with the Police Sword Corps unit, an elite force consisting of higher-ranking officers authorized to carry swords. Kenshin had been questioned by police officers about his violation of the sword prohibition. Just as he was about to surrender peacefully, the crazed Police Sword Corps, led by Assistant Inspector Ujiki, forced him to draw his sword, then used that as an excuse to attempt to legally kill him under the pretext of self-defense. At the time, Kenshin had been justifiably concerned that the Corps would involve the people of the city as well as his companion, Kamiya Kaoru. For their protection, Kenshin had reluctantly drawn his

sakabatô to accept the challenge. He then beat them down until they were unable to stand. Not much time had passed since then, but for a man like Kenshin, who was involved in many incidents, it was already long forgotten.

Was it that man? Kenshin finally placed the face as that of Ujiki, a coldhearted, merciless revolutionary patriot from Satsuma. He must have received some kind of punishment since their previous encounter, and surely his dissatisfaction and discontent had grown. In a way, the connection made sense. But the core issue was still unknown.

"Chief, I have a favor to ask of you. Could you quickly investigate the nishiki-e publisher Iroha-ya by this afternoon? This one would like to know what kind of person the owner is, and if he has any connection to the three groups of dissidents you have mentioned just now. Yes, by four o'clock if possible…"

Kenshin didn't mention that Iroha-ya was the publisher that sold Tsukioka Tsunan's nishiki-e artwork. To begin with, Kenshin had no idea that Tsunan had something outrageous planned. He thought if Tsunan were discovered to be a former Sekihô Army cadet, he could be viewed with prejudice, just like the time Kenshin was almost arrested for impersonating Hitokiri Battôsai.

Tsukioka-dono's name won't be mentioned, but still… The instincts of a former hitokiri were telling him that something was about to happen, but where? The thought that Sanosuke might be involved made the tea in his mouth taste bitter.

"I have no idea what this means, but since this urgent request comes from none other than Himura-san, I have no choice," the chief stated in a definite tone. Despite that, there were only a few hours left.

"Sorry to trouble you with this."

Seeing Kenshin bow his head in a truly apologetic manner, the chief's face immediately broke into a smile. As a man who rendered distinguished service during the Revolution, Kenshin could have assumed any government position. Instead, this man declared that he "did not wish for honorary or governmental positions," and lived a stoic life as a rurouni. The man before him was somewhat pitiable, yet endearing—qualities that could make one feel like reaching out with both arms to embrace him. A feeling of trust and affection filled the chief's heart.

"Um, about the ones you mentioned earlier, Assistant Inspector Ujiki and his men..." Kenshin asked about what happened to them after the incident.

"Oh, the Police Sword Corps. I may have told you this before, but the Corps was dissolved, and now they're scattered all over our Tokyo Prefecture jurisdiction. That said, we stationed half of the Police Sword Corps in the Takebashi area to guard the Imperial Palace alongside the Imperial Guard Regiment. The intention was to have the two groups keep an eye on each other. Instead, it brought dissatisfaction from both sides." At this point, the chief paused to moisten his mouth with tea before continuing. "On a day off like this, men like Ujiki should be spending their day at that billiard place near Takebashi called New York. It's the latest trend nowadays." The chief's words carried an obvious note of disapproval, but it wasn't clear whether it was from anger or grief. "Himura-san, is something about to happen here in Tokyo Prefecture?"

"Well..." Kenshin paused to consider his reply, then said, "Perhaps tonight, or at least within a day or two, a major incident that might spark the overthrow of the government could disrupt the city. Yes, if possible, it might be wise to choose two or three hundred reliable men and have them stand by—secretly—at the station."

Although based on guesswork, Kenshin was seized by his own words. Perhaps the former Sekihô Army's Tsukioka Tsunan was also a member of a rebel militia, and had recruited Sanosuke to join them. If that were the case, then it was difficult to imagine that they could have formed an alliance with the malcontents inside the government. After all, such a militia would contain remnants of the Sekihô Army, which suffered the dishonor of being branded a false imperial army by the same government.

Kenshin's doubts and suspicions boiled up and expanded, one after another. There was no end to it.

"Yes Chief, that would be best," Kenshin repeated. "This one has had a premonition that within three days—but most likely at midnight tonight—a major incident may well occur. Of course, if nothing happens, then so much the better."

"Himura-san." The two men smiled at each other. It was a silent understanding between men.

"This one is planning to go visit some of the places that come to mind. Apologies for the selfishness, but this one would like to call upon you once again around four o'clock." Kenshin straightened up and bowed, then grasped the sakabatô beside his knees with his right hand and stood up straight.

Thinking he probably hadn't had lunch yet, the chief invited Kenshin to at least have a tempura *chazuke*, a bowl of rice topped with tea and tempura, before leaving. But Kenshin politely declined and left the chief's home, heading once again toward the run-down row house.

If what Sanosuke said is correct, Tsunan should be out delivering his work to Iroha-Ya about now. Moreover, if he were truly the subject of the suspicious-looking man's surveillance, then that man probably won't be at the row house. These were Kenshin's thoughts as he hurried to the row house, but counter to his assumptions, a different man was casually watching Tsunan's residence. This man was dressed in a police officer's uniform, and Kenshin took cover to observe him.

Of course, with that uniform on, no one will grow suspicious of him wandering around the area. He looks as though he's been sword trained. Kenshin surmised that the man was most likely a former member of the Police Sword Corps. *Perhaps he was one of the men present at that incident.* Although it was a possibility, it was a risk Kenshin was willing to take. He assumed a slow, natural pace as he walked toward the officer. Luckily, the officer didn't seem to recognize him.

The First Stopover

"Just how far are we going?" the officer asked the man beside him, unable to contain his growing uneasiness. In the officer's eyes, the man who had hailed him had a gentle, almost feminine appearance, despite the large cross-shaped scar on his left cheek. His manner of speaking was also very polite.

"There is something this one would like you to hear. If you would be so kind...?" The officer had followed the man for some distance at his behest, but now the sword at the man's side began to worry him. Soon, the two men arrived at a canal, far from the back-alley row house.

"This place should do." Kenshin stopped in his tracks and looked around. The canal by their feet was brimming with water, brightly reflecting the spring sunlight. Riverboats weren't so common now that the new railways had been constructed, but the Tokyo waterways, which flowed in every direction, were still a very important part of life for the people of the city. Then again, today was Sunday. Pedestrian and cart traffic was sparse in this neighborhood, which normally bustled during weekdays. It was a clear, cloudless day.

"This concerns Tsukioka Tsunan-dono," Kenshin said, a statement that seemed out of place in the environment. He turned around to face the officer, and their eyes became locked in a fierce stare. "That should explain the reason you were lured here."

"Wh-what is this all about?" the officer sputtered, still gazing intently at Kenshin. "I have no idea what this is all about..."

"It's useless to play innocent," Kenshin replied coldly. He began to voice his speculation in an impassive tone. "You were spying on Tsukioka-dono's residence. There must be something inside that you need."

"Hmph. I was wondering what you were going to say, but that's absurd. You'll get yourself arrested for insulting a police officer with such nonsense," the man sneered, baring his white teeth. His attitude was cool and composed.

"No nonsense about it. All the evidence is inside that house." Kenshin watched the police officer's behavior with unblinking eyes. There were obvious signs of restlessness, but as if to cover it up, the officer spoke as though he were about to leave.

"So be it, then. Is that all you wanted to talk about?" the police officer said, turning away.

"Stop right there!" Kenshin shouted in a low, commanding tone. The police officer's face distorted into a hideous display of bare hatred. He drew the saber on his hip with surprising speed, slashing it toward Kenshin as he turned around. The strike harbored an intensity that could not be taken lightly. Kenshin warded off the blow with a light-footed retreat. The police officer didn't pause before striking out with his second attack. Kenshin leapt lightly to the right and then to the left as he deflected the blow. The officer repeated the same attack a third time.

It happened on the fourth blow, when Kenshin tried to dodge—his foot got caught in some underbrush and he landed on his right hand, momentarily disoriented.

"Oh, you're mine now...!" The police officer rushed forward, trying to seize the opportunity, but his foot became entangled in the brush as well. He staggered and tried to regain his balance. Meanwhile, Kenshin rolled over and extended his sword from his hip. The police officer, recovered from his stumble, held his saber in a unique overhead position.

Jigen-ryû. Just like Assistant Inspector Ujiki. Kenshin placed his left hand on the sakabatô at his hip, and waited for his opponent's next move.

"*Ches-to!*" The police officer let out a Jigen-ryû battle cry and moved forward with a broad step just as Kenshin leapt from his kneeling position. The two passed by each other, and at the moment they crossed paths, their bodies appeared to come into contact. "Ngh!" The officer's saber sparkled twice as it danced in the air. Then the police officer fell, shoulder first, toward the ground.

Kenshin had met the Jigen-ryû death blow from below, using the iai-nuki combat form. Normally, the iai move consists of drawing the sword in a flash, striking a killing blow, and then returning the blade to its sheath in one continuous motion. In this case, Kenshin had left the blade sheathed. Stepping closer to his opponent as he twisted his body in a half-turn, he had then struck the police officer's abdomen with the sheathed sakabatô. Of course, Kenshin's lightning skill was such that the sword was invisible to the naked eye until the sakabatô was resting once again at his hip. Kenshin glanced around once, then quickly left the bank of the canal.

Ten minutes later, the sound of thunder echoed through the clear skies, a sound not commonly heard in the spring. It woke the fallen police officer, and he managed to stand, using his saber as a crutch. The officer acted as if in a trance at first, but hearing the spring thunder a second time snapped him out of it. His body began to shake, and the expression on his face slowly changed. His eyes were consumed by fear.

"I-I remember now. That large cross-shaped scar...that man was the legendary Hitokiri Battôsai. He's strong, much too strong..." The police officer had forgotten all about the pain in his side, and simply trembled in fear for a while. His body looked shrunken and his face twitched as it turned red, then paled.

"I-I can't just stand here..." The officer muttered in a voice so low that it was almost a groan. He began to run, clutching his injured side. He crossed the bridge over the canal, passed several rows of houses, and emerged onto the main street in Ginza, lined with elegant Western-style homes. Soon, he turned onto a small street. Shops and residences were sparsely scattered along both sides of the narrow street. Soon, a storefront came into view, displaying a boldly lettered Billiards sign. The name of the hall was London.

The sun was still high above his head, and pale clouds floated across the otherwise clear blue sky, but the police officer had no time for noticing such things. He pushed open the Western-style door and entered the London, but never came out.

"So, the enemy is here, not at the New York in Takebashi," Kenshin muttered to himself as he looked up at the billiards sign.

A raid perhaps...? No, best to observe the situation for a little while. Kenshin cautiously checked his surroundings, paying close attention to the buildings within a few doors of the billiard hall. Just as he made up his mind to proceed, his stomach growled unexpectedly. *Oh, no, it probably would've been a good idea to have that tempura chazuke...* He regretted his decision, but it was too late now.

Kenshin stood beneath the eaves of the billiard hall. He could hear voices coming from inside. It was probably people in the middle of playing the game, for sometimes cheers were heard interspersed with the sound of billiard balls striking each other.

Kenshin placed his hand on the door and slowly pushed it open, then entered the shop and casually glanced around.

There were a total of twelve pool tables. Near each table were men in Western-style clothes, many of whom looked like government officials from some ministry or another. There were also young girls and wives from good families dressed in kimonos, and all seemed amused by this game imported from the Western world.

In spite of being repeatedly banned by the government, billiards popularity grew as government officials themselves took the initiative and started to bet on and compete in games. Because those who were to supposed to control the game had been influenced early on, it was gradually legalized by the ninth year of Meiji (1876). At this time, however, billiards was still illegal in this part of the country.

It goes without saying that Kenshin wasn't interested in the game. But it seemed rather strange that the games had continued after a police officer in uniform had barged in. There had been no signs of confusion, and nary a scream from the ladies. In other words, these people were familiar with the police officers who were regulars, and whose presence was not meant to control the situation.

Kenshin tried his best to walk at a casual, leisurely pace as he proceeded to the back of the hall. The eyes of a few people were focused on the sword at Kenshin's hip, but most of the men and women had no interest in this intruder. Soon, Kenshin reached the end of the first floor of the large hall, and noticed the stairs in the corner that led to the second floor.

Up there, most likely... Kenshin bent forward and climbed the stairs.

Deadly Combat

As he approached the opening at the top of the stairs, Kenshin peered up into the second floor to check his surroundings. A guard stood a short distance away near the corner of a hallway. The other hallway to the left of the top of the stairs was empty. The guard wore Western-style clothes, but he had a Japanese sword in his hand. The man appeared to be very alert, and had the same feel about him as Assistant Inspector Ujiki and the police officer Kenshin had followed into this place a moment ago.

So, how many steps to reach him...? Kenshin thought to himself, measuring the distance with his eyes.

"You stupid fool!"

The loud yell erupted from the room at the far end of the hallway, creating an unexpected opening. The guard turned toward the room and Kenshin slipped swiftly into the hallway on the left, out of sight. After pausing a moment to prepare himself, Kenshin leapt out and rushed the guard, delivering a powerful blow to the man's body. The guard's mouth gaped open, but he made no sound as he fell toward Kenshin's shoulder, his right hand barely touching the hilt of his sword. Cautiously, Kenshin dragged the man into the other hallway and out of sight, then strained his ears to hear what was going on inside the room.

"I'm sorry, I was careless," came a voice from inside the room. It sounded like the police officer from earlier. "That man is without a doubt Hitokiri Battôsai..."

Then a different, but still familiar, voice spoke. "All right, don't forget that we have important matters to deal with. The Ministry of Home Affairs will be attacked tonight, and there will be mass confusion. Presumably, the police will rush over, and then each cell will take action along with their comrades in the imperial guards. We'll take control of the imperial court and force the government to reconsider rewards for services rendered during the Seinan War...." The voice paused, followed by a brief, sharp order for silence. A moment later, with a thundering battle cry, the door was sliced diagonally in two, just as if someone was using it to test the sharpness of his blade. If Kenshin hadn't sensed the murderous aura coming from the room and thus stayed far from the door, he would have faced the same fate.

"Who's there?!"

"It's probably Hitokiri Battosai! He must have followed

Nakajima!" another voice shouted. The air crackled with tension, sending the second floor into an uproar. Two men sprang from the room, kicking down the door that had been mercilessly attacked a moment before. One carried a saber, the other a Japanese sword. Both moved with quick agility.

Kenshin's sword was already drawn. Goose bumps prickled across his entire body as he held his sakabatô ready. The two men attacking him were not ordinary street punks, but warriors who had spent years training. They took silent aim to cut Kenshin from the left and the right, and their cruelty and swiftness reminded him of wolves.

The ceiling was low, so the man with the saber adapted his technique from slashing to thrusting. His saber flashed as it moved horizontally, then thrust forward. Kenshin spread his arms to dodge the attack, then crouched down and sharply swung his sakabatô. The man dropped his saber and cradled his arm against his chest, then fell sideways onto the wooden floor. Kenshin turned swiftly and used the point of his sakabatô to force the man with the Japanese sword up against the wall.

Footsteps were soon heard from both the first floor and the room at the back of the hall. Encouraged by this sign of reinforcement, the man with the Japanese sword recklessly brought his blade down with all his might.

One of the men who had run up from the first floor wielded his sword relentlessly, clearly a veteran of many bloody battles. He kept a steady eye on Kenshin's movements, deftly exchanging blows and reversing their positions until Kenshin's escape route was blocked. The man moved with the lethal grace of a leopard, but still Kenshin managed to reel off his opponent's long sword and strike the man's shoulder as he passed. The man staggered and tumbled down the stairs to land with a thud that shook the floor. The women, who had until then been enjoying billiards, screamed in unison and began to scatter.

The man named Nakajima made no move to attack, though his sword was drawn. He appeared to have frozen when he found out his opponent was Hitokiri Battôsai.

Ujiki was the only enemy left, and he and Kenshin faced each other. Ujiki raised his naked blade into the *tombo* overhead position unique to Jigen-ryû, and watched for an opening. Ujiki had once been painfully and publicly defeated by Kenshin's Hiten Mitsurugi-ryû. Jigen-ryû, as a strike-to-kill technique, required no defense, but it was still unwise to attack recklessly. Just then, a tall man clad in Western-style clothing came up from the first floor and quickly pulled a pistol out of an inside jacket pocket.

"Ha ha. Ujiki, looks like you're having a tough battle. Allow me to back you up." The man wore a faint smile on his face. Judging from his obvious Satsuma dialect, he was an active or retired army officer from the same province as Ujiki, probably discontent with the reward for his services during the Seinan War. His thin lips looked profoundly cruel, and he gazed down on Kenshin as though he were a trapped bird or beast.

"I don't need any backup from you. I'll defeat this man myself." Ujiki, once the leader of the Police Sword Corps, still had his pride as a swordsman. Kenshin listened to their exchange carefully.

"Stop this armed uprising nonsense. Such recklessness will only cause the deaths of innocent people," Kenshin said, but the two men showed no emotion.

"What we do is none of your business," the man with the pistol replied. Kenshin slowly returned the sakabatô to its sheath at his waist.

"What do you think you're doing, Battôsai?! Your sword! Take up your sword!" Ujiki shouted.

The man with the pistol looked back and forth between Kenshin and Ujiki, the muzzle of his pistol pointed directly at Kenshin's chest. It was obvious he was willing to pull the trigger without a second thought at the first sign of any suspicious movement from Kenshin.

"I'll cut you up if you don't draw!" Ujiki exclaimed. But Ujiki, sword still held in the tombo position, seemed hesitant about closing the distance between them. Kenshin slowly moved forward a few steps, arms relaxed at his sides. He sensed someone moving downstairs.

Ujiki held his sword slightly flatter than the usual tombo position, likely due to the low ceiling. He was indeed a master, as expected from the previous head of the Police Sword Corps. He moved his body fluidly, controlling his breath and storming into his attack.

Kenshin stood still as he emotionlessly confronted Ujiki's sword. The muzzle of the pistol was still pointed at him from a short distance behind. The moment before Ujiki's lethal long sword touched him, Kenshin ducked down at blinding speed. The man with the pistol thought he heard the sound of the blade ripping through the air, and a sensation of a short, sharp swish. But he must have been mistaken, for Kenshin was still in the same position, arms at his sides. Somehow, Ujiki's sword had been knocked from his hand and into the air, where it had then incredibly passed through the arm of the man holding the pistol. Ujiki's shoulders slumped and he dropped to his knees. He stared up at Kenshin blankly.

"Assistant Inspector Ujiki, this one will withdraw for now. There is one more place that must be visited. However, you should heed this advice: Stop this meaningless riot. The people who have finally started to regain their peaceful lives could be exposed to the turmoil of the Revolution once again. If you insist on being unreasonable, then next time this one will not hesitate to kill you!"

Ujiki seemed to be at loss for words, and the man with the sword through his arm replied instead.

"Hmph. Try to stop us. The ones who are attacking the Ministry of Home Affairs aren't our comrades. It's hopeless to try to find them now. There are thirteen different hideouts in this city, and we won't give up their locations no matter how we're tortured. It would be impossible to gain control of all of them. By this time tomorrow, this city will be transformed into a hell of burning flames." The man laughed despite the pain that distorted his lips, his bravado unfazed.

Kenshin had been ready to leave, but those words awoke something dangerous deep inside of him—the madness of his hitokiri days.

Unforgivable.

Kenshin's mind was flooded with the images of chaos and destruction that he had participated in at the end of the Shogunate era. A path to the God of Death lay in those ruins. It was the lone path of the beast. A path for one who believed in living by the sword until his last breath, even if death in some gutter was the inevitable outcome.

Deep inside Kenshin's heart, his anger grew into a boiling rage and then transformed into a cold, chilling smile. The smile seemed to come from the joy of returning to his former hitokiri self. Or perhaps he was ridiculing his own worthlessness. Kenshin was confused by his unexpected smile, and tried to suppress it as he hung his head. The fact that such conflicting emotions even entered his mind made him resentful. Then the smile spread, expanding inside Kenshin. His shoulders quivered as he tried to contain the strong impulses buried deep in his heart. To a stranger's eyes, he may have looked as though he were crying.

Taking his eyes off the shattered men in the hallway, Kenshin descended the stairs with gentle steps. At times he was unable to hold back the chi that threatened to explode from him, and it escaped as wild laughter that spread throughout his body. Each time this happened, Kenshin smacked his fist against his forehead to suppress the madness, and one by one he visualized the faces of Kamiya Kaoru, Myôjin Yahiko, and Sagara Sanosuke.

Kenshin, please don't go back to being a hitokiri. Don't wield your killing sword... From somewhere beyond, he thought he heard Kaoru's sad, weeping voice. The laughter echoing from the depths of his dark soul gradually began to drift away, like a receding tide. Slowly, his heart warmed once again, and a sense of reality returned.

Ujiki's comrades disappeared quietly and in unison, leaving behind the "heart" of a rurouni, wandering in the wind.

Two-Man Army

"Okay, let's get started," Sanosuke said as he stood up. Kenshin, Yahiko, Kaoru, Tsubame, Tae, Sanosuke, and Tsunan were seated on cushions in a circle surrounding a spread of fancy sushi and bottles of saké. The party was being held on a wooden floor in the middle of a dojo, so some shabbiness was unavoidable. But luckily those who had gathered were all interesting and unique individuals. Although she had no objections to the location, Kaoru was already in the mood to vent at Sanosuke.

"So, this was what you meant when you said you'll take care of the money? In other words, this was about sponging off Tsunan-san. I can't believe it!"

"It's all right. See, as the saying goes..." Sanosuke continued after a pause, "What's mine is mine, and what's yours is mine..."

Kenshin looked appalled as he started to say something, but tonight Sanosuke was particularly full of vigor. As if to prevent Kenshin from talking, he proclaimed, "Don't sweat the small stuff. Let's drink and have fun until we pass out!" And so, the party to celebrate Sanosuke and Tsunan's reunion had begun.

In the beginning, the presence of popular artist Tsukioka Tsunan made the usual crowd nervous, but their mood changed as they sipped saké from their bowls and the bottle made the rounds. Even those who were usually quiet became talkative and surprised themselves with their own clever jokes. Their wit grew sharper, and they began to discuss their new insights into daily matters that normally went unnoticed.

Everyone chatted pleasantly about their high ideals, their hearts cheerful and open. There were no problems in this world. They couldn't help but laugh out loud. Kenshin and Kaoru both laughed a lot. Sanosuke cracked an unusual number of jokes as he happily held his bowl of saké.

Spirits high with some help from the alcohol, Tae and Tsubame grew bold enough to ask Tsunan, the artist they adored, to draw their portraits. Tae gazed in fascination at her own image. Her cheeks blushed cherry red in bliss, her radiance apparent to everyone. It was a happy moment, and no one could resist laughing—except Yahiko and Tsunan.

Yahiko had drunk too much too quickly. He had reached

his limit soon after the party began, and he was suddenly overwhelmed by some emotion that was either anger or sadness. Heaven and hell, comedy and tragedy. These feelings suddenly appeared to rock his existence, and Yahiko didn't understand why, or even where they came from. To everyone else, it simply looked as though Yahiko had suddenly fallen ill.

There was no way for Yahiko to know what happened after that. Not only did drowsiness overtake him, but the hangover demon ran rampant after he lost consciousness. In the morning, he wouldn't remember a thing, and all that would remain of the night would be a dull, heavy pain in his head. It was unclear if alcohol would be Yahiko's friend or foe in the future.

On the other hand, whether it was due to his personality or because of the important matters awaiting him, Tsunan did not show any signs of drunkenness no matter how many cups of saké he consumed. Even when pestered into drawing portraits of Tae and Tsubame, it was impressive to see that not a drop of ink went astray.

How much time had passed? The night winds blowing past the exterior of the Kamiya dojo could be heard faintly inside. Before anyone knew it, the noisy party had come to an end. Tae and Tsubame were cuddled up under a futon cover by the wall, Kaoru was lying on the floor using a *zabuton* cushion as a pillow, and Yahiko was sprawled out in a corner of the dojo, his whole body shivering. Kenshin leaned against the wooden wall in the corner of the dojo, sakabatô in his arms, fast asleep.

"All right, then…" Sanosuke whispered, his voice low so that only Tsunan could hear. He stood up suddenly, followed by Tsunan. "Well, shall we go now?"

"That was our final supper. Did you thoroughly enjoy yourself?" Tsunan asked.

"Not really. That wasn't why I planned this party. The Akabeko girls feed me quite often. It was the least I could do for them." Tsunan remained silent. "So, how was it for you? It must've been ten years since you've been to a rowdy party. Were you able to enjoy yourself a little?"

"Hmph. Not one bit."

"Tch. You're a cynic, through and through." The two men jokingly whispered, but their eyes met unexpectedly.

"Are you really okay with this, Sanosuke?" Because of the party, Tsunan had come to understand what Sanosuke had told him the previous night. "Well, I'm having a good time in my own way."

As former Sekihô Army cadets, the two men had witnessed the tragic death of Sagara Sôzô. But Sanosuke had also lived as Zanza, and through his encounter with Kenshin, had been able to escape the darkness of his past. On the other hand, Tsunan had blindly continued down the dark, damp path of revenge. He felt envious of the light he'd seen from the darkness, the glow he saw as Sanosuke mingled and laughed with Kenshin and the others.

Maybe it's wrong to involve my old friend in this outrageous plan to overthrow the government, Tsunan thought once again. As if Sanosuke had sensed those thoughts, he countered Tsunan's hesitation.

"You fool. It's not like me to be that sentimental."

"I see. I thank you from the bottom of my heart for choosing the Sekihô Army over the life you have now." Tsunan bowed his head slightly and cast off his concerns.

"Let's hurry. If we waste too much time, it'll be sunrise by the time we haul the grenades over to the Ministry of Home Affairs." Tsunan quietly opened the door to the dojo and led the way out.

As he followed, Sanosuke murmured softly, "Sorry, you guys. I'm not asking you to understand. But after all, the Sekihô Army is very special to me." He glanced at Kenshin slouched in the corner and whispered, "Kenshin, if I ever see you again, it'll be after I've become a felon. If you smack me down with your sakabatô, I won't hold it against you." Sanosuke left the dojo and closed the door gently behind him. No one was able to prevent the two men from leaving—they were all in an alcohol-assisted sleep. After Sanosuke and Tsunan's departure, the memory of the party still lingered gently in the dojo and the minds of those who rested, all unaware of the major event that was about to occur.

Kenshin slowly opened his eyes. Everyone else was still

asleep. He stood up briskly, sakabatô firmly in hand. *What a man that Sano is*, he thought. Soon, Kenshin too disappeared from the dojo, moving off into the starry night.

Approximately three hours later, under the halo of the new moon, the two men steadily made their way toward the main gate of the Ministry of Home Affairs. Surrounded by darkness, the two former Sekihô Army cadets had finally begun their own terrible uprising.

Although it was already spring, the night breeze was cold. Sanosuke and Tsunan had no time to notice, as they compared the hand-drawn map to the positions of the security guards guarding the main gate. They then placed grenades by the gate in several locations.

It was impossible for just the two of them to penetrate the main gate and enter the building by force, since it was protected by a number of police officers. Therefore, Tsunan had planned a diversionary tactic early on. The idea was to create time-delay explosives by adjusting the lengths of the fuses, then position them in previously scouted places, setting them to detonate one after another. Naturally, the police officers would gather where the explosions had occurred, moving about in confusion. The two men would seize that opportunity and slip inside the building.

The grenades went off in sequence with tremendous force. The network of guards was severed as many of the police officers rushed to the front of the main gate in a panic, just the way Tsunan had expected.

After gauging the situation, the two men ran to the wall near the towering Ministry of Home Affairs building. Tsunan folded his arms in front of his chest to form a foothold for Sanosuke, who used it as a springboard to launch himself onto the top of the wall. From his perch atop the wall, Sanosuke reached down to pull Tsunan up. The two men worked in perfect sync. But despite his decisive actions, Sanosuke still felt some mental hesitation.

Come to think of it, before the captain organized the Sekihô Army, he was manipulated into committing arson and robbery in order to stir up trouble for the Tokugawa government... To shake off his hesitation, Sanosuke looked at Tsunan, whom he had just pulled up to the top of the wall, but his normally resolute friend looked shocked.

"What's wrong? What are you standing around for?" he asked, eyeing Tsunan suspiciously. Sanosuke turned his gaze in the direction Tsunan was looking. Waiting there on the grounds of the Ministry of Home Affairs was Kenshin, sakabatô at his waist, ready to be drawn at a moment's notice.

The True Heart of the Sekihô Army

"Kenshin…" Tsunan's surprised voice was drowned out by the sound of explosions. "Don't tell me he entered the Ministry of Home Affairs before us. What kind of man is he?"

"Himura Battôsai, the legendary hitokiri," Sanosuke replied to the distressed Tsunan.

"I see. So he's the famous Hitokiri Battôsai…"

Without hesitation, Tsunan jumped down off the wall. The distance between them was seven or eight ken, but Kenshin refused to move. "Have you come to take Sanosuke back with you?" Tsunan asked as he landed.

"No," Kenshin replied curtly, then slowly drew his sakabatô. "This is a course of action Sanosuke has chosen as a man. It is not for this one to decide otherwise. Instead, this one has come to bring a halt to the violence that both of you are creating."

Tsunan was enraged by Kenshin's words. Ten years of resentment spilled out of him in a low voice. "An Ishin Shishi standing in the Sekihô Army's path once again. But I'm not going to lose this time!" Tsunan cried as he pulled grenades from his sleeves with both hands, lit them instantly with the spark-producing bands he wore on his fingers, and threw them without hesitation. "Take this!"

Kenshin refused to move. He gazed intently as the two grenades flew toward him, then casually flashed his sakabatô, as if in a practice swing. The grenades fell to the ground and rolled near Kenshin's feet, but they did not detonate. Kenshin had skillfully cut the fuses off in midair.

"Argh! You Ishin Shishi!" Instead of being intimidated by Kenshin's sword skills, Tsunan's fighting spirit had been heightened even more.

Adding fuel to the flames, Kenshin exclaimed, "As a former Ishin Shishi, this one is even less inclined to allow your 'Sekihô Army' to take such foolish actions."

Sanosuke, who had jumped down and was now at Tsunan's side, felt as though he had been pierced through the heart by Kenshin's words, and was even more enraged than his partner. "What makes you think you can talk to us like that, you lowly hitokiri?!"

Perhaps Tsunan was getting desperate as he took out

every grenade tucked inside his kimono, ignited them one by one, and threw them toward Kenshin.

One, two, three, four, five, six...none of the grenades that flew toward Kenshin detonated. Every fuse was cut off by Kenshin's sakabatô. Naturally, such a miracle was possible due to Kenshin's keen powers of observation and the swiftness of his Hiten Mitsurugi-ryû. To Kenshin, who could see a bullet shot from a pistol, severing the fuses of the much larger, slower grenades was not a difficult feat. In spite of the ease of the feat, Kenshin was actually being cautious—if more explosions were to echo in the night sky, it might trigger an uprising among the malcontent members of the government and military.

Every eventuality that came to mind has been taken care of, but there's always the slight chance that something could go wrong. And Kenshin was fighting against time as well.

"Rrraaaagh!" Instead of giving up, Tsunan was even more fired up, and prepared to throw more grenades. It was Sanosuke who stopped him.

"That's enough, Tsunan."

"Sanosuke!"

"You can't beat him that way. We've wasted too much time. The police will arrive soon." Suddenly, Sanosuke delivered a single blow to Tsunan's stomach. No match for Sanosuke, Tsunan started to pass out.

"Sa...no?"

"Don't misunderstand this," Sanosuke said to Tsunan,

and then turned toward Kenshin. "Sorry for the trouble. Hey, if I had continued to take his side, would you have pounded me down?"

"Yes," Kenshin replied decisively. "There is no room for half-hearted relationships. No mercy would have been given."

As a man, Sanosuke was pleased by Kenshin's words. "Thanks," Sanosuke said as he effortlessly lifted Tsunan's unconscious body and once again climbed the walls surrounding the Ministry of Home Affairs, this time to make his exit. It wasn't long before the police force arrived.

No other uprisings occurred anywhere in the city that night because after Kenshin left the billiard hall London, he had paid a visit to Minister of the Army Yamagata Aritomo's residence and requested that all army officers immediately return to their stations, to guard against their participating in the insurgency. Then, he returned to the police chief's residence at the agreed time.

"Himura-san, I've been waiting for you," the police chief said in greeting. "The publisher who owns Iroha-Ya was a former civilian patriot, and seems to have been an acquaintance of Sagara Sôzô's. However, after Meiji he proved to be an irresponsible man who used his political ties for business purposes." The chief paused for a moment before continuing. "I was surprised to discover that he has expanded his business holdings to include thirteen billiard halls in the city."

Kenshin guessed that the publisher had provided the gunpowder and other raw materials Tsunan had used to create the grenades. The publisher had tricked Tsunan into becoming the fuse to ignite the coup d'etat. The thirteen billiard halls, which included New York and London, matched up with the number of secret hideouts. Kenshin had requested that the police chief assign some of the recalled police officers to guard each of the thirteen locations. Having made these preparations, Kenshin had then attended Sanosuke and Tsunan's reunion party. But of course, the two men had no idea what he had been up to.

It was past three in the morning and Kenshin was standing before the gate of a large house in Koji-machi, owned by Army Major General Someya Shûzô, whose glamorous achievements during the Seinan War had elevated him to celebrity status. According to the police chief, this man was the mastermind behind the armed uprising.

This one will have a word with him.

Kenshin felt his anger stir toward Someya. The officers had risked their lives during the war, so it was not difficult to understand that they might harbor resentment about the repayment for their services. But just because the army's budget had been cut to help rebuild the nation's finances was no excuse to resort to an armed uprising. Moreover, this plot had involved Sanosuke and Tsukioka Tsunan. Kenshin was infuriated, his feelings boiling over. To make matters worse, the mastermind was hiding in the background, keeping his hands clean. In midst of a blinding rage, Kenshin decided he and Someya should have a discussion.

"I'm sure you know this, but please refrain from acting rashly and irresponsibly," the police chief had warned Kenshin after telling him about the existence of the mastermind. But Kenshin was no longer able to contain the emotions churning in his heart.

Naturally, he didn't assume that the Someya residence would be open and defenseless that evening. He might very well have to clash with guards, but Kenshin was determined to break through the security and force his way in. He had come here driven by a fury akin to that of a wounded beast. As expected, the front gate of the Someya residence was closed, and armed soldiers and officers camped by a fire beside it. The glow from the fire illuminated the street in the distance.

Kenshin observed the situation from afar for a short time, then partially drew his sakabatô and walked closer to the side gate. There were about fifty soldiers near the bonfire, all with a nervous look on their faces. Their mood implied that they already knew that the thirteen billiard halls were under surveillance by police officers. Two of the men were seated on folding stools, most likely the men's superior officers. At first, the two men appeared indifferent to Kenshin when they spotted him. It was clear that Kenshin was alone, and there were many armed men on guard, so it was natural for them to be at ease. But when they noticed the sword at Kenshin's waist, they grew agitated.

"You there, for what purpose have you come here?"

"This one needs to speak to Major General Someya."

"Wh-what?!" The voice carried an obvious tone of confusion and resentment. When Kenshin turned around, the shocked voice of one of the soldiers cried out.

"H-hey, could he be the one that appeared at the London?" The soldiers drew their weapons, but Kenshin raised his hand to calm them.

"Please be quiet. This one does not wish to hurt anyone— no grudge is held against any of you." But the soldiers started to slowly close in on Kenshin. "This one wishes only to speak to the major general. There is no intention of resorting to violence. Please allow this one to pass."

Kenshin's words only made the soldiers more tense. Eventually, one soldier ran behind Kenshin, attempting to block his escape route. When Kenshin turned to prevent this, the soldier suddenly curled his finger around the trigger of his gun. Kenshin immediately drew his sakabatô, flipped the blade so the sharp side faced forward, and slashed the gun in two with a single stroke.

A moment later, every gun barrel that had been pointed at Kenshin was cut off.

"Do you understand now?" Kenshin glared at the men surrounding him as he sheathed his sakabatô. The soldiers stiffened in fear, remaining rigidly in place, in a state of shock at the blinding speed of Kenshin's swordplay. No one tried to follow Kenshin as he turned his back and entered the side gate.

When Kenshin reached the entrance hall, a thuggish man who looked like a bodyguard stopped him in his tracks. The man had probably already heard every detail of the incident at the gate, for he spread his arms wide on the steps to the entrance hall, blocking the way.

"You are not allowed to pass."

Kenshin continued to silently advance.

"Do you know what time it is? His Excellency will not meet with you at such an absurd hour."

As Kenshin climbed the steps to the entrance hall in silence, the man rushed forward, trying to tackle him. Kenshin delivered a blow to the man's stomach, then caught him as he collapsed and laid him quietly on the floor, before heading inside the house. With no other people to interrupt him, Kenshin was able to make his way to Someya's living room. On the way, he heard the voices of young men talking nearby.

Kenshin opened the fusuma door to find Someya sitting at a Western-style desk. The man looked up at Kenshin suspiciously. There might have been complications if others had been in the room, but fortunately Someya was alone. Kenshin silently closed the fusuma door and stood about one ken away from the desk. Still, Someya did not utter a sound, holding back his shock as best as he could.

"You have failed," Kenshin said.

Someya remained silent. News of the evening's failure must already have reached the man, but there were no apparent signs of disappointment or discouragement. Perhaps he was confident of his safety as the mastermind of all this.

"Many people could have died needlessly," Kenshin continued in a low whisper. "This one's friend was involved as well."

"Wh-who are you?" Someya finally said.

"You should remain *silent*," Kenshin said in a low, sharp tone. Kenshin felt a murderous rage growing inside him. "The Revolution was built upon the bodies of many people. The New Government is not perfect, but that is why those who survived should not be obsessed with their own greed, and instead pray for the happiness of the survivors. Otherwise, all those deaths will have been for nothing. The hearts of those who perished before they could realize their dreams must be kept in mind." Kenshin slowly drew closer to Someya.

Someya pushed back his chair and stood halfway up, practically leaning backwards. Kenshin placed his hand on the hilt of his sword, his movement a fleeting flash of white light to Someya's eyes.

"Soon, you too will end up like this," Kenshin said as he sheathed his sword.

Someya thought he'd been cut. Although he didn't make a panicked attempt to escape, the color drained from his face.

"Beg your pardon." Kenshin bowed slightly and left without looking back. As he closed the fusuma doors behind him, the Western-style desk in front of Someya split in half and crashed onto the carpeted floor.

Kenshin looked up on his way home at the sky packed with stars. They looked as though they would fall if touched, but they shined brightly, boldly. A faint smell of flowers drifted in from a distance. "It's all over now," Kenshin said to himself, and felt the fierceness in his blood fade.

When Tsunan came to, he was in his own room. He hurriedly opened the closet and looked inside. Not a single device remained.

"If you're looking for the grenades, Kenshin took them all," Sanosuke said nonchalantly. "He said he'd bury them somewhere no one will notice."

"Damned government spy!"

Tsunan's anger was not surprising, but since he didn't know much about Kenshin, Sanosuke took it upon himself to clear up the misunderstanding.

"That's not it at all. He's just like us, unhappy with the current government. No, perhaps even more unhappy than us because he's one of the people who helped to establish it."

"Don't give me that nonsense. How can a lowly hitokiri understand us?!" Tsunan yelled, cutting him off. But Sanosuke didn't flinch.

"Sure he does, because he was a hitokiri thoroughly involved in a lot of dirty business, including all those assassinations he committed behind the scenes of the Meiji Revolution. As a result, he couldn't allow himself to see us—the Sekihô Army—behave immorally." Sanosuke slowly looked over at Tsunan and continued, "Hey, Katsu. They say the captain did some immoral things, but there's no way he wanted to. The Sekihô Army lived for the ideal of equality for the four classes. After all that, we can't act dishonorably."

"What's wrong with you? All this business about being clean or dirty has nothing to do with it! We need to do whatever it takes to accomplish our goals!" Tsunan was adamant. Sanosuke, not knowing what to do, put down his teacup and stood up.

"All right. Then that means the Sekihô Army will truly end up being a 'false army.'" Sanosuke turned his back and started to leave, but paused to offer his final words to Tsunan, who was still trying to grasp what Sanosuke was getting at. "Just because the government is playing dirty doesn't mean we have to be like them. I don't care if it takes a slow, deliberate effort—I'm going to do this in a way that will make the captain smile from his place in the afterlife." It was that kind of understanding that Sanosuke had gained

by meeting Kenshin.

"Captain..." Tsunan whispered to himself, but it was unclear if Sanosuke heard him.

A few days passed. While taking a walk in the city, Kenshin asked Sanosuke, "So, how is Tsukioka-dono these days?"

"Not sure. We parted ways during a disagreement, so it feels too awkward to go see him," Sanosuke replied with a sour look on his face. Then a voice called out to him—it was the owner of the picture book shop, the man who Sanosuke had shaken down for information some time ago. Kenshin and Sanosuke hadn't noticed that they had walked past the man's storefront.

"Oh, sorry about what happened before. What's up?" Sanosuke said bluntly.

The shop owner fumbled around for something as he replied, "Ah, there's something I was asked to give you, from Tsunan-san." The shopkeeper told them it was the final nishiki-e by Tsukioka Tsunan as he handed over a piece of artwork. "I don't know what's gotten into him, but he suddenly told me that he's starting up something called an 'illustrated newspaper,' to challenge governmental injustices. I told him not to do it, because they're strictly regulated. Oh well, what a shame to lose such a popular artist..." The owner sighed with disappointment.

Sanosuke looked at the final nishiki-e of Sagara Sôzô

and relished the joy welling up inside of him. "That's too bad, isn't it?" he quietly said.

Kenshin snuck a peek at the name of the publisher printed on the corner of the artwork, but it wasn't Iroha-Ya. Due to the prompt actions of the police chief, Iroha-Ya's owner had been taken into custody on Monday, the day after Sanosuke and Tsunan raided the Ministry of Home Affairs. Although all of the billiard halls were still open, there were no customers.

Kenshin had already obtained a promise from the police chief not to investigate matters surrounding Tsunan.

All is well... Kenshin thought to himself with relief. But another problem loomed on the horizon. Ahead lay a fierce competition between Tae, Tsubame, Kaoru, and even Yahiko to get hold of Tsukioka Tsunan's final nishiki-e, with Sanosuke caught in the middle. It was easy to imagine Kenshin's expression as he wondered what to do.

Katsu Kaishû, forty-five...Ôkubo Toshi-michi, thirty-eight...Saigô Takamori, forty-one...Katsura Kogorô, thirty-five...these were their ages in the first year of Meiji. Sakamoto Ryôma, thirty-three, and Nakaoka Shintarô, thirty, were slain by assassins and didn't live to see the end of the Revolution. Takasugi Shinsaku died at the young age of twenty-nine. During Meiji, Kondô Isami was executed at the age of thirty-five, and Hijikata Toshizô was thirty-four when he was killed in action. When reading the history of the end of the Shogunate era and the Revolution, we are surprised to see that so many young people were involved in the action. The Meiji Revolution was indeed a revolution accomplished by the young. Surely, that must be the main reason why that era still captivates us, even in this modern Heisei age.

It's been three years since I began drawing Rurouni Kenshin, and while it is based on historical fact, I aspired to draw freely, unrestricted by convention, in order for the characters to be just as attractive as the real-life heroes. In this novelization, Shizuka-sensei introduced Katsu Kaishû, and I feel the world of Rurouni has expanded once again. My only regret is that I was unable to draw as many illustrations as I had hoped, due to the problems associated with the weekly series schedule. I would like to use this page to offer my sincere apologies.

To those who have read this novel after reading the manga or watching the anime, or those who met Kenshin and the others for the first time through this novelized version, please continue to support them.

Finally, I would like to offer my gratitude to Shizuka Kaoru-sensei, who has done a magnificent job of novelization.

Watsuki Nobuhiro

POSTSCRIPT

GLOSSARY

The name means "Red Cow," an appropriate appellation for a beef-pot restaurant.	**AKABEKO**
A Samurai protest, 1876.	**AKIZUKI UPRISING**
The final, chaotic days of the Tokugawa regime.	**BAKUMATSU**
Direct Shogunate retainers of samurai rank.	**BAKUSHIN**
Fought in 1868 in the Kyoto suburb of Fushimi between the joint forces of the Satsuma, Chôshû, and Tosa and the Bakufu (Shogunate) forces.	**BATTLE OF TOBA AND FUSHIMI**
Literally means "red hollyhock." The hollyhock was the symbol of the Tokugawa.	**BENI AOI**
Saito Musashibo Benkei was a Buddhist warrior monk who served Minamoto no Yoshitsune and is legendary for his loyalty and prowess. He joined Yoshitsune's retinue when the warlord defeated him at Gojo Bridge.	**BENKEI**
Buddhism came to Japan from China and Korea between the sixth and eighth centuries AD, and shares many themes with Shintoism. In fact, Shintoists viewed Buddha as another kami while Buddhists viewed kami as manifestations of the Buddhas and Bodhisattvas.	**BUDDHISM**
The historic term for carbon dioxide.	**CARBONIC ACID**
The historic term for potassium hydroxide, also known as lye.	**CAUSTIC POTASH**

CHLORATE OF POTASH

The historic term for potassium chlorate, a compound of potassium, chlorine, and oxygen used in explosives and fireworks.

CHLORINE OF POTASSIUM

The historic term for chlorine of potassium, a compound of potassium and chlorine used in medicine, food processing, and lethal injection.

CHO

A Japanese measure of distance. One cho equals approximately 109 meters or 358 feet.

DOJO

Martial arts training hall.

-DONO

Honorific. Even more respectful than –san; the effect in modern-day Japanese conversation would be along the lines of "Milord So-and-So." As used by Kenshin, it indicates both respect and humility.

EDO

Capital city of the Tokugawa government. Renamed Tokyo ("Eastern Capital") after the Meiji Restoration.

FROM THE EARTH TO THE MOON

The original French title is *De la Terre á la Lune*, and the English title is a direct translation. The Japanese title is *Gessekai Ryoko*, or *Lunar Travel*.

FUROSHIKI

This literally means "cloth for the bath, " and the cloths were initially used to carry things to and from the bath houses. Later, furoshiki were used to wrap and carry all manner of items.

Sliding doors used to separate rooms constructed of lightweight wood and opaque decorative paper. The doors are set into tracks on the top and bottom, but can be easily removed.

FUSUMA

Lowest-ranking direct Shogunate vassals. In the late Edo period, some gokenin effectively sold their rank by adopting the sons of wealthy commoners for a fee.

GOKENIN

Also called nitrocellulose, trinitrocellulose, or cellulose nitrate. It is a mild explosive used in rockets, printing ink bases, and celluloid, which was the original material used to manufacture billiard balls. Guncotton is made by treating ordinary cotton with concentrated nitric and sulfuric acid. Guncotton can be stored underwater, where it will keep indefinitely.

GUNCOTTON

A Samurai protest, 1876. Sword bearing was prohibited when this rebellion was defeated.

Hagi Uprising

Traditional Japanese clothes that resemble long, pleated skirts. Hakama were originally worn by samurai to protect their clothing during horseback riding, much like Western chaps. Hakama are worn over kimono and are tied at the waist.

HAKAMA

The tenth of fifty-three checkpoints along the Tokaido highway between Edo and Kyoto during the Edo period, it was considered the gateway to the Kanto region. Government passes were required to pass each checkpoint, similar to modern passports.

Hakone Gateway

HAORI JACKET   Worn over a kimono for warmth or for formal occasions. Haori can be made of anything from cotton to brocade, and are secured with two ties at the front rather than a belt.

HATAMOTO   Elite Shogunate retainers. The hatamoto made up the official Shogunate guard and the armies under direct Shogunate command.

HITEN MITSURUGI-RYÛ   Kenshin's sword technique, used more for defense than offense. An "ancient style that pits one against many," it requires exceptional speed and agility to master.

HITOKIRI   An assassin, literally "person slayer." A term given to four different samurai during the Bakumatsu. The hitokiri were also referred to as "The Four Butchers" and "Heaven's Revenge Against the Enemies of Imperial Restoration." Kenshin is loosely based on the hitokiri Kawakami Gensai.

HITOKIRI IZO   Okada Izo, one of the four real hitokiri who fought as assassins against the Tokugawa shogunate in the Bakumatsu.

ISHIN SHISHI   Loyalist or pro-Imperialist patriots who fought to restore the emperor to his ancient seat of power.

JIKISHINKAGE-RYÛ   Also known as Kashima Shinden Jikishinkage-ryû. A style of sword fighting founded by Matsumoto Bizen-no-Kami Naokatsu in the late Muromachi or early Sengoku era, around 1570. Jikishinkage means "from the shadow of the heart."

Sword-arts or kenjutsu school established by Kaoru's father, who rejected the ethics of *Satsujin-ken* (swords that give death) for *Katsujin-ken* (swords that give life).	**KAMIYA KASSHIN-RYÛ**
Fabric that is woven from threads that are specially pre-dyed to create the final pattern. This technique has fallen out of style in Japan, but is still practiced as *ikat* in India.	**KASURI**
Japanese long swords with slightly curved, single-edged blades, traditionally worn by samurai. The combination of the katana and wakizashi is called daisho, and represents the honor of the samurai.	**KATANA**
Prior to the Meiji, most common people did not have a family name. Katsu, although of low rank, is from a samurai family and therefore has two names. After the Revolution, many ex-samurai like Katsu changed their first names to reflect the change in times or to resemble noble names. Yasuyoshi is formed by rearranging the kanji for Awa, the province where Katsu once held office.	**KATSU YASUYOSHI**
Japanese unit of measurement for distances. One ken equals approximately two meters or six feet.	**KEN**
The art of swordsmanship.	**KENJUTSU**
A way of measuring salary based on rice.	**KOKU**

-KUN	Honorific. Used in the modern day among male students, or those who grew up together. The historic form is "superior-to-inferior," intended as a way to emphasize a difference in status or rank, as well as to indicate familiarity or affection.
KYOTO	Home of the Emperor and imperial court from 794 AD until shortly after the Meiji Restoration in 1868.
LIEUE	An old French unit of measurement, equal to approximately 2.5 miles.
MARGARET HAIRSTYLE	A popular women's hairstyle of the time, the Margaret was a long center braid at the back of the head looped under and secured with a ribbon just above the nape of the neck.
MEIJI RESTORATION	1853-1868. Culminated in the collapse of the Tokugawa Bakufu and the restoration of imperial rule. Named after Emperor Meiji, whose chosen name was written with the characters for "culture and enlightenment."
MOON PRINCESS KAGUYA	A character from the Japanese fairy tale *The Tale of the Bamboo Cutter* or *The Tale of Moon Princess Kaguya*. The story is about a poor bamboo cutter who finds a baby girl in a stalk of bamboo who is actually a princess from the moon, and must one day return home.
OJÔ-SAMA	A term used to address a young woman from a good family; a more polite version of "young lady."

This slight student has a powerful sounding name. Okuma means "Big Bear" and Dai means "Great." Goro is a common Japanese boy's name.	**ÔKUMA DAIGORO**
A unit of measurement. One pyo equals one bale of rice.	**PYO**
Translation of Go-Isshin, or the coming of a new age after the Bakumatsu.	**REVOLUTION**
Wanderer, vagabond.	**RUROUNI**
Reversed-edge sword (the dull edge on the side the sharp should be, and vice-versa); carried by Kenshin as a symbol of his resolution never to kill again.	**SAKABATÔ**
Honorific. Carries the meaning of "Mr.," "Ms.," "Miss," etc., but used more extensively in Japanese than its English equivalent. Even an enemy may be addressed as -san.	**-SAN**
A monetary unit. One hundred sen equals one yen.	**SEN**
A title used for teachers, martial arts instructors, or professionals like doctors, lawyers, politicians, or other authority figures. It is also used to show respect to a person who has gained mastery of a certain skill or art.	**-SENSEI**
A bamboo practice sword. Shinai are constructed from four bamboo slats held together with leather strips, and while they can cause injury they have no cutting blade.	**SHINAI**

SHINPUREN UPRISING

A samurai protest, 1876.

SHINTOISM

An ancient Japanese religion that started around 500 BC. Shintoism is a shamanistic religion that includes nature and ancestor worship and includes many gods, or kami.

SHURIKEN

Throwing knives. Shuriken range from the single-pointed variety to the multi-pointed versions commonly called throwing stars in the West.

SUKIYAKI

A popular one-pot meal in Japan. High-quality beef is sautéed in a hot skillet with special sauce, vegetables, and other ingredients. The dish is usually cooked directly at the table and shared with a group.

TATAMI MAT

A standard way to measure room size in Japan. The size of a single square of tatami differ by region. In the Tokyo region, the traditional size is 90 cm x 180 cm x 5 cm, approximately 35 in x 71 in x 2 in.

USHIWAKAMARU

Later became known as Minamoto no Yoshitsune. A general in the Heian and early Kamakura eras.

WAKIZASHI

Japanese short swords, between twelve to twenty-four inches long and worn blade up. Samurai wore them in conjunction with the katana. Merchants, forbidden the longer katana, also used wakizashi.

ZANSHIN

Remaining completely wary even when your opponent has fallen.